Iraq at a Distance

THE ETHNOGRAPHY OF POLITICAL VIOLENCE

Cynthia Keppley Mahmood, Series Editor

A complete list of books in the series
is available from the publisher.

Iraq at a Distance

What Anthropologists
Can Teach Us
About the War

Edited by

Antonius C. G. M. Robben

PENN

University of Pennsylvania Press

Philadelphia

Published by
University of Pennsylvania Press
Philadelphia, Pennsylvania 19104-4112

Printed in the United States of America on acid-free paper

10   9   8   7   6   5   4   3   2   1

Library of Congress Cataloging-in-Publication Data
Iraq at a distance : what anthropologists can teach us about the war / edited by Antonius C. G. M. Robben.
    p. cm. — (Ethnography of political violence)
    Includes bibliographical references and index.
    ISBN 978-0-8122-4203-4 (alk. paper)
    1. War and society—Case studies.   2. Political anthropology—Fieldwork—Case studies.   3. War on Terrorism, 2001–   4. Iraq War, 2003– .   I. Robben, Antonius C. G. M.
GN497.I73   2010
303.6'6—dc22

                                                                    2009027546

Contents

Preface

This volume is not a typical anthropology book about Iraq. The essays were written in the midst of the Iraq War and lack, therefore, the hindsight that often benefits scholarly analyses. Moreover, the contributing authors did not conduct the long-term fieldwork that customarily underlies most anthropological studies. The physical danger to foreign civilians in Iraq was so great that even experienced war correspondents were for years able to leave Baghdad's Green Zone only on day trips surrounded by private security contractors or embedded in military units. This book shows, however, that the impossibility of conducting ethnographic fieldwork in war zones such as Iraq does not preempt anthropological interpretation.

This book arose from three pressing concerns in mid-2005: a moral outrage against the Iraq War, the absence of an anthropological voice in professional and public debates, and the similarities with previous armed conflicts worldwide (Robben 2005). The anger and dismay over the steeply rising number of dead as the Iraq War dragged on, the urbicide of Fallujah, the displacement of millions of citizens, the gruesome beheading of kidnap victims, the lethal roadside bombs, the mistreatment of Iraqi civilians—with the humiliation of inmates at Abu Ghraib prison as the first public jolt that there was something profoundly wrong with the war—and the terrible waste of resources in the mismanaged reconstruction of Iraq's infrastructure were felt by many people, not just anthropologists. Numerous anthropologists voiced their opinions at home, among friends and colleagues, and maybe in the classroom, but few brought their anthropological knowledge to bear on the issues discussed in the public domain. Some anthropologists with expertise in the Middle East wrote op-eds about the ethnocentrism of foreign troops fighting in Iraq and pointed out the blindness of our political leaders to Iraq's turbulent political history and ethnic-religious complexities, but these were lone voices among the political scientists, military historians, foreign affairs specialists, and opinion makers that dominated the media. The absence of an anthropological perspective was all the more surprising because anthropologists have since the 1980s been studying armed conflicts that have many similarities with the Iraq War.

These concerns resulted in the formation of the Iraq Research Project in early 2006, in which a group of anthropologists, seasoned in the ethnographic study of violence, suffering, and armed conflict, were invited to write about the Iraq War. Since then, the American Anthropological Association has examined the involvement of anthropologists in the U.S. military and has been reviewing its code of ethics (AAA Commission 2007). Furthermore, many anthropologists have pledged themselves to the opposition against research and service for the military initiated in 2007 by the Network of Concerned Anthropologists (Members 2007). Anthropological research about the Iraq War has concentrated mainly on the study of U.S. veterans and especially on the ethically questionable employment of anthropologists by the military. This book focuses on the plight of the Iraqi people in this devastating war, waged under the banner of freedom and democracy, through comparisons between Iraq and past and present armed conflicts in Cambodia, Israel, Palestine, Northern Ireland, Afghanistan, and Argentina. The introductory chapter conceptualizes the methodological approach to the study of inaccessible war zones and discusses the importance of comparative anthropology in interpreting the fragmentary, conflicting, and partisan information emerging from those fronts. The five ethnographic chapters analyze, respectively, the Manichaean discourse of the war on terror, the deterioration of women's rights in Iraq, the ethnic-religious partitioning of Baghdad, the loss of popular support for the U.S. and Coalition forces in Iraq and Afghanistan, and the counterinsurgency warfare in Iraq. The volume closes with an epilogue that discusses the anthropological findings from a historical perspective.

Acknowledgments

The Iraq Research Project could never have gotten off the ground without the intellectual generosity of its members. I want to express my warmest thanks to the contributors for putting their busy research agendas on hold to immerse themselves in the study of the Iraq War. My heartfelt gratitude goes to the University of Pennsylvania's editor-in-chief, Peter Agree, for making this book a priority in a tight production schedule and for maintaining his graciousness in an increasingly tough publishing business. Final thanks go to Ashley Nelson and Erica Ginsburg for efficiently guiding this book through the publishing process, and to Holly Knowles for preparing the index.

Bibliography

AAA Commission on the Engagement of Anthropology with the U.S. Security and Intelligence Communities. 2007. *Final Report*. http://www.aaanet.org/pdf/ FINAL_Report_Complete.pdf (accessed: December 17, 2007).

Members of the Network of Concerned Anthropologists. 2007. The Network of Concerned Anthropologists Pledges to Boycott Counterinsurgency. *Anthropology News* 48 (December):4–5.

Robben, Antonius C. G. M. 2005. Anthropology at War? What Argentina's Dirty War Can Teach Us. *Anthropology News* 46 (September):5.

Ethnographic Imagination at a Distance: An Introduction to the Anthropological Study of the Iraq War

Antonius C. G. M. Robben

Anthropology has had a long history of studying cultures at a distance. In fact, anthropology began in the nineteenth century with the study of travel and missionary accounts, memoirs of explorers and sailors, and surveys conducted by colonial administrators. This armchair anthropology made way for in situ research by the pioneering work of early ethnographers of Native American cultures such as Schoolcraft, Morgan, and Cushing, as well as the British Haddon expedition to Torres Straits. Anthropology professionalized under the domineering influence of Franz Boas and Bronislaw Malinowski, who turned ethnographic fieldwork into the discipline's defining research strategy. Their students traveled the world to conduct long-term fieldwork and write in-depth ethnographies.

World War II interrupted this ethnographic mapping of the world as parts became inaccessible to fieldwork. Anthropologists, however, did not sit around idly. Anthropologists in Nazi Germany carried out racial selections in one of the darkest chapters of the discipline (Schafft 2004), while many anthropologists on the other side of the moral divide offered their services to the Allied war effort. The study of culture at a distance was reborn, albeit with improved research methods, greater ethnographic knowledge, and more empirical experience than nineteenth-century armchair anthropology. British and American anthropologists assessed enemy strengths, instructed troops in cultural awareness, and contributed to propaganda campaigns (Yans-McLaughlin 1986). They also engaged in ethically questionable practices, such as informing on Japanese Americans in U.S. internment camps, examining the susceptibility of the Japanese people to certain diseases in case of biological warfare, exploring the transcontinental resettlement of postwar refugees to promote U.S. economic expansion, and gathering intelligence under the cover of fieldwork (Price 2008). The most

celebrated study of culture at a distance is Ruth Benedict's *The Chrysanthemum and the Sword: Patterns of Japanese Culture* (1974), which delineates
Japanese assumptions about war, hierarchy, education, ancestor worship,
virtue, duty, discipline, revenge, and the role of the emperor. This study
sought to help the war against Japan and smooth its occupation by U.S.
troops by trying to understand Japanese culture. Benedict (1974:5) was
keenly aware of her methodological problems: "I could not go to Japan and
live in their homes and watch the strains and stresses of daily life, see with
my own eyes which were crucial and which were not. I could not watch
them in the complicated business of arriving at a decision." She solved these
shortcomings by interviewing Japanese Americans, consulting the literature
about Japan, watching movies, and comparing and contrasting Japanese
and American cultures (1974:5–17).

The methodology of the study of cultures at a distance became most
clearly formulated when World War II evolved into the Cold War. Funded
by the Office of Naval Research, Benedict initiated the Columbia University
Research in Contemporary Cultures project to analyze societies inaccessible
to anthropologists. The empirical data derived from two sources: informants
and cultural material. The informants were preferably migrants and refugees
or American diplomats and professionals who had temporarily lived in those
societies. Five methods were used to study cultures through informants:
open interviews, life histories, projective techniques, focus groups, and the
unobtrusive observation of interviewees to discover gestures, moods, and
styles (Benedict 1974:5–8; Mead 1953:41). The cultural material was subjected
to a content analysis, and included novels, poems, memoirs, diaries, letters,
folktales, children's stories, songs, historical studies, newspapers, censuses,
propaganda, films, photographs, and works of art (Mead and Métraux 1953).
Researchers were conscious of the inevitable gaps of knowledge about the
imponderabilia of everyday life but believed that these indirect sources were
of sufficient quality to uncover structural regularities, patterned behaviors,
personalities, and cultural themes (Gorer 1953:57).

Another plea for anthropological studies at a distance was made in the
late 1960s by Kathleen Gough when anthropologists continued to be barred
from communist countries, and the rise of dictatorial regimes and revolutionary guerrilla and anticolonial insurgencies made fieldwork difficult elsewhere. Gough suggested that anthropologists should draw more on the
work of journalists and social scientists who had visited those countries and
conduct comparative studies of food production, foreign aid, and social in-
equality in capitalist and communist societies as well as processes of social

change set in motion by revolutionary movements. Research data could be gathered by international organizations and foreign researchers. Afraid of being associated with a conservative agenda, she concluded: "I may be accused of asking for Project Camelot, but I am not. I am asking that we should do these studies in *our* way, as we would study a cargo cult or kula ring, without the built-in biases of tainted financing, without the assumption that counter-revolution, and not revolution, is the best answer, and with the ultimate economic and spiritual welfare of our informants and of the international community, rather than the short run military or industrial profits of the Western nations, before us" (1968:407).

Today, parts of the world are once more becoming inaccessible to fieldwork due to the so-called war on terror declared by the U.S. government after the terrorist assaults in Washington and New York on September 11, 2001. This war is reterritorializing the world into security zones, danger zones, and war zones whose borders are drawn by increasing surveillance measures and armed conflicts that inhibit anthropologists from traveling unimpeded to desired field sites. This is not to say that anthropologists cannot work in trouble spots, such as Colombia, Sri Lanka, Lebanon, Israel, and Palestine, but that certain places and regions are for the time being inaccessible to research, such as parts of Iraq, Pakistan, Somalia, Sudan, and Congo, because of the intensity of the violence, the unpredictability of the combatants, and the suspicion of working undercover for foreign intelligence services. Iraq is a case in point. Hypothetically, anthropologists might enter less dangerous provinces, cities, and neighborhoods, but the dangers are considerable. The ethnographic returns will diminish as the violence increases, and the risks to fieldworkers and research participants will become so great that empirical research will be impossible.

This book has been written as war and violence still rage through the lives of the Iraqi people. With the exception of Nadje Al-Ali and Ibrahim Al-Marashi, none of us has been to Iraq since the overthrow of Saddam Hussein because of the ongoing violence. We have therefore resorted to ethnographic imagination at a distance to analyze the consequences of the war on Iraqi society. Ethnographic imagination at a distance is the leap of analytic and interpretive faith required to explain phenomena that cannot be studied directly through ethnographic fieldwork. Ethnographic imagination transcends empiricist realities, and anthropological interpretations at a distance should not be withheld because of methodological standards that can never be met in war zones. The lack of studies about the Iraq War seems to suggest that anthropologists have lost the boldness of earlier generations in overcoming the methodological problems of studying cultures at a distance. Still, we are in a better position today than they were then because of the many ethnographies of violence and social suffering that give us a heightened understanding of inaccessible war zones. We would do a disservice to anthropology if we felt we could not measure up to our disciplinary standards or are in doubt about the unique anthropological perspective we can contribute about the Iraq War without conducting the ethnographic fieldwork that has been our professional trademark.

What contribution can anthropologists make to the understanding of a war-torn Iraq? Here, I am thinking of a perspective that has been brewing inside anthropology since the mid-1990s that Jeffrey Sluka and I have named "the compassionate turn" (Sluka and Robben 2007:22). The compassionate turn began as a reaction against the negativism of postmodern anthropology and comprises approaches such as militant anthropology, public anthropology, the anthropology of social suffering, and the ethnography of everyday violence. This palette of approaches ranges from a radical militant anthropology that pursues "a politically committed and morally engaged anthropology" (Scheper-Hughes 1995:410) to a less partisan focus on social suffering that "brings into a single space an assemblage of human problems that have their origins and consequences in the devastating injuries that social force can inflict on human experience" (Kleinman, Das, and Lock 1997a:ix). The common denominator is the importance of empathy both as a methodological technique to grasp the Malinowskian native point of view and as an epistemological approach to understand people's subjectivity. Such empathy turns into compassion when the ethnographer has a clear awareness of the moral, ethical, and political implications of the ethnographic knowledge. Practitioners become implicated in the lives of their research participants, engage in social advocacy as witnesses, or, as the authors of this volume have done, bring their scholarly expertise to current events. They try to influence public debates and at times encourage social and political changes that will lessen the violence and suffering inflicted on societies, as has been done successfully in the collections by Ahmed and Shore (1995) and Besteman and Gusterson (2005).

The compassionate turn differs from the action anthropology of the 1970s, although the political activism of militant anthropologists such as Nancy Scheper-Hughes (1995) comes close by urging anthropologists to take sides against oppression and put the discipline at the service of the oppressed. It is obvious that such politico-moral choices are seldom clear-cut. Should an anthropologist choose the side of Shi'is, brutally oppressed for many years by Saddam Hussein, who pursue a government of national alliance to overcome ethnic-religious tensions but will need the long-term assistance of U.S. forces resented by many Iraqis? Or should one cast one's lot with equally oppressed Shi'is who oppose such foreign presence and desire more political autonomy, even at the risk of civil war?

The essays in this book have moral implications. We as authors have political standpoints, and our interest in the Iraq War has for some of us been sparked by outrage, but our shared concern is compassion with regard to the everyday experiences, realities, hardships, and struggles of the Iraqi people. We want to contribute our anthropological understanding to the foreign policy studies, political analyses, military assessments, human rights reports, newspaper dispatches, and book-length chronicles about the war in Iraq. Our anthropological perspective capitalizes on an ethnographic imagination of the everyday realities endured by the Iraqi people and how they are affected by political forces beyond their reach. We want to show that their lives matter within the larger framework of geopolitical forces, ideological and religious conflicts, international oil interests, and global military strategies. We want to emphasize their shared humanity with so many other people whose past has been burdened by violence and suffering, and thus demonstrate that we "are imaginable to each other and that we may conjoin in a shared standard of justice from diverse rationales; in short, that we are equally human beyond our diverse vocabularies" (Hastrup 2002:40). Our ethnographic imagination about the Iraq War derives from our fieldwork in other conflict areas and is contextualized and influenced by, but does not emerge from, our politico-moral convictions.

Although fieldwork remains firmly at the heart of anthropology and is the professional foundation from which we start, we believe that the insights of existing ethnographic studies about violence and suffering, our own field experiences of conflict areas, the example set by multisited research, extensive interviews, and cross-cultural comparison give us sufficient research tools to analyze current events in Iraq in a responsible way. Once Iraq becomes safer, ethnographic fieldwork will become possible again and will allow researchers to pursue in more depth some of the issues raised in this volume.

Ethnographic Imagination and Comparative Anthropology

The awareness of globalization as a process penetrating and connecting the farthest regions of the world liberated anthropology in the 1990s from the century-old research practice of long-term fieldwork in one location. The anthropological attention turned from the study of society, culture, and identity within one circumscribed space to interconnections, chains, paths, and bridges among multiple locations and dimensions. Multisited fieldwork arose as the research practice most suited for understanding global linkages (Marcus 1995). The geopolitical reality of the 1990s was favorable for this fieldwork approach. The Cold War had ended, the Warsaw Pact and the Soviet Union had disintegrated, China was opening its borders, and anthropology had become receptive to new types of ethnography, thanks to the postmodern turn and the emphasis on narrative ethnography. Anthropologists were researching transnational phenomena, following their interconnections, and reporting the findings in innovative ways.

The ethnographic study of globalization, multisited fieldwork, and an epistemological critique of the unity of time, space, culture, and identity emerged together. Gupta and Ferguson (1992) wrote about the despatialization of culture due to globalization and interconnectedness, and urged anthropologists to study boundaries, breaks, borderlands, and discontinuities for a better understanding of the construction of cultural difference (see also Appadurai 1996; Hannerz 1996; Herzfeld 2001). The fall of the Berlin Wall in 1989 symbolized this process of deterritorialization, and there was even talk of the end of history as the world came under the sway of democracy and neoliberalism.

Unexpectedly, this symbol of unity and freedom was toppled by two hijacked planes flying into the World Trade Center in New York on the morning of September 11, 2001: 9/11 became the world's new symbol, one that replaced the optimism of 1989 with the anxieties of 2001. U.S. president George Bush declared a war on terror couched in a Manichaean discourse of cultural difference that reordered the world into security zones and danger zones. This division was reinforced by increased border controls, the exchange of hitherto confidential information about airline passengers, biometrics and body scans, the monitoring of financial transactions and electronic mail, and a host of other surveillance measures. The war on terror turned borderlands into no-man's-lands and was rapidly cutting many post–Cold War linkages. The unimpeded flow of goods, people, finances, and ideas that characterized the last decade of the twentieth century became replaced by inclusionary and exclusionary zones during the first decade of the twenty-first century. Appadurai (2006:29) speaks therefore of a "crisis of circulation" because of the disjunctures erected within such flows.

These disjunctures have also been interrupting the movement of anthropologists. Single-sited and especially multisited ethnographic fieldwork are becoming harder to conduct as a result of strictly enforced national boundaries, the multiplication of danger zones, and the emergence of new war zones. War and danger zones in Iraq, Afghanistan, Pakistan, Somalia, Sudan, Congo, and the Caucasus are off-limits to ethnographers. A few anthropologists with previous fieldwork experience might still venture into these places, but new field research has become impossible. Which countries will follow? It is conceivable that Iran, Lebanon, and Indonesia as well as diaspora communities in the Western world may be added to the list.

The creation of inclusionary and exclusionary zones is mirrored in this book's attention to the spatialization of conflict. Alexander Laban Hinton demonstrates how President Bush's representation of the war on terror as a fight between those on the side of Western life, freedom and democracy, and Islamist terrorists intent on creating a global caliphate under sharia legislation divided the world into zones of good versus evil. In a comparison with Cambodia, Hinton demonstrates how such Manichaeism led the Khmer Rouge to distinguish between degenerate cities and an enlightened countryside with tragic consequences for urban residents. Nadje Al-Ali describes how the movement of Iraqi women is increasingly restricted through overall insecurity and the imposition of gender boundaries by Islamist groups. It has become dangerous for women to visit the marketplace unescorted by men, drive a car, or attend classes together with male students. Julie Peteet delineates the parallels between the sociospatial separation of Israelis and Palestinians with the physical barriers and partitions emerging in Baghdad. Increasing numbers of Sunnis and Shi'is are living in exclusive enclaves, and many throughways have become too dangerous to travel. Jeffrey A. Sluka demonstrates, in a comparison between the U.S. occupation of Iraq and the conduct of British troops in Northern Ireland, that counterinsurgency wars are disputed in four interlocked spaces (war zones, states, home fronts, and the media-globalized world) whose complex interaction determines which warring party wins the hearts and minds of the civilian population. Finally, I describe in my essay how the latest counterinsurgency tactics turned both public and domestic spaces into confusing war zones for Iraqi civilians with checkpoint killings, random arrests, intrusive house searches, abusive detention regimes, and unpredictable conduct by troops, insurgents, and terrorists. I compare these tactics to Argentina's dirty war practices and conclude that this sociospatial chaos makes human rights violations inevitable.

The freedom of anthropologists to conduct fieldwork is restricted not only by the spatialization of conflict but also by the enlistment of anthropologists in the war on terror. As Sluka remarks in this volume, anthropologists have become targets in the hearts and minds strategy of a Western military eager for their ethnographic knowledge. General David Petraeus (2006:51), a key thinker on counterinsurgency and the 2007–8 commander of the Multi-National Coalition Force in Iraq, has stated that "knowledge of the cultural 'terrain' can be as important as, and sometimes even more important than, knowledge of the geographic terrain. . . . the people are, in many respects, the decisive terrain, and . . . we must study that terrain in the same way that we have always studied the geographic terrain." The Human Terrain System, launched in 2005, operationalizes such cultural intelligence gathering by embedding anthropologists in combat brigades (González 2009; Kipp et al. 2006; Rohde 2007). It has also been suggested that military ethnographers be stationed at U.S. embassies to try to attain a "near-total immersion in the local population" and use social network analysis to collect cultural intelligence (Renzi 2006:184).

Whatever one's politics and professional ethics, the posting of security anthropologists in war zones will make ethnographic fieldwork more difficult by independent academics, if not outright dangerous (see González 2007; McFate 2005; Selmeski 2007). Just as happened in the 1960s and 1970s, ethnographers will be questioned by local populations about their political agendas. The suspicion of being a CIA spy will be replaced by accusations of supplying cultural knowledge and language skills to the U.S. military in the global war on terror. Ethnographic study at a distance may then be a possible option, instead of simply abandoning former research sites altogether, when fieldwork is no longer possible.

The contradiction in conducting anthropological research about a place one cannot visit is less obvious than it seems at first sight. Anthropologists during World War II studied people without participant observation, as have anthropologists working in the anthropology of violence and suffering. All the contributors to this book have done the same; they seldom witnessed the human affronts they studied. The reason is that "the field" is as much a mental space as a location, and the two do not necessarily overlap. The anthropology of globalization began to disengage the two when it relied on telecommunications, the Internet, and the media to supplement data about flows and interconnections collected through participant observation. Ethnographic research about areas simply too dangerous to live in, such as Iraq, will have to draw on newspaper articles by war correspondents written with the help of local stringers, status reports by international

NGOs and local human rights groups, communiqués by insurgent groups and the military, blogs by civilians and soldiers (see Brown and Lutz 2007), interviews with refugees, and radio broadcasts, television programs, and camcasts available on the Internet. Like the witness and victim testimonies used by anthropologists studying political violence, these multiple sources provide important causeways into the fields and spaces where participant observation has become impossible.

Unlike World War II and Cold War anthropologists who often lacked any fieldwork experience in violent societies, today's anthropologists can draw on the ethnographic findings, understandings, and theories from the anthropology of violence and social suffering for their studies at a distance (see, e.g., Gusterson 2007; Kleinman, Das, and Lock 1997b; Scheper-Hughes and Bourgois 2003). Many ethnographies have been published on violence, repression, and suffering during the past two decades that allow us to study new situations with improved concepts, methods, narrative techniques, and analytical approaches.

These studies have the additional advantage of offering insight into inaccessible societies through comparative methods. I do not refer to the statistical comparisons of large samples, structural-functionalism, structuralism, or neo-evolutionism that aim at constructing grand theories or general laws, but to the controlled "macrocomparison of distant case studies" (Gingrich 2002:229; see also Bowen and Petersen 1999; Fox and Gingrich 2002; Holy 1987). Yengoyan (2006:25–26) calls this "comparative contextualization" and argues that "Although we start from the particular and the local, contextualizations do render parallel pathways of convergence and divergence; thus unique or obscure events within one context are visible in other cases." The obscure and ill-understood phenomena in an inaccessible war zone are thus exposed and clarified by a comparison with a war zone whose violence has been studied in-depth through fieldwork.

The comparative approach used by the contributors to this volume is heuristic rather than explanatory and aims at improving the understanding of culturally specific meanings, experiences, practices, events, and processes that influence the lives of the Iraqi people. For example, Sluka's analysis of processes of political violence, armed resistance, counterinsurgency, and popular mobilization in Northern Ireland allows him to better interpret current events and unfolding developments in Iraq: "The function of comparison then is not so much to determine, from scratch as it were, the similarities and differences between phenomena . . . but to illuminate one set of ill-understood phenomena by reference to another set more clearly comprehended" (Howe 1987:136). The comparative method employed in this volume consists of examining side by side "processes of change as they go along" (Moore 2005:1) in the awareness that similar processes generate culturally specific meanings, practices, discourses, and understandings (see Gingrich 2002; Hannerz 1992; Lock 2002; Wolf 1999). Multisited fieldwork has added a new dimension to comparative methods with its emphasis on connections and imaginative influences between different places and disjunctive sites (Marcus 1995, 2006). These insights help the ethnographic imagination of possible connections between a field site and an inaccessible site.

The essays in this collection draw on processes of change discovered during long-term fieldwork in conflict sites other than Iraq. Alexander Hinton (2005) takes his analysis of the ideological manufacturing of fundamental social difference and its gruesome consequences for the Cambodian people to the Manichaeism and binary oppositions of Bush's war on terror, and warns about the ensuing dehumanization of an enemy believed to pose an existential threat. Julie Peteet's (2005) fine-grained ethnohistorical research into the relationship of place and identity in Palestinian refugee camps allows her to be particularly attentive to the spatial dimensions of the Iraq War and the emerging territorialization of ethnopolitical conflicts between Sunnis and Shi'is. Jeffrey Sluka (1989) uses his multilevel understanding of civilian support during three decades of violent conflict between British Security Forces and Nationalist Northern Irish guerrillas to identify similar processes in Iraq where U.S. troops were losing the Iraqi people's hearts and minds in their fight against insurgents and foreign mujahideen. I use the concept of mimesis developed in my ethnography about guerrilla and dirty warfare in Argentina (2005) to critique the latest fashion in U.S. counterinsurgency tactics. Finally, Nadje Al-Ali's essay about gender and women's rights in post-Saddam Iraq shows another approach to the study of inaccessible field sites. She has conducted extensive interviews with Iraqi refugees in London, Amman, and Dearborn (Michigan), and women's rights activists in northern Iraq.

These approaches help identify particular processes amid the diverse sources of information available about Iraq's war zones and allow us to contribute our ethnographic imagination to places where participant observation is impossible. This ethnographic imagination is steered by a compassionate attention to the violence and suffering endured by the Iraqi people since the overthrow of Saddam Hussein's dictatorial regime, and provides an anthropologically informed critique of Iraq's occupation by Western military forces.

The Iraq War in Comparative Perspectives

In " 'Night Fell on a Different World': Dangerous Visions and the War on Terror, a Lesson from Cambodia," Alexander Hinton interprets the good-versus-evil ideology justifying the war on terror and compares it to a similar Manichaeism employed by the communist Khmer Rouge in Cambodia during the 1970s. Manichaeism is a structural dichotomy that often underlies genocides and massive violence. Hinton demonstrates how the Manichaean discourses in such different societies as the United States and Cambodia address comparable issues.

When Islamist terrorists used passenger planes as missiles to demolish New York's Twin Towers on September 11, 2001, this incomprehensible event was immediately framed by the news media under the headline "America under Attack." But who attacked America and why on earth would they do so? Hinton demonstrates that President Bush provided a narrative and an ideological framework to understand these urgent questions. Hinton immediately recognized the similarities between Bush's political convictions and the Khmer Rouge rationalization of the 1975–79 Cambodian genocide about which he was writing a major study (2005). In less than four years, almost one-quarter of Cambodia's population of eight million had died from starvation, disease, exploitation, and summary execution in a radical experiment in social engineering intended to transform the country into an egalitarian utopia. This ideological agenda required the purge of counterrevolutionary forces to cleanse the Cambodian state of class enemies and traitors. This mission was undertaken with unusual cruelty and disproportionate revenge, justified by a Manichaean perception of Cambodian society as divided into self-righteous "old people" (exploited peasants, the illiterate) and despicable "new people" (city dwellers, landlords, the educated).

The war on terror in general, and the war in Iraq in particular, are taking place in another geopolitical and historical context and do not have genocidal proportions, yet Hinton perceives parallels between the ideological framing of the violence in Cambodia and Iraq. Both organize their worlds into "we" and "them," or good against evil, to legitimate the use of violence. Hinton found a potent discursive expression in Bush's September

20, 2001, address to a joint session of Congress and the American people that ritually celebrated the country's unity against the existential threat from abroad. Hinton analyzes Bush's speech together with the Khmer Rouge ideology through four rhetorical questions: Who attacked our country? Why do they hate us? How will we fight and win this war? What is expected of us?

The Khmer Rouge felt threatened by an amorphous enemy hidden within their revolutionary ranks. These counterrevolutionary forces were mainly found among the alienated "new people" who had been perverted by urban life and were thus expelled from Cambodia's cities to the countryside, only to die working the land. America's enemies are the Islamist terrorists affiliated in the loosely structured al Qaeda network, supported by rogue states, and sheltered as dormant terrorist cells by diaspora Muslim communities in the Western world. The enemies of Cambodia and the United States were both defined as personifications of evil that deserve to be eliminated. Cambodia's enemies hated Pol Pot's Khmer Rouge for trying to create a just, egalitarian communist society without exploitation and class antagonism. The Islamist enemies hate the United States because of its way of life, freedom, democracy, progress, and civilization.

Both enemies were believed to be so powerful that they had to be fought with all means available. The Khmer Rouge emptied cities, held endless purges, forced suspected traitors to confess under torture, and resorted to boundless revenge. They expected all Cambodians to be vigilant and to denounce even family members. President Bush also proclaimed a total war on the terrorists, employing all of America's resources to hunt them down. He asked the American people to overcome all fears, unite, and participate in this epic fight of civilization against savagery portrayed with Christian overtones as an Armageddon. Hinton shows that Osama bin Laden used a structurally similar Manichaean dichotomy as did Bush to divide the world into "good" Muslims and "evil" infidels, and into the pious defenders of Islam's holy places and the immoral imperialist Western crusaders.

Hinton's comparison of these Manichaean frameworks exposes the construction of difference in a demonizing discourse, the differentiation between "us" and "them," and dehumanizing practices, thus giving a better understanding of 9/11, the armed resistance against U.S. and Coalition troops in Iraq, the beheading of journalists and civilian contractors, the continued support for the Taliban in Afghanistan, and the globalization of enmity along the lines of Christianity versus Islam. Equally important, he exposes these Manichaean frameworks, used by leaders such as Pol Pot,

George W. Bush, Tony Blair, and Osama bin Laden for their political and ideological ambitions, as narrative constructions that dehumanize enemies and impose much suffering on ordinary people and their families.

The media attention to Iraq's death counts and military operations has been so obsessive that the plight of Iraqi women has remained underreported. Still, women constitute 55–65 percent of a total population of twenty-four million inhabitants. They suffer proportionally from the lethal violence and bear the daily hardships of maintaining family life under dangerous circumstances. Nadje Al-Ali concludes in her essay, "The War on Terror and Women's Rights in Iraq," that the participation of women in Iraq's public life improved briefly after the 2003 invasion but deteriorated rapidly after 2004. There is a tragic irony here: even though the emancipation of Iraqi women was one of the justifications for the war on terror—with the mistreatment of women by fundamentalist Taliban as a nightmarish prospect—women's rights have declined steadily since the initial upsurge.

The emancipatory rhetoric of the U.S. and Coalition governments argued that women would benefit from a regime change in Iraq by spreading what Tony Blair triumphantly called "the values of freedom, democracy, the rule of law, religious tolerance and justice for the oppressed" (2005:350). Several pro-invasion women's organizations run by Iraqi returnees from exile denounced the Ba'thist regime for trampling women's rights and tried to conquer a political space in the new Iraq. They propagated women's rights and founded grassroots organizations critical of the foreign occupation. They tried, inter alia, to prevent the erosion of existing family law, acquire a women's quota of political representation, and deter the advance of Islamism and sectarian violence.

Al-Ali paints a sobering portrait of the illusory pre-invasion expectations and the optimism about women's emancipation. Instead, women have been systematically denied access to the public, economic, and political domains of Iraqi society. They have been kidnapped for ransom by criminal gangs and abducted abroad for sexual exploitation. They have been killed, beaten, tortured, raped, and taken hostage by members of the foreign occupational forces and the array of nonstate armed groups. Even a short trip to a store or market exposes women to numerous threats from roadside bombs, makeshift checkpoints, suicide bombers, and fire exchanges between troops and assailants.

The public movement of women is hindered further by the emergence of Islamist groups that try to impose their religious and moral standards on gender relations and women's lives. Women have been sprayed with acid for not wearing headscarves and attacked because of their Western-style clothing. More than one million widows can hardly move about if not accompanied by male relatives, and universities have been bombed to implement a strict separation of male and female students. Fundamentalist leaders have also been trying to change Iraq's progressive family laws to a sharia-based jurisdiction, thus undermining women's legal rights and confining women to the home by forbidding them from working or even driving a car.

These fundamentalist pressures have also been occurring in other Muslim societies, such as Afghanistan and Indonesia, as means to construct an ethnic or religious identity in a world experienced as hostile to Islam. Revealingly, Nadje Al-Ali demonstrates how this conservative religious consciousness has been given distinct local meanings in Iraq by its troubled foreign occupation. The Islamization of gender is imposed by certain Iraqi leaders to emphasize the break with Saddam Hussein's secular regime, which did not exclude women from the public sphere, and to resist the emancipatory gender politics of the foreign administrators.

The collapse of Iraq's infrastructure has hit women disproportionally hard because the burden of running the household often falls on them. Electricity and running water have often been unavailable, and health and educational services are inadequate. Malnutrition, disease, child mortality, and school dropout rates have increased significantly. Iraqi women have taken the initiative to relieve some of the most urgent needs not met by Iraq's social services by founding local aid organizations, but these fail to stop the deterioration of women's rights because of the terrible security situation and the rise of Islamism.

In "The War on Terror, Dismantling, and the Construction of Place: An Ethnographic Perspective from Palestine," Julie Peteet draws on extensive fieldwork in Palestinian refugee camps to contribute a spatial understanding of the Iraq War. Since the 1940s, Israeli-Palestinian relations have been dominated by spatial separation and control that have provoked periodic outbursts of violence and imposed much suffering. In fact, spatial politics have characterized Middle Eastern history since the Crusades, and this historical knowledge has informed armed resistance against foreign domination, whether in Palestine, Afghanistan, Iraq, or Algeria. As Peteet argues, Middle Easterners regard today's war on terror as a ploy to change the region's warden: the American superpower is replacing Europe as the key political force in the Middle East. U.S. troops are stationed in many Middle

Eastern countries run by allied governments. Iran is the only major exception. Iraq is a glaring example of spatial politics and American hegemony. The tried Roman practice of divide-and-rule is being used again in Iraq which, according to some U.S. politicians, should be carved up into three semi-autonomous ethnic-religious parts.

Peteet perceives in Iraq a similar process of dismemberment that has been plaguing Israel-Palestine for over six decades. She discerns emergent properties to the foreign occupation of Iraq that have already crystallized in Israel-Palestine. The Coalition's fortified nerve center or Green Zone in Baghdad, the concrete walls around Sunni neighborhoods, frequent curfews, the many fixed and shifting checkpoints, and the foreign controlled oil terminals in the Persian Gulf are some of the most visible outcrops of spatial domination with counterparts in Israel-Palestine. Spatial segregation, ethnic separation, and political disintegration and compartmentalization are matters of fact in Israel-Palestine that are becoming a reality in Iraq.

This process of dismemberment and territorialization is partitioning the world into exclusionary zones of distinction and indistinction, argues Peteet. Democracy, civilization, and the law are reproduced in the first—even though executive privilege and a siege mentality can suspend them when threats are felt imminent—while terror, militant Islam, and a lawless state of exception reign in the latter zone. Israeli, U.S., and Coalition troops act with impunity because the war on domestic and global terror is believed to be of such existential magnitude that it cannot be hindered by unrealistic legalities and due process formalities. This politics of enclosure is preventing the physical mobility of Palestinians by denying them passage at checkpoints and roadblocks, confining them to exclusionary zones with walls, trenches, and barbed wire, and controlling their presence through permits, passes, visas, and identity cards. Mobility is a scarce good exploited by the Israeli government for political and military purposes. Several of these mobility problems are occurring in a city like Baghdad where Sunnis and Shi'is are segregated by checkpoints, barriers, walls, and the interethnic and interreligious violence that draw invisible but deadly boundaries among ethnic-religious enclaves.

The draconian system of Israeli surveillance and subjugation, multiplied by a conscious policy of changing rules and regulations at will to enhance the chaos, anxiety, and unpredictability of the daily regime, has led to deteriorating health, employment, education, and religious and family life among the Palestinian people. More than five hundred barriers and a four-hundred-mile concrete wall are preventing Palestinians from reaching hospitals in life-threatening situations, as well as preventing men and women from arriving at work on time or finding employment at all. Enclosure prevents children from going to school, students from attending university, families from meeting each other, and the faithful from visiting their holy sites on important religious days. Similar developments are occurring in Iraq. The politics of space and enclosure deprives the excluded from familiar spaces and meanings, and imposes desolate landscapes and bounded spaces. The regional, national, and ethnic partitions may eventually materialize as people are expelled from familiar places and memories and emotions of past homes dissipate, argues Peteet, were it not for acts of memory and resistance and, paradoxically, by the violence and humiliation that maintain such dismemberment.

Pre-invasion critics warned that Iraq would become America's second Vietnam. There are of course many differences in the geopolitical context, the underlying ideological motives, the geographic terrain, the cultural complexities, and the military strategies of both wars, but they share a similar combat situation of American ground troops fighting a tenacious insurgency. Jeffrey Sluka argues in "Losing Hearts and Minds in the 'War on Terrorism'" that the United States has unlearned the counterinsurgency lessons drawn after its ouster from Vietnam in 1973 and that the same mistakes appeared again in Iraq. These mistakes were also made by the British army against the IRA (Irish Republican Army) and the INLA (Irish National Liberation Army) in Northern Ireland. Sluka (1989) draws on years of fieldwork in a Catholic neighborhood in Belfast to critique the current U.S. and British counterinsurgency tactics in Iraq and Afghanistan.

Counterinsurgency warfare revolves around winning the hearts and minds of the civilian population, according to classic military doctrine, so that the people will withdraw their support from the embedded combatants. While carrying out research in Northern Ireland, Sluka arrived at the conclusion that repressive counterinsurgency tactics breed community support for insurgents. British troops and the local police, the Royal Ulster Constabulary, fired into Catholic protest crowds, used excessively high concentrations of tear gas, interned suspected Nationalist combatants without a trial, tortured suspects, harassed, threatened, and verbally abused civilians, broke into homes, and created a surveillance chokehold with checkpoints, observation posts, identity checks, body searches, closed-circuit television cameras, and helicopters with high-intensity spotlights. The suffering of many civilians unrelated to the armed confrontation made the Catholic population turn against the British army and local police, and thus raised their sympathy for the IRA and INLA. Civilian casualties, extrajudicial killings, and human rights violations made the counterinsurgency forces lose the moral high ground to the guerrillas and nurtured popular support. Sluka argues that precisely these same expressions of state terrorism have involved the U.S. and Coalition forces in hopeless wars in Iraq and Afghanistan. The moral authority, which the U.S. possessed after 9/11, was wasted in Iraq and Afghanistan by overaggressive operations against unexpected armed insurgencies. The number of deadly casualties among U.S. and Coalition troops, and especially Iraqi and Afghani civilians, has been rising constantly and the approval rates of the foreign military presence have been declining steadily among the local population.

Sluka provides an important analytical framework to understand and diagnose the winning of the hearts and minds of a population facing guerrilla and counterinsurgency warfare. He distinguishes four levels to earning popular support: (1) the population living in the war zone; (2) the national population; (3) the foreign troops' home front; and (4) the international community. Sluka documents how U.S. and Coalition forces were progressively losing the multilayered support for the wars in Iraq and Afghanistan after the initial sympathy for overthrowing Saddam Hussein and the Taliban. Local populations turned against the foreign troops because of the indiscriminate counterinsurgency warfare and were increasingly supporting revengeful attacks on the liberators-turned-occupiers. The Iraqi people saw the destruction of their country's infrastructure and the decline of security, while the Afghan people have seen little economic improvement and have suffered under the military efforts to defeat a Taliban resurging in southern Afghanistan. The rising number of troops killed by roadside bombs and suicide attacks turned the home fronts in Great Britain and the United States against their political leaders, Blair and Bush, and large popular majorities wanted the troops to come home. Finally, the international community was feeling deceived by the false grounds on which the Iraq War was waged. It became also disillusioned by the torture and abuse in prisons like Abu Ghraib and at Guantánamo Bay and Bagram airbase. It has become skeptical about a durable solution to the quagmire in Afghanistan and is becoming convinced that the military strategy against terrorist networks such as al Qaeda has backfired, spurred the growth of Islamist organizations, and made the world a more dangerous place. In sum, the hearts and minds of the people locally, nationally, and internationally have been lost on all four counts.

The fundamental mistake in Iraq and Afghanistan, as earlier in Vietnam and Northern Ireland, has been that the response to insurgents is 80 percent military and only 20 percent political. An important lesson drawn from the Vietnam War, namely that these figures should be the other way around, was unlearned during the Reagan administration with its arms race to win the Cold War. The tendency to solve political problems with military force can be witnessed again in the Iraq War by the use of ruthless tactics, thus ignoring the fundamental lesson that repression breeds resistance or, in the words of Sluka, "that fighting terrorism by employing terrorism (creating innocent victims) creates more terrorism." Sluka concludes, therefore, that the war on terror failed by late 2006 after losing its two main fronts in Iraq and Afghanistan. He expects that the Iraqification of the war will have the same disastrous outcome as the Vietnamization of the Vietnam War because people's hearts and minds are never won militarily but only politically, economically, and socially.

The aggressive counterinsurgency warfare employed by U.S. troops against Iraqi insurgents is described in my contribution, "Mimesis in a War Among the People: What Argentina's Dirty War Reveals About Counterinsurgency in Iraq." Based on extensive research in Argentina (Robben 2005), I draw parallels between the counterinsurgency-cum-dirty war against the Argentine guerrilla insurgency during the 1970s and the swarming tactics employed by U.S. counterinsurgency units in Iraq. Swarming is the latest innovation in counterinsurgency, yet follows dutifully the basic rule that a guerrilla force is best beaten by imitating its tactics. The elusiveness of insurgents fighting among the people in the cities of Iraq, just like urban guerrillas under civilian guise in Argentina, prompted the U.S. military to use equally evasive tactics. Swarming maximizes the tactics of surprise and mobility through connectivity. Small combat units roam independently in a particular urban area in the hope of a chance meeting with insurgents, while being aware of each other's coordinates through high-tech communication equipment. When one unit makes fire contact with irregular combatants, other combat units in the vicinity converge on the scene, engage the enemy, and redisperse once the fighting is over.

The Argentine military developed their own swarming tactics in the 1970s. Combat units cruised the streets of Argentina's cities, took up position at harbors and airports, and pored over the address books of captives in search of new targets. The Argentine counterinsurgency quickly turned into a dirty war in which combatants and political opponents were abducted, tortured, disappeared, and eventually assassinated. Human rights violations were an integral part of Argentine state terrorism and created a culture of fear that involved the entire society.

I argue that the war in Iraq underwent a similar process of abusive counterinsurgency operations that evaporated the initial popular support for U.S. and Coalition troops. Numerous innocent civilians were killed at makeshift checkpoints, suspects were abused in large numbers at several prisons, of which Abu Ghraib was only the most notorious, and U.S. soldiers have raped, beaten, and executed civilians, carried out indiscriminate house raids, and attacked neighborhoods and entire cities with excessive military force to eliminate insurgents and foreign mujahideen while disregarding the safety of civilians. These abusive and deadly operations were fed by a Manichaean perception of the global war against Islamist terrorism and rebounded on the people of Iraq. The political rhetoric of fighting a war against a truly evil enemy intent on destroying a Western way of life triggered a demonization process that influenced the on-the-ground conduct of the average U.S. soldier who noticed a passenger car ignoring his misunderstood stop signs or whose buddies were killed by an improvised explosive device.

Swarming tactics enhance the risks to the civilian population because of their emphasis on surprise and mobility in an urban environment. The combat units have become just as unpredictable as the insurgents they are imitating. Intentionally, their operations are impossible to fathom and therefore create chaotic public and domestic spaces in which bewildered civilians are easily harmed. Furthermore, if troops have been primed with just war thinking, believe they are fighting evil, and are convinced that coercive interrogations are needed to identify the elusive insurgents, then the possibility of human rights violations is more than real. Young officers commanding the swarm units have to make split-second decisions with deadly as much as strategic consequences. The accidental killing of bystanders, revenge on civilians for a roadside bombing, and the abusive detention and on-the-spot mistreatment of suspects will make the host population turn rapidly against the foreign troops and reap sympathy for the insurgents. A comparison of the Argentine dirty war and U.S. swarming operations in Iraq yields the lesson that the mimesis of the unpredictable surprise tactics of Iraqi insurgents, operating in a war among the people, by counterinsurgency forces steeped in good-versus-evil thinking will result in high civilian casualties and alienate the population whose hearts and minds are at stake.

Ibrahim Al-Marashi was invited to write the epilogue to this volume because we do not want to preach to the converted nor exclusively to our own disciplinary parish. As a historian and Iraqi scholar who has conducted extensive research on Iraq's armed forces, he is ideally suited to take the measure of our work on the Iraq War and gauge its wider appeal and relevance.

Final Remarks

Anthropology has occupied a marginal place in debates about the war in Iraq for at least four reasons. First, anthropological perspectives are increasingly used by other disciplines (journalism, history, cultural studies, political science, peace and conflict studies). Second, anthropologists define ethnographic research narrowly as participant observation, feel therefore unable to address issues beyond their empirical experience, and thus leave public and scholarly debates in the hands of less self-conscious disciplines. Third, the slow production of ethnographic knowledge (because of long-term fieldwork and the time involved in writing up results) causes anthropologists often to run behind the pace of current affairs. Fourth, anthropologists have a tendency to ignore as non-anthropological, and thus not deserving of ethnographic attention, issues and topics that cannot be studied through fieldwork. However, "As anthropologists, our job is to make another sense of the world, another kind of order. If our notions of fieldwork restrict our possibilities of accessing the social world, and hence our understanding of that world, we must find other ways of doing ethnography while still acknowledging the important influence fieldwork has had on anthropological reasoning" (Melhuus 2002:79).

In this volume we want to demonstrate the importance of using our ethnographic imagination to study war-torn societies at a distance and to emphasize the relevance of anthropology in understanding current affairs by reawakening "a comparative consciousness that illuminates connections—between local and global, between past and present, between anthropologists and those they study, between uses of comparison and implications of its uses" (Nader 1994:86). In-depth interviews and controlled macrocomparisons, as have been done in this book, are only two approaches to the study of inaccessible war zones. Methodological alternatives are telephone interviews with people living in war zones; media analyses; and content analyses of newspapers, broadcasts, and blogs. This volume encourages anthropologists to look at today's world and see where their ethnographic imagination can yield new insights to current debates. We make this call in the conviction that anthropology has much to offer because of the substantial scholarly work done by the anthropology of violence and social suffering, the accumulated ethnographic experience about fieldwork in conflict zones, the development of comparative multisited methodologies, and the occurrence of a compassionate turn in anthropology that emphasizes the empathic understanding of people whose lives are weighed down by social, political, and global forces.

Bibliography

Ahmed, Akbar, and Cris Shore. 1995. *The Future of Anthropology: Its Relevance to the Contemporary World*. London: Athlone.
Appadurai, Arjun. 1996. *Modernity at Large: Cultural Dimensions of Globalization*. Minneapolis: University of Minnesota Press.
———. 2006. *Fear of Small Numbers: An Essay on the Geography of Anger*. Durham, N.C.: Duke University Press.
Benedict, Ruth. 1974 [1946]. *The Chrysanthemum and the Sword: Patterns of Japanese Culture*. New York: New American Library.
Besteman, Catherine, and Hugh Gusterson, eds. 2005. *Why America's Top Pundits Are Wrong: Anthropologists Talk Back*. Berkeley: University of California Press.
Blair, Tony. 2005. The Threat of Global Terrorism. In *A Matter of Principle: Humanitarian Arguments for War in Iraq*, ed. Thomas Cushman, 340–51. Berkeley: University of California Press.
Bowen, John R., and Roger Petersen. 1999. Introduction: Critical Comparisons. In *Critical Comparisons in Politics and Culture*, ed. John R. Bowen and Roger Petersen, 1–20. Cambridge: Cambridge University Press.
Brown, Keith, and Catherine Lutz. 2007. Grunt Lit: The Participant-Observers of Empire. *American Ethnologist* 34 (2):322–28.
Fox, Richard G., and Andre Gingrich. 2002. Introduction to *Anthropology, by Comparison*, ed. Andre Gingrich and Richard G. Fox, 1–24. London: Routledge.
Gingrich, Andre. 2002. When Ethnic Minorities Are "Dethroned": Towards a Methodology of Self-Reflexive, Controlled Macrocomparison. In *Anthropology, by Comparison*, ed. Andre Gingrich and Richard G. Fox, 225–48. London: Routledge.
González, Roberto J. 2007. Towards Mercenary Anthropology? *Anthropology Today* 23 (3):14–19.
———. 2009. *American Counterinsurgency: Human Science and the Human Terrain*. Chicago: Prickly Paradigm Press.
Gorer, Geoffrey. 1953. National Character: Theory and Practice. In *The Study of Cul-*

ture at a Distance, ed. Margaret Mead and Rhoda Métraux, 57–82. Chicago: University of Chicago Press.

Gough, Kathleen. 1968. New Proposals for Anthropologists. *Current Anthropology* 9 (5):403–35.

Gupta, Akhil, and James Ferguson. 1992. Beyond "Culture": Space, Identity, and the Politics of Difference. *Cultural Anthropology* 7 (1):6–23.

Gusterson, Hugh. 2007. Anthropology and Militarism. *Annual Review of Anthropology* 36:155–75.

Hannerz, Ulf. 1992. *Cultural Complexity: Studies in the Social Organization of Meaning*. New York: Columbia University Press.

———. 1996. *Transnational Connections*. London: Routledge.

Hastrup, Kirsten. 2002. Anthropology's Comparative Consciousness: The Case of Human Rights. In *Anthropology, by Comparison*, ed. Andre Gingrich and Richard G. Fox, 27–43. London: Routledge.

Herzfeld, Michael. 2001. *Anthropology: Theoretical Practice in Culture and Society*. Malden: Blackwell.

Hinton, Alexander Laban. 2005. *Why Did They Kill? Cambodia in the Shadow of Genocide*. Berkeley: University of California Press.

Holy, Ladislav. 1987. Introduction: Description, Generalization and Comparison: Two Paradigms. In *Comparative Anthropology*, ed. Ladislav Holy, 1–21. Oxford: Basil Blackwell.

Howe, Leo. 1987. Caste in Bali and India: Levels of Comparison. In *Comparative Anthropology*, ed. Ladislav Holy, 135–52. Oxford: Basil Blackwell.

Kipp, Jacob, Lester Grau, Karl Prinslow, and Don Smith. 2006. The Human Terrain System: A CORDS for the 21st Century. *Military Review* (September/October):8–15.

Kleinman, Arthur, Veena Das, and Margaret Lock. 1997a. Introduction. In *Social Suffering*, ed. Arthur Kleinman, Veena Das, and Margaret Lock, ix–xxvii. Berkeley: University of California Press.

———, eds. 1997b. *Social Suffering*. Berkeley: University of California Press.

Lock, Margaret. 2002. *Twice Dead: Organ Transplants and the Reinvention of Death*. Berkeley: University of California Press.

Marcus, George E. 1995. Ethnography in/of the World System: The Emergence of Multi-Sited Ethnography. *Annual Review of Anthropology* 24:95–117.

———. 2006. What Is at Stake—and Is Not—in the Idea and Practice of Multi-Sited Ethnography. In *Anthropology in Theory: Issues in Epistemology*, ed. Henrietta L. Moore and Todd Sanders, 618–21. Malden: Blackwell.

McFate, Montgomery. 2005. Anthropology and Counterinsurgency: The Strange Story of Their Curious Relationship. *Military Review* (March–April):1–46.

Mead, Margaret. 1953. The Study of Culture at a Distance. In *The Study of Culture at a Distance*, ed. Margaret Mead and Rhoda Métraux, 3–53. Chicago: University of Chicago Press.

Mead, Margaret, and Rhoda Métraux, eds. 1953. *The Study of Culture at a Distance*. Chicago: University of Chicago Press.

Melhuus, Marit. 2002. Issues of Relevance: Anthropology and the Challenges of

Cross-Cultural Comparison. In *Anthropology, by Comparison*, ed. Andre Gingrich and Richard G. Fox, 70–91. London: Routledge.

Moore, Sally Falk. 2005. Comparisons: Possible and Impossible. *Annual Review of Anthropology* 34:1–11.

Nader, Laura. 1994. Comparative Consciousness. In *Assessing Cultural Anthropology*, ed. Robert Borofsky, 84–96. New York: McGraw-Hill.

Peteet, Julie. 2005. *Landscape of Hope and Despair: Palestinian Refugee Camps.* Philadelphia: University of Pennsylvania Press.

Petraeus, David H. 2006. Learning Counterinsurgency: Observations from Soldiering in Iraq. *Military Review* (special edition: Counterinsurgency Reader) (October):45–55.

Price, David H. 2008. *Anthropological Intelligence: The Deployment and Neglect of American Anthropology in the Second World War.* Durham, N.C.: Duke University Press.

Renzi, Fred. 2006. Networks: Terra Incognita and the Case for Ethnographic Intelligence. *Military Review* (special edition: Counterinsurgency Reader) (October):180–86.

Robben, Antonius C. G. M. 2005. *Political Violence and Trauma in Argentina.* Philadelphia: University of Pennsylvania Press.

Rohde, David. 2007. Army Enlists Anthropology in War Zones. *New York Times*, October 5.

Schafft, Gretchen E. 2004. *From Racism to Genocide: Anthropology in the Third Reich.* Urbana: University of Illinois Press.

Scheper-Hughes, Nancy. 1995. The Primacy of the Ethical: Propositions for a Militant Anthropology. *Current Anthropology* 36 (3):409–20.

Scheper-Hughes, Nancy, and Philippe Bourgois, eds. 2003. *Violence in War and Peace: An Anthology.* Malden: Blackwell.

Selmeski, Brian R. 2007. Who Are the Security Anthropologists? *Anthropology News* 48 (5):11–12.

Sluka, Jeffrey A. 1989. *Hearts and Minds, Water and Fish: Support for the IRA and INLA in a Northern Irish Ghetto.* Greenwich, Conn.: JAI Press.

Sluka, Jeffrey A., and Antonius C. G. M. Robben. 2007. Fieldwork in Cultural Anthropology: An Introduction. In *Ethnographic Fieldwork: An Anthropological Reader*, ed. Antonius C. G. M. Robben and Jeffrey A. Sluka, 1–28. Malden: Blackwell.

Wolf, Eric R. 1999. *Envisioning Power: Ideologies of Dominance and Crisis.* Berkeley: University of California Press.

Yans-McLaughlin, Virginia. 1986. Science, Democracy, and Ethics: Mobilizing Culture and Personality for World War II. In *Malinowski, Rivers, Benedict and Others: Essays on Culture and Personality*, ed. George W. Stocking Jr., 184–217. Madison: University of Wisconsin Press.

Yengoyan, Aram A. 2006. Introduction: On the Issue of Comparison. In *Modes of Comparison: Theory and Practice*, ed. Aram A. Yengoyan, 1–27. Ann Arbor: University of Michigan Press.

Chapter 1
"Night Fell on a Different World": Dangerous Visions and the War on Terror, a Lesson from Cambodia

Alexander Laban Hinton

Most of us try not to think it: the sky raining paper and ashes; a couple holding hands as they step off the ledge of a skyscraper; sleek modern towers billowing fire, smoke, debris, and human bodies; rescue workers climbing stairs to their end; a skyline gouged by an atomic plume; an unmatched shoe lying on the ground; survivors suited in dust and blood, the living dead; a crushed stroller; the smoldering graveyard of twisted steel and debris that became "Ground Zero"; unclaimed cell phones used by air passengers making their last calls; the smell and taste of the acrid air; and, perhaps most terrifying, the thoughts of the doomed in the moments before they jumped or were incinerated or crushed to death. These images are difficult to contemplate, let alone write about. Words come up short against a void, a rupture of the ordinary that seems almost unimaginable, the stuff of books and novels that does not belong in our everyday life.

When the first plane hit, I was at a Queens gym using the Stairmaster, trying to get some exercise after caring for my nine-month-old daughter, who liked to rise at 4:45 A.M. each day. Looking up at the gymnasium television, I saw smoke pouring out of the North Tower. I left quickly. On the way home, I stopped at the local bagel store, where the manager was telling another patron, "I hope we bomb the hell out of them." By the time I reached home, the second plane had hit the South Tower.

When the first tower imploded, people didn't know what to say. Even the normally unruffled news anchors sat stunned and speechless, like their viewers, for a moment. When they found words, they could only say the obvious, "The tower just collapsed."

That day was like no other I can remember, when icons of routine, control, and order, like these normally stoic newscasters, disheveled. Like a taut spring, our government unraveled: a president in flight, senators on the run, and panic-stricken staff fleeing the White House. All the while, as the arteries leading out of New York City constricted, the television provided two constants that heightened an already intense state of anxious anticipation: replay after replay of the towers being struck and collapsing, and a "zipper" at the bottom of the screen, under the headline "America under Attack," flashing rumors of additional targets hit, hijacked planes in the air, and the whereabouts of the government of the world's superpower, which had been sent into hiding by nineteen men armed with box cutters. We seemed to be becoming one of those distant stricken lands we prefer to pity, frightening places safely contained in newspaper headlines and brief television stories.

For a day or two, we lived in the rawness of this moment. The day after, newspapers, while beginning to get their bearings, ran stories with headlines like those of the September 12 edition of the *New York Times*: "When the Unimaginable Happens, and It's Right Outside Your Window," "A Different World," and "An Unfathomable Attack."[1] Breaking from the more typical mode of address connoting confidence and certainty, many of these articles acknowledged that the events of 9/11 pushed the limits of language, leaving us with words that could only point toward the void of the towers' ruin as something "incomprehensible," "unbelievable," "unthinkable," and "inexpressible," terms disfavored in a forward-looking land that celebrates rationality, science, achievement, and progress.

We don't like such voids and turn from them quickly. But in that moment, many of us directly confronted our own mortality, a taken-for-granted sense of safety in the routine, and the limits of meaning and comprehension. If, on a crystal clear day in September as we went about our everyday lives, planes could be flown into the World Trade Center and bring it down, then anything might be possible. Most of us could place ourselves in the picture of that day: a passenger making the last call, a day trader staring at the plane coming in, a mother pushing a stroller on the ground below, a dishwasher in Windows on the World wondering what had happened below, a secretary forced to jump by the intense heat. It could happen to any of us, anywhere, at anytime.

Such thoughts are intensely disconcerting, producing the fear and anxiety that are the stuff of terror. In response, we try to suture the gaps of meaning, stitching them closed with more familiar threads of narrative, metaphor, lexicon, and ritual. By September 12 "the event," so difficult to describe, began to be encased by a date, "9/11," and a series of plotlines. If many people initially described "the event" through inadequate similes ("It was like a movie" or "like Pearl Harbor"), 9/11 was scripted like a cinematic or historical drama, a story with victims and survivors, heroes and villains: firefighters and rescue workers climbing into an inferno to help others; evil terrorists slaughtering the innocent; Mayor Giuliani's heroic "last stand" in his headquarters near the towers and his almost magical ability to be everywhere in Manhattan at once, his manner calm and reassuring; a planeload of passengers who wouldn't go down without a fight. And now, of course, we have TV shows and movies that re-create this narrative at a further remove: the movie *Flight 93*, the television series *24*, the docudrama *The Flight That Fought Back*, a mini-series based on the 9/11 report, and Oliver Stone's *World Trade Center*. What "seemed like a movie" has now become a movie, pushing it more safely into the distance.

Violence is like that, something we often try to encase in more comfortable narratives, explanatory or otherwise, that reduce what seems overwhelming and inexplicable to something that can be controlled and understood. Of course, such efforts are in some ways useful, providing us with meaning, transforming what is existentially horrifying into a less threatening form and helping us try to comprehend and perhaps even prevent violence. The problem, however, is that so much is lost in this narrative process, as a cross-check of *World Trade Center* or *Flight 93* against the voice recordings of the firefighters, passengers on Flight 93, and cell phone calls of people in the towers will quickly reveal.

If President Bush initially dimmed in the backdrop of 9/11, he quickly regained his footing. As people asked, "Who did this?" "How could this happen?" "How could someone hate us so much?" and, most ominously, "Could it happen again?" President Bush began to provide answers through a larger political narrative centered on war and terror. This narrative was told in a language of powerful abstractions and was accompanied by a set of potent images, ranging from pictures of heroic firefighters to Congress singing "God Bless America" on the steps of the Capitol. It was centrally focused on an "us" and a "them" bound in an epic battle, whose contours were already taking shape on the night of September 11, when President Bush told the nation that the country was confronting an "evil" enemy that had attacked "*our* way of life" and that, in the battle to "bring *them* to justice," "*We* will make no distinction between the terrorists who committed these acts and those who harbor them."[2]

With these words that spelled out the first crude version of the "Bush Doctrine," the nation stepped toward the shadows of preemption and unilateralism and began speaking the language of fear and terror, cast in oppositions of "good and evil" and "civilization and barbarism" and grounded in a new vocabulary of color-coded terrorist alerts, sleeper cells, anthrax attacks, Taliban, disaster kits, Ground Zero, and, of course, the "war on terror." We also developed new habits such as keeping disaster kits, planning escape routes, procuring secret stores of Cipro, learning how to seal our windows with duct tape, and purchasing gas masks.

This language was not unfamiliar to me. At the time, I was working on a book on the genocide that took place in Cambodia from 1975 to 1979, when Cambodia was ruled by Pol Pot and his Khmer Rouge radicals (Hinton 2005). When the Khmer Rouge took Cambodia's capital, Phnom Penh, on April 17, 1975, many Cambodians greeted the communist rebels with a cautious optimism, weary from five years of civil war that had torn apart their lives and killed hundreds of thousands of Cambodians. All of the city dwellers were sent to live and work in the countryside, joining the peasantry in what would be one of the most radical revolutions in history.

Over the next three years, eight months, and twenty days, life in Cambodia was radically transformed. Economic production and consumption were collectivized, as Pol Pot and his circle mobilized the entire population to "launch offensives" on the agricultural "front lines" to initiate a "super great leap forward." The labor demanded in this "battle" against nature was backbreaking, monotonous, and unceasing. Everyday freedoms were abolished. Buddhism and other forms of religious worship were banned. Money, markets, and media disappeared. Travel, public gatherings, and communication were highly restricted. Contact with the outside world vanished; only a trickle of news filtered through monotonous propaganda broadcasts.

In addition, the state tried to control the minds and bodies of the masses, determining what they ate and did each day, pronouncing whom they would marry, constraining how they spoke, insisting upon what they should think, and, most insidiously, deciding who would live and die. In the Khmer Rouge world, everyone had to display a proper revolutionary consciousness; thinking about the past was a sign of subversion or, even worse, treason. "To keep you is no gain," the Khmer Rouge warned. "To destroy you is no loss."

Most Cambodians dwelt in an emotionally numbing world of terror, uncertain if they would suddenly be accused, unsure if they would awaken from the night. Not surprisingly, Cambodians still refer to the Khmer Rouge era as "Hell on Earth," "The Prison without Walls," or "The Fire without Smoke." As one man explained to me, "Everyone suffered as if they were in jail. We were ordered around and watched closely like prisoners. We were forced to work extremely hard, yet given little food. . . . There was no freedom. We weren't allowed to speak or move about freely. And, if there was a problem, a person would be killed and discarded. You always had to be prepared for death" (Hinton 2005:2). In the end, more than 1.7 of Cambodia's 8 million inhabitants, almost a quarter of the population, perished from disease, starvation, overwork, or outright execution in one of the most notorious genocides of the twentieth century.[3]

Thirty years stand between the violence and terror of this past and that of the present. Clearly, there are many differences in terms of historical context and in terms of the extremity of the violence and suffering: genocide, for example, is not taking place in Iraq, though the potential has been there. Nevertheless, the war on terror has strong echoes with the Cambodian case, resonances that should give us pause to consider what lessons can be learned from the Cambodian genocide. In this essay, I trace one of these echoes, the dangers of Manichaean visions (particularly those that emerge in the aftermath of socioeconomic upheaval), which became clear after the attack on the World Trade Center.

On 9/11 I was in the midst of analyzing a Khmer Rouge tract that asks "Who are we?" Written at a time when political paranoia was rampant, a series of brutal purges were under way, and military conflict with Vietnam was escalating, the text attempts to elucidate the boundaries of the political community. It begins, "It is necessary to draw a clear line between us and the enemy and stand on our side to make the revolution. . . . let us determine who we are." If "we" included "our nation, people, worker-peasant class, revolution, [and] collective system," the "enemy" encompassed "imperialist aggressors and lackeys of all stripes" and "the enemy which is planted within our revolutionary ranks."[4] The speech crystallized divisions that ran rampant in the Khmer Rouge vision of the world, which depicted everything in Manichaean terms: as a pure "we" that was under extreme threat by an impure enemy ("them") that both threatened from without and was insidiously "burrowing from within." Ultimately, the tract differentiates "us" and "the enemy" in terms of "political, ideological, organizational, sentimental and traditional views and politics."[5] The key to distinguishing between friends and enemies was political consciousness, or the extent to which a person was "mindful" of the party "line" and "standpoint." Group traits followed this premise. "Enemy" groups, ranging from imperialist lackeys to the "feudo-capitalist/landowning class," were those having a strong "private stand."

On the surface, identifying these enemies was relatively easy. When cadre received orders to purify the cooperative by killing members of the "feudal-capitalist/landowning" class, they could check local registers and see who belonged to this crystallized category of difference. Party documents and speeches defined each of these classes roughly as follows: feudalists (royalty, former ministers, provincial governors, high-ranking Lon Nol military officials), capitalists (businessmen, particularly those with foreign trading connections), petty capitalists (high civil servants, "intellectuals," teachers, hairdressers, tailors, craftsmen, small businessmen, low-ranking civil servants, employees, clergy), and landowners (rich peasants who used modern equipment and employed laborers and upper-middle-class peasants who hired laborers to do over 60 percent of their work) (Summers 1987:14–15).[6]

In practice, however, the identification of "enemies" was more difficult. For, given their premise that everything changes, the Democratic Kampuchea (DK) regime also allowed for the possibility that some of these former enemies might transform themselves and become revolutionaries. Therefore, cadre were instructed to examine the extent to which people exhibited "antiproletarian" sentiments and traits. While the "Who Are We?" broadcast did not go into detail about what these traits were, the "Sharpen the Consciousness" tract did. A key trait of an enemy was a strong private stand, which was reflected in "worldview, life-view, economy, morality" and "living and working habits" (Jackson 1989:272, 284). Those having this private stand were drawn to private property, thought primarily of themselves and their families, followed "personal sentiments," tried to oppress others, yearned for the old society, or opposed the party's collective line.

The "we" that belonged in DK society exhibited opposing traits on the collectivist side of the "dividing line"—a "proletarian class worldview," collective stand, renunciation of private property and personal attachments, enthusiasm for the new society, and revolutionary sentiments. The 1978 radio broadcast also explained that a person who "sharpened and clarified" this collective stand would come to feel "a constantly seething hatred for the enemy; a profound revolutionary sentiment toward the oppressed classes; a powerful love for the nation, revolution, collective system and party. These three emotions constitute the basis of the daily fighting spirit."

It is precisely this sort of a Manichaean vision that has too often been used to legitimate mass violence and, in the extreme, the attempted annihilation of entire groups of people—particularly after episodes of sociopolitical upheaval that generate a crisis in meaning and enhance the appeal of reductive visions that provide seemingly clear answers to the existential questions that have been raised.[7]

In Cambodia, the Khmer Rouge came to power after a period of extreme socioeconomic upheaval: the economy broke down in the wake of the Vietnam War; the United States intensively bombed parts of the Cambodian countryside, killing thousands, destroying homes, and inciting many youths to join the antigovernment movement; foreign troops moved at will through strategic areas; Prince Sihanouk was overthrown in a coup headed by pro-U.S. elements; and the country was rocked by a civil war in which as many as six hundred thousand people died. As their lives were torn apart, tens of thousands of Cambodian peasants—particularly the extreme poor and the young—joined the Khmer Rouge in order to restore their king to power, to seek vengeance against the corrupt "oppressors" who were responsible for their impoverishment and for the bombing of their homes, and to find meaning in a chaotic and violent world.

At such moments, people are often drawn to movements and ideologies that promise renewal. Upheaval exacerbates existential anxiety and meaninglessness, contributes to cognitive constriction, and increases the appeal of more simplified schemas for thought and behavior. Genocidal ideologies tap into this anxiety, discontent, and meaninglessness by promoting a blueprint that will lead to a more satisfactory way of life—including the elimination of elements of the population portrayed as the cause of social woes or as a threat to this new social order. Charismatic leaders are often central to this process, as they espouse a certainty and purpose to which their followers are drawn and with which they want and need to identify (see Lindholm 1990). Not all modern genocides are full-fledged revitalization movements, but most contain the notion that the annihilation of a threatening or impure group will help create the preconditions for a better life. As I discuss below, the rhetorics of Osama bin Laden, while sharing themes with some of the Bush administration narratives, more closely resemble that of a revitalization movement and at times border on suggesting genocidal intent in legitimating the indiscriminate destruction of U.S. civilians. A case could even be made that the attack on the World Trade Center was a "genocidal massacre."[8]

A similar sort of vision—not genocidal but certainly Manichaean—emerged in wake of 9/11, as the world was reduced to an epic struggle between good and evil that allowed no shades of gray and demanded that everyone take sides. This Manichaean vision was prevalent after 9/11, particularly in the discourse of the Bush administration, which was often tinged with a cinematic quality that resonated with epics like Star Wars, a John Wayne western, and Orientalist movies such as *The Mummy* (both the original and the remake). President Bush's landmark September 20, 2001, "Address to a Joint Session of Congress and the American People"[9]—which provided an explanation for what had happened on 9/11, who did it, why they did it, and what the United States would do about it—provides a clear example of the Manichaean thought embedded within the political narratives of the Bush administration.

Like the "Who Are We?" speech, much of President Bush's speech is concerned with making abstract distinctions between "us" and "them" and distinguishing each group's characteristics. As a ritual event, a "state of the union" address—held before members of the Congress representing every part of the country, members of the president's cabinet, Supreme Court justices, the Joint Chiefs of Staff, and, through television, the Internet, and radio, the entire nation—is an exercise in *communitas*, one that, in the aftermath of 9/11, was particularly weighted with emotional force and a sense of liminality, or momentous passage into a new mode of national being that had been "brought upon us in a single day—and night fell on a different world."

President Bush attempts to further amplify this sense of national community through the constant use of first-person plural ("we") and possessive plural pronouns ("our"), by making reference to key national symbols (the flag, the national anthem, Republicans and Democrats joining to sing "God Bless America"), communal activities ("the lighting of candles, the giving of blood, the saying of prayers"), shared emotions ("Tonight we are a country awakened to danger. . . . Our grief has turned to anger, and anger to resolution"), and a common purpose ("we are a country . . . called to defend freedom . . . [and] bring our enemies to justice"). His speech immediately creates an isomorphism between the "state of the union" and the strength and "courage" of the heroes, singling out Todd Beamer, the United Flight 93 passenger who is said to have led the passenger revolt with the yell "Let's roll," "the rescuers, working past exhaustion," and George Howard, a decorated police officer who was buried under the avalanche of debris when the second tower fell and whose mother had given President

Bush his police shield. Heroism was further personified by the presence of Mayor Giuliani in the audience.

As the "Who Are We?" speech so clearly brings into focus, group identity is predicated on contrasts: an "us" requires division from a "them" against whom given attributes are asserted, projected, or denied. In the context of mass violence, such oppositions often involve naturalizing or organic claims, as the "sacred" soil or social body is constructed as under dire threat—just as the Khmer Rouge tract warns that the revolutionary collective is threatened by "the enemy which is planted within our revolutionary ranks" and the "expansionist, annexationist Vietnamese enemy," a warning echoed elsewhere by the omnipresent Khmer Rouge discussion of the dangers of "counterrevolutionaries," "microbes," "plant parasites," and "hidden enemies burrowing from within." Feelings of stress and anxiety, such as those that arose in the context of the Khmer Rouge revolution and after 9/11, may be assuaged by locating the source of the threat in such a seemingly tangible enemy "other," though, ironically, such assertions of certainty are undercut by more complex realities on the ground.

A key way in which organic and naturalized national identifications are asserted is through metaphor and metonymy, as the nation is depicted as a body and parts come to stand for wholes. September 11 reverberated with such connotations, with the World Trade Center standing as a symbol of capitalism, modernity, progress, globalization, civilization, and U.S. world domination. In a straightforward manner, then, the attacks constituted an assault on these key U.S. identifications. On a deeper embodied level the towers themselves, through a common metaphor that likens a building to a body and especially the head (buildings have "faces" and windows that look like eyes and are sometimes even represented as alive in popular culture), may stand for the American social body, an association that resonates with each person's sense of bodily being.

The linguist George Lakoff has argued that part of the symbolic power of the attack on the World Trade Center thus comes from its likeness to someone being shot in the head, with the planes as bullets and the fireball that burst upon impact resembling blood spurting out the building "head"; in other words, it connotes an assassination with the fall of each tower resembling the collapse of the person who has metaphorically been shot (Lakoff 2001). In a similar vein, Galway Kinnell ends perhaps the most famous poem written about 9/11 to date, "When the Towers Fell," with these lines: "As each tower goes down, it concentrates / into itself, transforms itself / infinitely slowly into a black hole / infinitesimally small; mass / without space, where each light, / each life, put out, lies down within us" (Kinnell 2002).

The collapse and ruins of the towers are also highly evocative, conjuring images of death and mass annihilation. Kinnell places 9/11 in "a lineage / in the twentieth-century history of violent death" that includes the castration and lynching of black men, trench warfare in World War I, the Holocaust (invoking Paul Celan's famous image of "black milk at daybreak" from his poem "Death Fugue"), state murder,

"atomic blasts wiping cities off the earth, firebombings
    the same
death marches, starvations, assassinations, disappearances,
entire countries turned into rubble, minefields, mass graves.
Seeing the towers vomit these black omens, that the last century
    dumped into
this one, for us to dispose of, we know
they are our futures, that is our own black milk crossing the
    sky.

As we shall see, President Bush invokes a similar sort of genealogy of twentieth-century violence but frames it in a very different way.

Other people interpreted the destruction of the towers in more biblical terms as a sort of twenty-first-century Armageddon. The ash covered survivors; fire and smoke, excruciating pain and suffering, and twisted molten conjured images of hell; and some even claimed to have seen the faces of the devil or other evil visages in the conflagration.[10] Still others saw signs of Christian healing and redemption, such as the steel beams forming crosses that were discovered in the rubble of Ground Zero, one of which, standing twenty feet tall and weighing two tons, became a powerful landmark at the site. It served as a place for rescue workers to pray and as a backdrop for religious services at Ground Zero, and was blessed by a Franciscan priest, inscribed with religious graffiti, featured in a poster, and left standing on the site for years until it was temporarily removed to nearby St. Peter's Church (it will become part of the 9/11 memorial).[11] President Bush evoked this spirit of Christian redemption in his September 11, 2001, address to the nation, which invoked Psalm 23: "Even though I walk through the valley of the shadow of death, I fear no evil, for You are with me."[12]

On yet another level, 9/11 and Ground Zero signified a sort of twenty-first-century Armageddon in terms of an epic battle between the forces of good and evil that was inflected by Christian idioms and symbolism. Per-

haps the most overt expression of this framing emerged in informal remarks President Bush made on the South Lawn on September 16, 2001—
"on the Lord's Day," he noted—when he referred to the war on terror as a
"crusade" ("This crusade, this war on terrorism is going to take a while"),[13]
a term that many viewed as directly invoking the violent medieval campaigns Christians waged against Muslims. One of President Bush's close
friends told the *New York Times* that the 9/11 attacks gave the president a
"wholly transformed sense of himself and his presidency. . . . Mr. Bush
clearly feels he has encountered his reason for being, a conviction informed
and shaped by the president's own strain of Christianity. 'I think, in his
frame, this is what God has asked him to do,' the acquaintance said. 'It
offers him enormous clarity'" (Bruni 2001). This sense of renewed Christian purpose in the midst of a Manichaean-like struggle pervades President
Bush's post-9/11 speeches, ranging from his September 16, 2001, assertion
that his administration would "rid the world of the evildoers" to his September 20, 2001, address in which he stated that "in our grief and anger we
have found our mission and our moment" and that "God is not neutral"
in the eternal war between "freedom and fear, justice and cruelty" and, by
implication, good and evil.[14] In fact, until recently, President Bush's top
speechwriter was Michael Gerson, an evangelical Christian known to infuse
Bush's speeches, including those written after 9/11, with religious allu-
sions—though President Bush was also heavily involved in the process of
editing and redrafting his speeches (Rutenberg 2006).

President Bush's constant abstract invocations of "evil" ("Today, we
saw evil"), "evil acts," or "evildoers" resonates with conservative Christian
conceptions of evil as an inherent force in the world against which "good"
must eternally struggle (Lakoff 2001). Along these lines, the forces of
"good" have a moral right to strike back against "evil," a notion that un-
derpins President Bush's implicit calls for righteous retribution or retalia-
tion in the name of justice (Lakoff 2001). It is implicit in President Bush's
September 20 address, which defines what happened as an act of war ("On
September the 11th, enemies of freedom committed an act of war against
our country"). In the midst of chaos and upheaval, which were powerfully
symbolized by the attack on and collapse of the towers, these sorts of defi-
nitions and framings provided answers that helped fill in the gaps of meaning and rub away the dark edges of fear, grief, anxiety, and terror (replacing
them with "courage," "endurance," "strength," "anger," and so forth—
"Our grief has turned to anger, and anger to resolution").

The need for answers is implicit in the structure of the September 20 address, in which President Bush notes that "Americans have many questions tonight" and then goes on to rhetorically pose four of these questions, the first of which, like the "Who Are We?" speech, was concerned with defining the enemy: "Americans are asking: Who attacked our country?" The explanatory narratives that followed had a cinematic quality. Like a movie, the plot has a villain, "a collection of loosely affiliated terrorist organizations known as al Qaeda" who "practice a fringe form of Islamic extremism" and are led by "a person named Osama bin Laden." The goal of this group of "murderers," President Bush notes, is "remaking the world—and imposing its radical beliefs on people everywhere." To this end, "the terrorists' directive commands them to kill Christians and Jews, to kill all Americans, and to make no distinction among military and civilians, including women and children." "Trained in the tactics of terror," these diabolical figures are "sent to hide in countries around the world to plot evil and destruction" in order to implement their "vision for the world," which is exemplified by Afghanistan, where people are "brutalized" and "starving," women are repressed, television is banned, and basic liberties are curtailed ("A man can be jailed in Afghanistan if his beard is not long enough"). For these reasons, "we are in a country awakened to danger and called to defend freedom. . . . All of this was brought upon us in a single day—and night fell on a different world, a world where freedom itself is under attack." This "war on terror begins with al Qaeda, but it does not end there. It will not end until every terrorist group of global reach has been found, stopped and defeated."

"Americans are asking: Why do they hate us?" What could motivate someone to do something like this? President Bush's speech constructs the motives of al Qaeda primarily in two ways: first, as an inversion of American values and the American "way of life" ("They hate our freedoms—our freedom of religion, our freedom of speech, our freedom to vote and assemble and disagree with one another"); and second, as "murderous ideologues" who kill in the name of their "radical visions." In perhaps the most memorable phrase of the speech, President Bush states, "We have seen their kind before. They are the heirs of all the murderous ideologies of the 20th century. By sacrificing human life to serve their radical visions—by abandoning every value except the will to power—they follow in the path of fascism, and Nazism, and totalitarianism. And they will follow that path all the way, to where it ends: in history's unmarked grave of discarded lies."

"Americans are asking: How will we fight and win this war?" With the characters and motives in place, President Bush's speech provides a script for the future, one that assuaged the feelings of fear and terror. The government would mobilize "every resource at our command"—diplomatic, financial, intelligence, and military—to defeat "the global terror network." On the domestic front, President Bush announced the creation of the Office of Homeland Security, an agency devoted to taking "defensive measures against terrorism to protect Americans." More broadly, President Bush put the military and nation on alert for not just one battle "but a lengthy campaign, unlike any other we have ever seen. It may include dramatic strikes, visible on TV, and covert operations, secret even in success. We will starve terrorists of funding . . . drive them from place to place, until there is no refuge or no rest." He warned, "the only way to defeat terrorism as a threat to our way of life is to stop it, eliminate it, and destroy it where it grows."

This battle would be epic, pitting good against evil, freedom against terror, civilization against barbarism—key terms that recur again and again in public statements about the new "war on terror." It was also a battle in which everyone had to choose sides. To this end, President Bush issued an ultimatum that he would often repeat: "Every nation, in every region, now has a decision to make. Either you are with us, or you are with the terrorists." For this was "not, however, just America's fight. . . . This is the world's fight. This is civilization's fight. This is the fight of all who believe in progress and pluralism, tolerance and freedom." Just days earlier, President Bush and Secretary of State Colin Powell had proclaimed that as a result of this "assault . . . against civilization," the strength of "every civilized nation in the world" would be brought to bear against the "evildoing" "group of barbarians" who, like wild animals, committed "barbaric acts" and lived in "holes" in the "hills" from which they needed to be "smoked out."[15]

Less than a year later in a speech given at a dinner for a Republican Senate candidate, he would refer to this choice between being "with us or against us" as "doctrine,"[16] noting that "Either you love freedom or you stand against the United States of America. . . . history has called us into action. History has given us the opportunity to defend freedom." Such statements also exemplify another theme often found in President's Bush's statements, the sense of being invested with a monumental, almost divine mission (here "history" could easily be replaced with the word "God"), one that, by being fulfilled, will lead to positive transformation and perhaps even transcendence. Thus, President Bush notes several times in this speech that "out of the evil done to America will come some incredible good." As an example, he cites the actions of the passengers on United Flight 93 as "perhaps the most significant moment . . . during 9/11" in the sense that they provide an "example of serving something greater than themselves as we join this war against evil."

"Americans are asking: What is expected of us?" Each American had a role to play in this epic. Like a hero-in-the-making who has been wounded and wrestles with conflicting emotions, Americans would overcome their fears and rise to meet the dark forces allied against them. As President Bush stated in his September 20 address, "Great harm has been done to us. We have suffered great loss. And in our grief and anger we have found our mission and our moment. Freedom and fear are at war. The advance of human freedom . . . now depends on us. Our nation—this generation—will lift a dark threat of violence from our people and our future. . . . We will not tire, we will not falter, and we will not fail." In so doing, each person would achieve a sort of transcendence as they "served something greater than themselves" in the battle of good against evil, freedom against fear, justice against cruelty, civilization against savagery—as had the courageous heroes of 9/11 like Flight 93 passenger Todd Beamer, George Howard the policeman, and Mayor Giuliani. Each person would return to the routines of life, but even as they grappled with their grief and fear during this war against terror, they would always "remember what happened that day" and remain "calm and resolute," patient, patriotic ("uphold the values of America" in this "fight for our principles"), and united with their fellow Americans as evinced by "the unfurling of flags, the lighting of candles, the giving of blood, the saying of prayers," and even the "touching" sight of "Republicans and Democrats joined together on the steps of this Capitol, singing 'God Bless America.'"

As time has passed, we have all watched the war unfold like a drama with sudden plot twists, resurgences of fear and terror, and a surfeit of blood and tragedy. At times it has had the tone of a western, such as when, after being asked if he wanted bin Laden dead, President Bush replied, "I want justice. There's an old poster out west, as I recall, that said, 'Wanted: Dead or Alive.'"[17] And, within a month, the White House released a "Most Wanted Terrorist" list of twenty-two suspects headed by Osama bin Laden, who was profiled by "America Fights Back," a special episode of *America's Most Wanted*, and had a $25 million bounty on his head by November.[18] In a speech announcing the creation of this list, President Bush stated that "the calling of the United States of America" was to "draw the line in the sand against," to wage "war against," and to "round up" these "evildoers."

This statement is strongly reminiscent of the Khmer Rouge "Who Are We?" tract, which asserted that it "is necessary to draw a clear line between us and the enemy." In fact, Khmer Rouge ideology was replete with such spatial and structural metaphors, which were often invoked in terms of construction, as in the constant DK invocation of the importance of "building" the country. Like an engineer's blueprint, Khmer Rouge discourse is filled with the terminology of "lines," "borders," "bases," "stands," "standpoints," and "dividing lines." Ultimately, the DK party "line" delineated a "base" upon which the revolution generally, and individual consciousness in particular, could be "built" or "stand." The true revolutionaries who stood on the proper side of this line would be filled with hatred toward the enemy "counterrevolutionaries," "feudalists," "capitalists," "colonialists," "imperialists," "oppressors," and "traitors" who threatened the DK social community.

As we have seen, a huge rupture of meaning emerged after 9/11, one that the Bush administration attempted to suture with a Manichaean vision that explained what had happened and what would be done about it. If this vision was predicated on a set of structural oppositions and imbued with Christian overtones, it also drew on longstanding constructions of the Oriental "other" that were epitomized by the figure of the Muslim fundamentalist terrorist and most acutely condensed in the figure of Osama bin Laden and his al Qaeda network.

Most broadly, the use of language of animality, savagery, and "the hunt" to describe "terrorists" invokes the trope of the "wild man" that, dating back at least to the Middle Ages, is encountered at the edges of the "civilized" world. Both held in awe and feared, the "wild man" is paradoxical, a being who is necessary for the cohesion of community (by the "wild man's" very opposition to it) while at the same time constituting a dire threat to the social order against which it brushes (through the "wild man's" difference and the exotic and dangerous powers this being contains) (Zulaika 1993). The very notion of the "wild man" helps stabilize categories of group identity, which are always tenuous because of the diversity they contain, and fixes fear and anxiety in a place that, through "the hunt," is ritually vanquished (but then must be re-created anew since this feared and impure "other" is necessary for social cohesion). In other words, the other is the Janus face of identity, a "them" that is necessary for "us" to cohere. Such imagery has been prevalent in the post-9/11 rhetorics of the Bush administration, ranging from the constant description of terrorists as "evil savages" to the assertions of a national community that was coming together to combat a dangerous threat—just as the evils of communists were constantly invoked during the Cold War.

As Edward Said (1994) has argued, such depictions of terrorists have been bound up with a related cluster of ideas about "the Orient" that coalesced after Napoleon's invasion of Egypt in 1798. Like images of the "wild man," these ideas about the Orient have emerged on the cusp of the familiar and the bizarre, as a dizzying array of human complexity is reduced to a set of essentialized stereotypes that ultimately say more about "us" than a "them" represented through half-truths, broad generalizations, and outright fictions. Moreover, this set of ideas has provided a legitimization for colonial and imperial ambitions, as "savage" or "backward" locals are conquered in the name of the "white man's burden" or "civilizing mission." The Middle East, in particular, has come to represent the antithesis of the "modern" West in the current historical moment, as Arabs and Muslims are associated with the following characteristics:

- barbarity (versus civilization)
- backwardness (versus progress)
- superstition (versus science)
- tyranny (versus democracy and freedom)
- femininity (versus the masculine West)
- irrationality (versus rationality)
- being childlike (versus adult)
- emotion and sensuality (versus having control over baser drives)
- undeveloped (versus developed)
- stasis (versus advancement).

Said argues that these oppositions are embodied in and perpetuated through a variety of institutions, such as the academic discipline of "Oriental studies," literature, and the media.

For example, the movie *The Mummy*, set in Egypt, which is often depicted as the epicenter of the Orient, is structured around the tension between science and superstition in an encounter with the "bizarre," as the "rational," "scientific" archaeologists, who are symbolically domesticating and bringing modernity to the Middle East, dredge up "the mummy," a symbol of superstition, danger, backwardness, stasis, sexuality, irrationality, tyranny, and evil. In the original version (1932), the mummy, the ancient Egyptian high priest Imhotep who has been revived, is even portrayed by Boris "the bizarre" Karloff; in the 1999 remake, this role is played by Arnold

Vosloo, who was later featured as the Arab terrorist mastermind Habib Marwan in the 2004 season of *24*, the Fox television series starring the (anti)hero counterterrorism agent Jack Bauer. A similar set of Orientalist tropes are manifest in numerous other movies, including *Lawrence of Arabia*, *300*, *Ali Baba and the Forty Thieves*, and even *Aladdin*.

These images circulate throughout President Bush's statements, such as his September 16, 2001, reference to the war on terrorism as a "crusade" and the terrorists as "barbaric," "evil people" who "can't stand freedom" and whose "widespread organization [is] based upon one thing: terrorizing."[19] President Bush's September 20 speech depicts the terrorists in a similar fashion. If the United States believes in "progress and pluralism, tolerance and freedom,"[20] the terrorists implicitly manifest the opposite qualities, such as regression, absolutism, intolerance, and tyranny. They are of a "kind" and are the "heirs" of "fascism" and "totalitarianism," radicals who "hate our freedoms" and want to create a fundamentalist regime along the lines of that imposed by the Taliban in Afghanistan. Even as President Bush commendably distinguishes between Muslims in general and terrorist "radicals," his use of the term "terrorist" is vague and open-ended enough to cause slippage. Moreover, his assertion that "we have found our mission and our moment" in the struggle to "destroy [terrorism] where it grows" and to "advance human freedom—the great achievement of our time" suggests a legitimating warrant to bring freedom and democracy to the Middle East, a "civilizing mission" that would be elucidated more clearly after the start of the war in Iraq.

Through the use of such dehistoricized Orientalist and "wild man" imagery, the Bush administration has been able to depict terrorists in a reductive manner that fits more easily into the Manichaean visions it has been asserting. Doing so explains away the violence since, according to our folk conceptions, it is self-evident and "natural" that evil, irrational, savage, hateful, animal-like people, such as Osama bin Laden and his terrorist network, do things like brutally murder innocents. Implicit within this conception is a broader suggestion of American innocence and victimhood—that without provocation or reason (beyond their evil nature), *they* attacked *us* and we must respond and destroy this threat if we are to protect our "way of life."

Such reductive explanations are quite thin and redirect our attention from a deeper understanding of the roots of 9/11 and Osama bin Laden and his al Qaeda network. Instead of asking "why do they hate us," a question that rhetorically splits the world into the us/them divides of the all-too-often invoked "clash of civilizations" framework, we should ask, "What motivated Osama bin Laden and his followers to destroy the towers?" even as we firmly condemn their violent actions. An obvious place to look would be the many interviews and statements that Osama bin Laden and his associates have made. The detailed content of these texts, however, has been almost completely ignored by the Bush administration which, with considerable success, asked U.S. media outlets to self-censor such statements for fear that they might contain hidden messages to launch attacks: "At best, Osama bin Laden's message is propaganda, calling on people to kill Americans. At worst, he could be issuing orders to his followers to initiate such attacks."[21] Fifty-two percent of the Americans interviewed in a Pew Research Center poll agreed that censorship was legitimate to safeguard national security.[22] Even as Osama bin Laden's statements began to be excerpted and summarized in much of the media, they remained available on the Internet and, more recently, a few books (Hamud 2005; Lawrence 2005b).

A reading of Osama bin Laden's interviews and statements reveals a Manichaean vision of the world that, while deplorable in its advocacy of violence, is not "irrational." In fact, there are some interesting parallels to the rhetorics of the post-9/11 Bush administration. While shifting according to the historical moment, bin Laden's statements, which draw extensively but selectively on Koranic scripture and exegesis (Gwynne 2006), center around a core set of themes. Several of these are manifest in one of bin Laden's earliest statements, a 1996 fatwa, "Declaration of War Against the Americans Occupying the Land of the Two Holy Places."

As the title suggests, one of bin Laden's primary complaints is about U.S. foreign policy in the Middle East, which he views as part of a long-standing attempt by the West to gain control over the Middle East that dates back to the Crusades. This perception was galvanized after the first Gulf war when, long after the conflict had ended, U.S. troops remained in Saudi Arabia, where "the two Holy Places," Mecca (Islam's holiest city and destination during the annual hajj) and Medina (the burial site of Muhammed), are located. Invoking scripture that justifies defensive struggle (jihad) against invaders who have attacked the Islamic community (*ummah*), bin Laden argues that this "occupation"—along with a host of other acts of aggression—gives the mujahideen the "legitimate right" to "carry arms against the *Kufr* [non-believers] until they are expelled, defeated, and humiliated. . . . While you carry arms on our land, our legitimate and moral duty is to terrorize you."[23]

Bin Laden's list of complaints about the United States is a long one. He condemns U.S. hypocrisy in supporting Saudi Arabia, which he refers to as "the land of the two holy places" since he views the Saudi government as illegitimate and corrupt. Despite its claims to advocate for human rights, bin Laden states, the United States has supported a government that has repressed and jailed Muslim scholars and other opposition figures while tightly controlling media outlets. Moreover, because they have generally advanced policies—such as allowing the "American Crusader forces . . . to occupy the Kingdom for many years" and setting the price of oil at levels that are far too low—that are against the interests of Muslims and because it has "man-made law instead of Sharia," the Saudi rulers have committed one of the "ten voiders" that "strip a person from his Islamic status and convert a Muslim into a *Mushrik*, a non-believer" (Hamud 2005:38, 36, 38).

Similarly, bin Laden condemns U.S. support of the Israeli "occupation" of Palestine and Jerusalem, the site of the third holiest site in Islam, Al-Aqsa mosque. As part of its "Zionist-Crusader alliance," bin Laden asserts, the United States has supplied the Israelis with money and munitions that have been used to massacre Palestinians. Such violence is part of a larger pattern of U.S. "aggression, inequity, and injustice" against the Islamic nation (*ummah*), one that can be seen in a host of other locales, ranging from Iraq (where UN sanctions were responsible for the deaths of hundreds of thousands of Iraqi children) to Algeria (where an Islamic party intending to impose sharia law after winning an election was violently repressed) to "massacres of Muslims that send shivers throughout the body and shake the conscience [that] also occurred in Tajikistan, Burma, Kashmir, Assam, the Philippines, Fatani, Ogadin, Somalia, Eritrea, Chechnya, and Bosnia-Herzegovina" (Hamud 2005:33). In his post-9/11 statements, bin Laden adds Afghanistan and Iraq (again) to this list.

Two points emerge clearly as one reads bin Laden's statements: in contrast to the reductive "wild man" and Orientalist rhetorics that have been used to describe him, bin Laden is not "irrational" and his actions are directly linked to a history of perceived wrongs. Bin Laden even complained about the way in which the actions of his group had been depicted in a dehistoricized manner after 9/11, stating, "Those who condemned the [9/11] attacks viewed them in isolation and failed to connect them to past events. They looked at the result, not the causes. . . . The blessed and successful strikes [on 9/11] were but reactions to what has happened in our lands—in Palestine and in Iraq, and in other places. . . . 9/11 was the response."[24] More broadly, bin Laden, who took notice of President Bush's September 16,

2001, reference to the war on terror as a "crusade" ("before the whole world he clearly described this as a crusader war"), situates American foreign policy as a continuation of the Crusades ("These battles cannot be viewed in any respect as isolated. Rather, they are part of a chain of the long, fierce, and ugly Crusader war") that are now being led by President Bush, who "carries the cross, raises its banner high, and stands at the front of the line" of the "new Crusaders."[25]

In another attempt to explain his motives, bin Laden issued an October 26, 2002, "Statement to America" that, ironically, was not widely broadcast in the United States because of the media's self-censorship policy. Noting that people in the United States were asking about the motives of his group, bin Laden explains, "we fight you because you attacked us and continue to attack us" in places like Palestine, Iraq, and the "Arabian gulf."[26] Despite its claims to be a "land of freedom" and to uphold international law, bin Laden asserts, the United States has repeatedly acted in a contrary manner, thus legitimating acts of "revenge" like 9/11: "We have the right to destroy the villages and towns of whoever has destroyed our own villages and towns. We have the right to destroy the economy of whoever has stolen our wealth. We have the right to kill the civilians of whoever has killed our civilians" (Hamud 2005:97). Updating his critique of U.S. hypocrisy about human rights, bin Laden argues that after 9/11, the United States became exactly like the governments it condemns in its annual human rights reports: "You then used the methods of the repressive countries you used to criticize," including torture and the arrest of "thousands of Muslims and Arabs" who were "held in secret custody without reason or trial." Guantánamo, in particular, "is a historical embarrassment to America and its values. It screams 'hypocrites' in your faces. What is the value of your signature on any agreement or treaty?" (Hamud 2005:101).

Even if they are not "irrational" or dehistoricized, bin Laden's statements are nevertheless premised on a violent Manichaean vision, one that divides the world into an us (the *ummah* or Islamic nation) versus a them (the Western "crusaders" and *Kufr*)[27] who are invested with contrasting qualities of purity and goodness (the Faithful who follow the Prophet) versus contamination and evil (the "evil" infidel; "friends of Satan"). Indeed, bin Laden lambastes the United States at every turn. In his "Statement to America," for example, bin Laden "invites" the people of the United States to Islam, which he characterizes as the religion of "sincerity, manners, righteousness, mercy, honor, purity, and piety," one that "enjoins good and forbids evil with the hand, tongue, and heart" while valuing "the equality of all people without regard to color, sex, or language."[28] The United States, in contrast, is "the worst civilization in the history of mankind," characterized by "oppression, lies, immorality and debauchery," including the "immoral acts of fornication, homosexuality, intoxicants, gambling, and [usury]." Governed by man-made laws (versus sharia), the United States "permits immorality as a pillar of personal freedom" that has led to incest, gambling, drug use, sexual diseases, and the exploitation of women (Hamud 2005:98–99). All of this is in addition to the "many acts of oppression, tyranny, and injustice" (Hamud 2005:100) that the United States has carried out in the Middle East and elsewhere.

Besides this basic Manichaean structure that divides the world into the forces of good and evil, bin Laden's Manichaean vision has several striking similarities to that of President Bush. Both claim to be acting because of a wrong (the 9/11 attacks versus U.S. foreign policy in the Middle East), as when bin Laden explains that "September 11th was but a reaction to the continuing injustice and oppression."[29] Each asserts the legitimacy of his (violent) actions as a necessary response to forces of evil that have attacked and threaten a "way of life" (American "freedoms" versus Islamic values). Bush and bin Laden both draw on scripture to depict their actions as an almost divine mission. And both claim to be acting in the name of a broader cause (the fight of "civilization" against barbarity as opposed to the Islamic jihad against the Crusader invaders). It is crucial to acknowledge these parallels in order to understand, at least partly, why bin Laden's message is attractive to many Muslims.

At the same time, there are also some crucial differences in bin Laden's messages that further enhance their appeal to Muslims. Bin Laden's rhetorics are much more explicitly and deeply enmeshed in scripture, even if he uses it selectively and at times out of context (Gwynne 2006). Moreover, he tries to define the conflict in explicitly religious terms whereas President Bush disavows that the war on terror is a war on Islam (though his religious overtones implicitly suggest that it is). Thus, bin Laden argues for the "fundamentally religious nature of the war. The people of the East are Muslims. They sympathize with the Muslims against the people of the West, who are the new Crusaders."[30]

Here his remarks echo Samuel Huntington's popularized argument about the "clash of civilizations," which asserts that in the post–Cold War era, the fault lines of conflict will run along the lines of the cultural differences of various civilizations (Huntington 1993). This argument is problematic in a number of respects, such as its failure to account for the diversity that exists within the "civilizations" Huntington asserts, its inability to explain the frequent "clash within civilizations," and its ignorance of what we might call the "click of civilizations"—the many ways in which cultural groups are deeply interlinked in the global world, often in ways that explicitly work against conflict (for example, common interest in not upsetting global economic flows).[31] What is perhaps most troublesome about Huntington's argument is the way in which it provides people with a buzzword—one that can be heard in the media, Congress, and governments around the world—to explain away the complexities of conflict and how it divides up the world in a simplistic manner that accords with the sort of Manichaean vision that bin Laden espouses.

Issues of shame and humiliation are also much more foregrounded in bin Laden's statements. Most of his speeches at some point touch upon this theme, usually in relation to the perceived abuses that Muslims have endured at the hands of the United States and its allies, such as massacres, imprisonments, and attacks, the defilement of "the Two Holy Places," and the repressive policies of pro-U.S. governments in the Middle East. In a related way, bin Laden legitimates his actions through a logic of reciprocity, arguing that 9/11 was but a minor act of payback for past abuses: "The blood spilling from Palestine must be reciprocated," or "What America now tastes is insignificant compared to what we have tasted for scores of years. Our *Ummah* has been tasting humiliation and contempt for more than 80 years."[32] Along these lines, for bin Laden, the 9/11 attacks were ritual acts of revenge that symbolically transformed the United States into the condition—defeat, shame, humiliation, and violation—of the people it has abused and oppressed in the Middle East. Even as we condemn such horrific practices, the beheadings of Daniel Pearl, Nicholas Berg, Paul Johnson, Kenneth Bigly, and so many others cannot simply be explained away as "natural" expressions of the "savage" or "wild man": such decapitations are also highly ritualized acts that symbolize, in part, revenge and the casting off of shame and humiliation. In fact, bin Laden directly refers to this symbolic link in a speech: "When the pagan King Amroo ibn Hind tried to humiliate the pagan Amroo Ibn Kulthoom, the latter cut the King's head with his sword, rejecting aggression, humiliation and indignation."[33] When the decapitation videos are played, they are also sometimes accompanied by political diatribes that include discussion of alleged abuses perpetrated against Muslims in the Middle East.

This sense of humiliation and wounding is part of another difference between the visions of bin Laden and Bush: bin Laden's utterances are more reminiscent of those associated with a classical revitalization movement. After comparing a wide range of social movements advocating for substantive cultural change, ranging from cargo cults to millenarian movements to revolutions, Anthony Wallace has argued that these "revitalization movements" followed a pattern: in the midst of stressful social change and upheaval, revitalization movements may emerge, often headed by charismatic leaders, that combine the old and the new in advancing a "revitalizing" vision for social life (1956). Osama bin Laden, who is a skilled orator and known for his probity, humble lifestyle (despite his enormous personal wealth), and courage, is a charismatic figure who has become, for people around the world, an Islamic hero who has dared to battle a mighty giant, the U.S.A. (Lawrence 2005a). Playing on a sense of unease and dissatisfaction—about economic woes, corruption, and rapid changes associated with modernity—in parts of the Middle East, bin Laden, as we have seen, provides both a diagnosis (for example, U.S. aggression in the region and the decadence of Middle Eastern governments) and a cure (defeating these corrupt forces and creating a global Islamic community [ummah] that will be governed by sharia law). This will take place, bin Laden argues, "under the banner of the blessed awakening of the Ummah that is sweeping the world in general and the Islamic lands in particular"[34] as a struggle (jihad) is waged to "expel the occupying enemy" and thereby "re-establish the greatness of this Ummah."

Finally, Bush and bin Laden differ, though not in a straightforward manner, in how violence should be used. Both legitimate violence using the rhetorics of victimhood (being harmed/attacked first) and morality (having the right to respond to this harm/attack with violence). Even as he constantly speaks of waging a war against terrorism and hunting down and destroying the savage, evildoing, "wild man" terrorists, however, President Bush is often careful to distinguish this enemy from the majority of Muslims. By doing so, he narrows the potential target base. Bin Laden, in contrast, specifically broadens his range of targets to include citizens of the United States who, he argues, "freely chose their government—a choice that demonstrates agreement with its policies." Using a rhetoric of revenge, bin Laden states, "Almighty God legislated permission for us to take revenge. If we are attacked, then we have the right to respond. We have the right to destroy the villages and towns of whoever has destroyed our own villages and towns. . . . And we have the right to kill the civilians of whoever has killed our civilians."[35] Ironically, the number of civilians killed in Afghanistan and Iraq—not to mention the numerous deaths related to the long and violent history of U.S. foreign policy in the Middle East—vastly dwarfs the number of people killed by Osama bin Laden's plots. Even so, a note of caution is warranted as bin Laden's rhetorics clearly imply a willingness and desire to kill massive numbers of U.S. civilians, an intent that is much more reminiscent of Pol Pot's genocidal logics than is Bush's more narrow targeting of terrorist groups.

After 9/11 the Bush administration continued to assert its Manichaean vision and associated tropes of savagery and the "wild man," though these shifted with the historical moment and redirections of the war on terror. If the "savage" bin Laden escaped after being cornered in the caves of Tora Bora and was never found, the figure of the nemesis reappeared, transformed, in the guise of a disheveled, shaggy, dirty, and disoriented Saddam Hussein being pulled, animal-like, from a "rat hole" in Tikrit on December 13, 2003. Major General Raymond Odierno explained, "He was in the bottom of a hole with no way to fight back. He was caught like a rat."[36] The evil archenemy and "wild man," who was the "ace of spades" in the government-issued deck of fifty-five cards of the "most wanted" Iraqi leaders and upon whose head a $25 million bounty had also been placed, had finally been "smoked out." Of course, an epic drama with heroes requires villains, and so we have seen them sprout anew like the heads of a hydra, ranging from Abu Masab al-Zarqawi and his successor, Abu Ayyub al-Masri, to the leaders of the other two members of the "axis of evil," President Mahmoud Ahmadinejad and President Kim Jong-il of North Korea.

The epic war on terror has not lacked dramatic moments: the capture of the traitorous "American Taliban" John Walker Lindh, reports from embedded journalists that seemed like a cross between real-time reality TV and a video game, election days in Afghanistan and Iraq, the fireworks of "shock and awe," Colin Powell's presentation "proving" the existence of Iraqi weapons of mass destruction, jubilant crowds toppling an enormous statue of Saddam Hussein at Fardus Square upon the "liberation" of Baghdad, the heroism and rescue of Private Jessica Lynch, President Bush landing a plane on the USS *Abraham Lincoln* against the backdrop of a sign reading "Mission Accomplished," color-coordinated terrorism alerts, and, of course, Saddam Hussein's capture, trial, and hanging.

Even as these epic moments seized our attention and framed our understandings of the war, lesser-known controversies have often arisen on the border of fact and fiction. If Paul Bremer famously announced, "Ladies and gentlemen, we got him," and the government heaped praise upon the efforts of U.S. intelligence operatives, reports began to emerge that Saddam Hussein had actually been captured by Kurdish commandos, drugged, and then placed into the "spider hole" for U.S. troops to pick up.[37] Though this story was never confirmed, an army report admitted that the decision to topple the statue of Hussein was made by a Marine colonel and staged by a psychological operations unit.[38] Photos taken by international journalists residing at the nearby Palestine Hotel and circulated on antiwar Web sites show a backdrop of a small crowd of Iraqis, U.S. soldiers, and journalists in a largely empty Fardus Square ringed by U.S. military vehicles—a stark contrast to the close-ups that circulated in the media that gave the appearance of a joyous act spontaneously performed upon "liberation" by a huge Iraqi crowd.[39]

The Jessica Lynch saga, which in many ways resembled a colonial captivity narrative in which a woman is kidnapped by savage Indians (here, the "savage" Fedayeen who brutalized her) only to be heroically rescued,[40] has similarly come under question. "U.S. officials" provided the details and the headline for a *Washington Post* article titled "She Was Fighting to the Death: Details Emerging of W. Va. Soldier's Capture and Rescue," which reported how, after her company was ambushed, Jessica Lynch "fought fiercely and shot several enemy soldiers . . . firing her weapon until she ran out of ammunition . . . even after she had sustained multiple gunshot wounds . . . [and had been] stabbed" and later slapped and interrogated in her hospital bed. Her rescue, depicted as equally heroic on a grainy video, was a "classic Special Operations raid, with U.S. commandos in Black Hawk helicopters engaging Iraqi forces on their way in and out of the medical compound."[41] A picture of Private Lynch, covered with an American flag and lying on a stretcher in a rescue helicopter, was beamed around the world, and the story of her dramatic rescue was subsequently glorified by a country song and depicted in a prime-time television movie, *Saving Private Lynch*.

The details of this narrative, however, soon came into question. In a BBC news article, John Kampfner, who helped produce a BBC documentary on the rescue called *War Spin*, claimed that the Jessica Lynch story was "one of the most stunning pieces of news management ever conceived" and suggested that the Pentagon was directly influenced by Hollywood, in particular by Jerry Bruckheimer, the producer of *Black Hawk Down*.[42] (Indeed, in many ways the rescue of Private Lynch constituted an inversion of the debacle in Somalia.) To support this argument, Kampfner notes that the Pentagon's storyline was never based on substantiated information, that Private Lynch's wounds were the result of a car accident (as opposed to her having been shot or stabbed), and that the Iraqi hospital staff claim there were no Iraqi soldiers in the hospital when the U.S. military arrived. As one of the doctors explained, "We heard the noise of helicopters. . . . It was like a Hollywood film. They cried, 'Go, go, go,' with guns and blanks and the sound of explosions. They made a show—an action movie like Sylvester Stallone or Jackie Chan, with jumping and shouting, breaking down doors."[43]

For her part, Private Lynch had no memory of her immediate capture but described her ordeal in interviews and a book.[44] She does remember that she "did not fire a shot and spent most of her time in the humvee huddled in a protective ball."[45] She also claims that she was never interrogated and that the hospital staff treated her well and even made an unsuccessful attempt to turn her over to U.S. forces. After returning to the United States, Private Lynch initially couldn't even brush her teeth, had to spend over eleven hours a day doing rehabilitation and continues physical therapy, which is ongoing, took a variety of medications for pain and nerves, and lost control of her bowels and bladder.[46] A Web site devoted to Private Lynch, which is titled "Jessica Lynch—American Hero and First POW/MIA Rescued from Iraqi Freedom" and has a background of stars, stripes, and bald eagles, updates the story, reporting that she is pregnant but has had to go off her pain medication.[47]

It is at such points of disjuncture between dominant narratives of war and the far more complex realities on the ground that anthropologists have something important to say. For we tend to talk to the people who stories are forgotten, excluded, or erased from the privileged storylines that claim to provide a universal account of the events of war. How, we must ask, do the stories we hear and events we observe on the ground relate to the truths espoused by government officials and mainstream media commentators? While we have such material from many locales, doing fieldwork during the peak of the conflict was obviously quite difficult. Nevertheless, we can catch glimpses of counternarratives and alternative views from other sources: al-jazeera.net, pictures of Fallujah after the siege, the Haditha massacres, the cells of Abu Ghraib, reports on the lives of injured U.S. soldiers after they return home, the debate over whether pictures of the coffins of U.S. soldiers should be shown, estimates that the war has taken hundreds of thousands of Iraqi lives (Burnham et al. 2006), reports that, at times, dozens of Iraqis are being tortured and killed each day, sometimes with drills, and admissions that for long stretches most Western reporters in Iraq had to get their stories from stringers and official government press releases.

Equally important, anthropologists are well placed to unpack the constructions of difference that are invoked in war narratives. As we saw earlier, the narrative that the Bush administration promulgated after 9/11 is replete with binary oppositions of good versus evil, civilization against barbarism, freedom fighting tyranny, modernity and tradition, secularism versus fundamentalism, rationality against irrationality, and so forth. Such discursive strategies are paired with highly symbolic symbols and events: Saddam's animal-like capture in a rat hole, the technological display of "shock and awe," the use of "smart bombs," infrared vision, and other high-tech optics reported on by embedded journalists, Private Lynch's ravaging by the "savage" Fedayeen (one medical report speculated that she had been anally raped) and heroic rescue, a pilotless Predator drone killing a carload of al Qaeda terrorists driving in the desert, depictions of "radical" and often scowling Muslim clerics such as Muqtada al-Sadr and Abu Hamza al-Masri, the burned and mutilated bodies of four Blackwater security contractors hanging from the top of a bridge in Fallujah, and grainy footage of jihadis decapitating Daniel Pearl, Nicholas Berg, Paul Johnson, Kenneth Bigly, and so many others.

Such brutal acts deserve our firm condemnation. But here, as in the representation of violence in many more "backward" places in the world, the acts were explained away through the use of descriptive labels such as "savage" or "barbaric." And, of course, the use of such descriptors implied a legitimacy to the Bush administration's broader war on terror—regardless of the brutality of violence that it waged against these subhuman "savages" and the unfortunate bystanders who were themselves relabeled "collateral damage" as they were all too often injured or killed in the process. By moving beyond such an essentialized construction of the demonic other, anthropologists can probe more deeply into the reasons why such violence is taking place and why it takes certain ritualized and symbolic forms that are otherwise thrown into the "savage slot."

Turning the lens back home to the war on terror, we can do a similar analysis of what Neil Whitehead (2004) has called the "poetics of violence." If the other is constructed as "barbaric" through certain discourses, images, and practices, an identity as an "us" is manufactured through both structuring absences (if they are "this way" then we, by implication, are the opposite) and a related set of discourse, images, and practices. "High-tech warfare" itself is an assertion of the "modern," and the entire premise of the war on terror is that it is a battle for the survival of "civilization." If the "savages" have certain spaces like decapitation in which they both assert and are slotted into given forms of identity, so too does the United States assert an identity in spaces such as detention centers, where the evil and contaminating "savages" are safely contained and placed into a set of conditions that transform them—through dehumanizing practices—into the identity tokens for which they are supposed to stand. Abu Ghraib (and many other sites of detention and redention) provided a vivid illustration of this process, as prisoners were thoroughly degraded and even bodily transformed into one of the key icons of the Orient, a pyramid.

It is through the analysis of such spatial practices and related discourses that we can begin to further develop larger explanations for how such violence arises, unfolds, and perhaps even is impeded. In considering the resonances between the war on terror and the Cambodian conflict— and there are many—I see strong parallels in terms of a situation of socioeconomic upheaval, a crisis of meaning, the promulgation of a Manichaean vision dividing the world into forces of good and evil, and proclaiming the need for a purification process. With regard to the war on terror, I think one could further point toward globalization as a possible facilitating factor, as global processes tend to heighten a crisis of identity and shake up the foundations of the nation-state, including the crucial sense of national belonging. At least those who walk more directly in the waves of globalization have radical possibilities of reimagining themselves as the nation-state often finds itself unable to control the flow of electronic media, ideas, and capital and is increasingly faced with resident "others" who are needed but whose presence subverts the idea of an ethnicized national space. Returning to President Bush's September 20, 2001, address, I think we can view the war on terror he proposed and initiated not just as a response and necessity but also as an opportunity to make people effervesce, to light candles, to wave flags, to jointly sing "God Bless America" through their representatives, and to wage war against "evil" forces that threatened this now united (or at least much more so than before) national community.

In conclusion, then, while a much more extreme case of violence, the Cambodian genocide holds a critical lesson for the present moment: the dangers of Manichaean visions, particularly during times of upheaval, when traditional structures promoting nonviolence may be undermined and when, critically, people may search for explanations, new meanings, and greater certainty. If Pol Pot's Khmer Rouge provided such a vision to its followers in the midst of a civil war and a world rocked by the Vietnam

War, so, too, did we see President Bush offering given narratives and explanations that helped fill in the gaps of meaning that had been rent by 9/11. In both cases, a "dangerous vision" was promulgated that divided the world into black and white, with an "evil" other—in this case often inflected by the trope of barbarism and the "wild man"—that was counterposed to a "good" us and, in so doing, reasserted the cohesion of a social community under threat. Osama bin Laden's rhetoric proceeds along similar lines except that, like the Khmer Rouge, he asserts a potentially more violent set of arguments that, ultimately, could be used to legitimate genocide.

In Iraq we see where our post-9/11 dangerous visions have taken us, as war is waged against an often amorphous enemy that appears to be at once everywhere and nowhere. As car bombs explode, innocent civilians are shot down by nervous contractors, American soldiers are blown up in their Humvees, tens of thousands of suspected Iraqi insurgents are imprisoned, and combatants, filled with a sense of wounding, rage, and moral righteousness that comes with Manichaean visions, threaten, attack, torture, and kill one another. The result is always the same, whether in Pol Pot's Cambodia or Osama bin Laden's and George Bush's post-9/11 world: innocent people are wounded and die, their families and communities are torn asunder, and no end to their suffering seems in sight. Cambodia and the other conflict zones in this book offer one lesson in common about such conflicts, which can drag on for years or abruptly end. A first step toward ending the hostilities is a willingness to accept that the enemy is not a "counterrevolutionary," a "wild man," or an "infidel" but a fellow human being who is attempting to live meaningfully in a world filled with hues of gray.

Notes

1. *New York Times*, September 12, 2001.
2. "Statement by the President in His Address to the Nation," September 11, 2001, http://www.whitehouse.gov/news/releases/2001/09/20010911-16.html (accessed March 12, 2007; italics mine).
3. On the definition of genocide, see Hinton 2002.
4. The first two paragraphs of the text read:

It is necessary to draw a clear line between us and the enemy and stand on our side to make the revolution. First of all, let us determine who we are. "We" means our nation, people, worker-peasant class, revolution, collective system of the proletariat, cooperatives, trade unions, Revolutionary Army and KCP. The "enemy" includes imperialist aggressors and lackeys of all stripes; the enemy has the intention of annexing and swallowing our territory; the enemy which is planted within our revolutionary ranks; the enemy in the for[m] of the feudal-capitalist and landowner classes and other oppressor classes; the enemy in the form of private and individualist system; and particularly, the expansionist, annexationist Vietnamese enemy.

It is absolutely necessary to distinguish clearly between patriotism and treason, between love for the nation and people and betrayal of the nation and people, between worker-peasant class and the feudal-capitalist landowner and other oppressor classes, between revolution and counter revolution, between the collective system of the party's proletariat and the private system of the antiproletarian classes, and between the KCP and another antinational and counterrevolutionary sham party. It is essential that we draw a clear-cut line in terms of political, ideological, organizational, sentimental and traditional views and politics. This is the initial and fundamental stand necessary for conducting the revolution to the end. (U.S. Foreign Broadcast Information Services, Asia and Pacific 1978:H3; a roughly similar version appeared in *Revolutionary Flags*, July 1977)

5. Some of the text about DK that follows is taken from Hinton 2005.

6. According to Summers (1987), the DK regime further divided the peasant class into mid-level middle peasants (landowners hiring laborers to do 20–60 percent of their farming work), lower-level middle peasants (subsistence smallholders with enough to eat), and poor peasants (those lacking the means of production, having to work the land of others, and periodically lacking enough to eat). The working class, in turn, was divided into independent laborers (construction workers, pedicab drivers, plumbers), industrial workers (those working in rubber plantations, shipyards, factories), and party workers (those working in mobile brigades, the revolutionary army, or the revolutionary government).

7. See Hinton 2005, from which material in the next two paragraphs is drawn.

8. Leo Kuper (1981) distinguishes between full-fledged genocides and genocidal massacres.

9. "Address to a Joint Session of Congress and the American People," September 20, 2001, http://www.whitehouse.gov/news/releases/2001/09/20010920-8.html (accessed November 8, 2006).

10. See, for example, "September 11 News.com, Mysteries—Faces and Crosses," http://www.september11news.com/Mysteries1.htm (accessed March 16, 2007).

11. "Ground Zero 'Cross' to Join Memorial," Associated Press, March 14, 2006, http://www.msnbc.msn.com/id/12778974/ (accessed March 16, 2007). According to a September 23, 2001, *New York Post* article, the born-again rescue worker who found an area with several crosses "marked the site by spray-painting on a nearby wall 'God's House,' and a directional arrow." He said that when he first found the crosses, they "took my heart, and made me cry for about 20 minutes. It helped me heal the burden of my despair, and gave me closure on the whole catastrophe" (http://www.september11news.com/Mysteries1.htm [accessed March 16, 2007]).

12. "Statement by the President in His Address to the Nation," September 11, 2001.

13. "Remarks by the President upon Arrival: The South Lawn," September 16, 2001, http://www.whitehouse.gov/news/releases/2001/09/print/20010916-2.html (accessed November 9, 2006).

14. Ibid.; "Address to a Joint Session of Congress and the American People," September 20, 2001.

15. "President Urges Readiness and Patience," September 15, 2001, http://www.whitehouse.gov/news/releases/2001/09/20010915-4.html (accessed November 9, 2006). Later on, President Bush made this analogy explicit while meeting with the governor of Louisiana: "I know the Governor likes to hunt rabbits down in Louisiana. Sometimes those rabbits think they can hide from the Governor. But, eventually, he smokes them out and gets them. And that's exactly what is happening to Mr. bin Laden, and all the murderers that he's trying to hide in Afghanistan" ("President Thanks Louisianans for Building Fire Truck for New York," December 19, 2001, http://www.whitehouse.gov/news/releases/2001/12/20011220-15.html [accessed November 9, 2006]).

16. "President Bush Speaks at Talent Dinner," June 11, 2002, http://www.whitehouse.gov/news/releases/2002/06/20020611-13.html (accessed November 9, 2006).

17. "Guard and Reserves 'Define Spirit of America,'" September 17, 2001, http://www.whitehouse.gov/news/releases/2001/09/20010917-3.html (accessed November 7, 2006).

18. "President Unveils 'Most Wanted' Terrorists," October 10, 2001, http://www.whitehouse.gov/news/releases/2001/10/20011010-3.html (accessed November 11, 2006). This bounty was doubled by the Senate on July 13, 2007; see Stephen Collinson, "Senate Doubles bin Laden Bounty to 50 Million Dollars," July 13, 2007, http://news.yahoo.com/s/afp/20070713/pl_afp/usattackscongress (accessed July 19, 2007).

19. "Remarks by the President upon Arrival: The South Lawn."

20. "Address to a Joint Session of Congress and the American People."

21. "Press Briefing by Ari Fleischer," October 10, 2001, http://www.whitehouse.gov/news/releases/2001/10/20011010-9.html#Rice (accessed June 16, 2007).

22. "Censoring the Enemy," PBS NewsHour with Jim Lehrer, http://www.pbs.org/newshour/bb/media/july-dec01/cens_10–15.html (accessed June 16, 2007).

23. "Declaration of War Against the Americans Occupying the Land of the Two Holy Places," in Hamud 2005:52.

24. "Third Statement Regarding Afghanistan, December 27, 2001," in Hamud 2005:87.

25. "Second Statement Regarding Afghanistan, November 3, 2001," in Hamud 2005:70, 73, 70, 69.

26. "Statement to America, October 26, 2002," in Hamud 2005:94.

27. For example, "These events divided the world into two sides—the side of Faith free of hypocrisy and the side of the infidels." "Statement Regarding Afghanistan, October 7, 2001," in Hamud 2005:65–66.

28. "Statement to America, October 26, 2002," in Hamud 2005:98–99.

29. "Third Statement Regarding Afghanistan, December 27, 2001," in Hamud 2005:86.

30. "Second Statement Regarding Afghanistan, November 3, 2001," in Hamud 2005:69.

31. There are also, however, ways in which the global economy profits from violence and conflict, as vividly demonstrated by Nordstrom (2004).

32. "Statement to America, October 26, 2002" and "Statement Regarding Afghanistan, October 7, 2001," in Hamud 2005:94, 64.

33. "Declaration of War Against the Americans Occupying the Land of the Two Holy Places," in Hamud 2005:49.

34. Ibid., 33, 45.

35. "Statement to America, October 26, 2002," in Hamud 2005:97.

36. "Saddam 'Caught Like a Rat' in a Hole," December 14, 2003, http://www .cnn.com/2003/WORLD/meast/12/14/sprj.irq.saddam.operation/index.html (accessed November 11, 2006).

37. "Was It Really the U.S. That 'Got Him'?" *Christian Science Monitor*, December 30, 2003, http://www.csmonitor.com/2003/1230/dailyUpdate.html?s = entt (accessed November 12, 2006).

38. "Army Stage-Managed Fall of Hussein Statue," *Los Angeles Times*, July 3, 2004, http://www.commondreams.org/cgi-bin/print.cgi?file = /headlines04/0703-02.htm (accessed November 12, 2006).

39. "The Photographs Tell the Story. . . ," Information Clearing House, April 14, 2003, http://www.informationclearinghouse.info/article2842.htm (accessed November 12, 2006).

40. I would like to thank Nicole Cooley for making this connection. See also McAlister 2003.

41. "She Was Fighting to the Death: Details Emerging of W. Va. Soldier's Capture and Rescue," *Washington Post*, April 3, 2006, p. A01, http://www.washington post.com/ac2/wp-dyn/A14879–2003Apr2?language = printer (accessed November 12, 2006).

42. "Saving Private Lynch Story 'Flawed,'" BBC News, May 5, 2003, http:// news.bbc.co.uk/2/hi/programmes/correspondent/3028585.stm (accessed November 12, 2006). Kampfner published a longer version of this essay in a *Guardian* article titled "The Truth About Jessica," http://www.guardian.co.uk/Iraq/Story/0,2763, 956255,00.html (accessed November 12, 2006). The Pentagon rejected this story and the documentary *War Spin* as "void of all facts and absolutely ridiculous" ("U.S. Rejects BBC Lynch Report," BBC News, http://news.bbc.co.uk/1/hi/world/americas/ 3043115.stm [accessed November 12, 2006]).

43. "The Truth About Jessica."

44. Bragg 2003.

45. "The Private Jessica Lynch," *Time Magazine*, http://www.time.com/time/ magazine/article/0,9171,1101031117-538846,00.html (accessed November 12, 2006).

46. Ibid.

47. http://www.jessica-lynch.com/ (accessed November 15, 2006). See also "Jessica Lynch Expecting a Baby Girl," Macon Morehouse, People, http://people .aol.com/people/article/0,26334,1546059,00.html (accessed November 15, 2006).

Bibliography

Bragg, Richard. 2003. *I Am a Soldier, Too: The Jessica Lynch Story*. New York: Knopf.

Bruni, Frank. 2001. For a President, a Mission and a Role in History. *New*

York Times, September 22. http://query.nytimes.com/gst/fullpage.html?sec = health&res = 9A07EEDF163AF931A1575AC0A9679C8B63 (accessed March 19, 2007).

Burnham, Gilbert, Riyadh Lafta, Shannon Doocy, and Les Roberts. 2006. Mortality After the 2003 Invasion of Iraq: A Cross-Sectional Cluster Sample Survey. The Lancet 368 (October 21):1421–28.

Gwynne, Rosalind W. 2006. Usama bin Ladin, the Qur'an and Jihad. Religion 36:61–90.

Hamud, Randall B. 2005. Osama Bin Laden: America's Enemy in His Own Words. San Diego: Nadeem Publishing.

Hinton, Alexander Laban, ed. 2002. Genocide: An Anthropological Reader. Berkeley: University of California Press.

———. 2005. Why Did They Kill? Cambodia in the Shadow of Genocide. Berkeley: University of California Press.

Huntington, Samuel. 1993. The Clash of Civilizations. Foreign Affairs 72 (3):22–49.

Jackson, Karl D., ed. 1989. Cambodia, 1975–1978: Rendezvous with Death. Princeton, N.J.: Princeton University Press.

Kinnell, Galway. 2002. When the Towers Fell. The New Yorker, September 16. Reprinted in http://www.legacy-project.org/index.php?page = lit_detail&litID = 95 (accessed April 8, 2009).

Kuper, Leo. 1981. Genocide: Its Political Use in the Twentieth Century. New Haven, Conn.: Yale University Press.

Lakoff, George. 2001. Metaphors of Terror. September 16. http://press.uchicago.edu/News/911lakoff.html (accessed February 26, 2007).

Lawrence, Bruce. 2005a. Introduction to Messages to the World: The Statements of Osama Bin Laden, ed. Bruce Lawrence, xi–xxiii. London: Verso.

———, ed. 2005b. Messages to the World: The Statements of Osama Bin Laden. London: Verso.

Lindholm, Charles. 1990. Charisma. Malden: Blackwell.

McAlister, Melani. 2003. Saving Private Lynch. New York Times, April 6. http://query.nytimes.com/gst/fullpage.html?res = 9F03E2DA1438F935A35757C0A96 59C8B63 (accessed December 16, 2008).

Nordstrom, Carolyn. 2004. Shadows of War: Violence, Power, and International Profiteering in the Twenty-First Century. Berkeley: University of California Press.

Rutenberg, Jim. 2006. Advisor Who Shaped Bush's Speeches Is Leaving. New York Times, June 15.

Said, Edward W. 1994. Orientalism. New York: Vintage.

Summers, Laura. 1987. The CPK, Secret Vanguard of Pol Pot's Revolution: A Comment on Nuon Chea's Statement. Journal of Communist Studies 3 (March): 5–18.

Wallace, Anthony F. C. 1956. Revitalization Movements. American Anthropologist 58 (2):264–81.

Whitehead, Neil L. 2004. On the Poetics of Violence. In Violence, ed. Neil L. Whitehead, 55–106. Santa Fe: School of American Research Press.

Zulaika, Joseba. 1993. Further Encounters with the Wild Man: Of Cannibals, Dogs, and Terrorists. Etnofoor 6 (2):21–40.

Chapter 2
The War on Terror and Women's Rights in Iraq

Nadje Al-Ali

Introduction

Women's rights and women's liberation have been part and parcel of the justifying rhetoric of proponents of the so-called war on terror. The U.S.-led interventions in Afghanistan and Iraq have similarly identified the need to "liberate" women from the barbaric practices of the Taliban and the Saddam Hussein regime, respectively. Simultaneously, women have been promoted as the "heroines" of the reconstruction of post-Taliban and post–Saddam Hussein societies (Pratt 2005). The concern for women implicitly justifies military intervention in these countries. Yet the degree to which this rhetorical support is translated into actual support for women's involvement in reconstruction is brought into question by the U.S. pursuit of its "national strategic interests" in both countries. In the case of Iraq, what needs to be explored are the ways in which U.S. support for its local political allies has operated to encourage the fragmentation of the state and political authority (Herring and Rangwala 2006) in ways that undermine women's participation and women's rights. In this sense, the promotion of women's participation in peace-building and reconstruction cannot be separated from larger international processes of imperialism and global capitalism.[1]

Despite the fact that women constitute the majority of the twenty-four million Iraqis (about 55–65 percent) who suffer from the lethal violence and bear the daily hardships of maintaining family life under difficult circumstances, the media as well as academic writings have paid only little attention to their plight. But how have Iraqi women actually fared in the aftermath of the invasion of 2003? Have they won their rights, freedoms, and social justice? In exploring these questions in the context of post-invasion Iraq, I examine issues related to the range of activities that can be subsumed under the label of women's rights activism; tensions between feminism and nationalism; contestations between secular and Islamist constituencies; and accusations leveled against women's rights activists of "aping the West."

Since the turn of the twentieth century, Middle Eastern women activists have had to struggle on many fronts: against legal restrictions and political barriers, against colonial occupation and ongoing imperialist encroachment, and against conservative patriarchal values. Despite the historical link between the women's and the nationalist movements, the charge of emulating "Western thought" and thereby betraying "authentic culture" has been a continuous challenge for Middle Eastern feminists. From its very beginnings, various constituencies opposed to the struggle for women's rights (Islamists as well as nationalist-leftists) have engaged in an evaluation of women activists with regard to their level of "authenticity" or "Westernness" (Al-Ali 2003:217). The context of a military occupation that is partly justified by the rhetoric on women's liberation has not only worsened the accusations hurled against Iraqi women's activists but also resulted in a great backlash against women's rights.

In what follows, I present some of the major developments with respect to women and gender relations as they have been unfolding since the fall of the Ba'th regime in 2003. I will explore the humanitarian crisis, changing gender ideologies and relations, and the violence experienced by women at the hands of the occupation forces, Islamist militants, insurgents, criminal gangs, and their own families. I will also discuss the implications of foreign intervention on women and women's rights in the context of the "war on terror."

Ethnography from afar in the context of my work does not relate to comparative research but to research among the older diaspora community as well as among recent Iraqi refugees after the invasion of 2003. The research for this chapter has mainly taken place among the Iraqi diaspora in Amman, Dearborn (Michigan), and London. Because of the ongoing lack of security I have not been able to carry out research inside central and southern Iraq, but I visited Iraqi Kurdistan in April 2007 where I carried out research among women's rights activists. In Iraqi Kurdistan as well as in Amman, I was able to talk to Iraqi women who continue to live inside southern and central Iraq but who were only temporarily outside to visit relatives, obtain medical treatment, or attend workshops and conferences.

The Climate of Fear

During the initial period of lawlessness after the invasion in 2003, women started to experience the insecurity, threats, fear, and violence that have circumscribed their lives ever since. Just a few months after the invasion, Human Rights Watch published a revealing report about the climate of fear among Iraqi women and girls. At the time the report was published in July 2003, incidents of kidnappings, abductions, and sexual violence were not widely reported and possibly not that widespread. However, the knowledge about these acts of violence targeting women and girls prevented many from leaving their homes and from going to work, to school, or to university. Neither occupation forces nor the debilitated Iraqi police were preventing or properly investigating these crimes (Al-Ali 2007:226).

Some families associate rape and the abduction or kidnapping of female family members with shame and the violation of family honor. Incidents of so-called honor killings have risen dramatically. According to several women activists who are working with victims of violence, some women who were abducted begged the police to keep them in police stations or prisons so as not to be killed by their families. Some women's rights activists have been trying to set up safe houses for women survivors of abductions as well as kidnappings. Kidnappings, unlike abductions, involve the demand of a ransom and might or might not involve sexual violence. There are also some accounts of families not paying the ransom demanded by the kidnappers as they fear the shame attached with the perceived loss of honor.

In addition to abductions with the intent to sexually assault a woman, there has also been an increase in the number of abductions in the context of sex trafficking. Although the actual number of trafficked women and girls is difficult to estimate, according to Iraqi NGO activists and even the U.S. State Department's June 2005 trafficking report (see Bennett 2006), sex trafficking is an increasing problem as young women are being abducted and sent to Yemen, Syria, Jordan, and the Gulf countries for sexual exploitation.

None of the women I talked to experienced sexual violence themselves but everyone had heard stories or knew someone who had been abducted or kidnapped. Despite the ongoing climate of fear and the underlying dangers, many women and girls started to venture out to schools, to university, and, to some extent, to workplaces in the fall of 2003. According to a Human Rights Watch report that refers to an assessment conducted by Save the Children U.K., school attendance increased from 50 percent in May 2003 to an estimated 75 percent in June 2003. However, girls' school attendance was often dependent on the availability of male relatives to accompany the girls to and from school (Human Rights Watch 2003:9).[2] Several women told me that after several months they could not sit at home anymore and that they started to venture out. Although living in fear, many families tried to create a sense of normality and started to try to pursue education, work, and even political mobilization. This trend has been reversed since 2005, however, in light of the increasing violence and lawlessness that forces many parents to keep their children at home instead of sending them to school (Al-Ali 2007:228–29).

At the time Human Rights Watch published its report in July 2003, most of the sexual violence experienced by women was carried out by criminal gangs taking advantage of the general lawlessness and chaos. However, since late 2003, more politically motivated groups, remnants of the past regime, and Islamist militia and terrorist groups have also contributed to the general climate of fear through kidnappings and bomb attacks targeting Iraqi civilians. As I will show later, women and children, just like men, have not only been victims of bombings, including suicide bombings, but have been targeted by Islamist militias and extremist organizations as symbols of a radical break with the previous regime and the resistance to the occupation. Women's dress codes, mobility, participation in political and public life, and legal rights are all contested issues and used in the power struggle between different forces in society.

In the early days after the invasion, the campaign to win hearts and minds by occupation forces succeeded to some extent, especially since there was much good will and hope in large parts of the population who were grateful to have been rid of a ruthless dictator. However, the failure to improve everyday living conditions as well as the deteriorating security situation, an array of human rights abuses, and escalating violence by occupation forces led to a shift in the general attitude toward American and British troops among the majority of women I talked to. The Human Rights Watch report of July 2003 mainly focuses on the failure of the occupying forces to prevent abductions and sexual violence against women, stating that many of the problems "derive from the U.S.-led Coalition forces and civilian administration's failure to provide public security in Baghdad. The public security vacuum in Baghdad has heightened the vulnerability of women and girls to sexual violence and abduction." This resonates with Iraqi women's rights activists who chided Coalition forces for their failure to protect women in postwar Iraq.

The police have also not been able to prevent violence, including gender-based violence. Because the police force is considerably smaller and relatively poorly managed, there is limited police street presence. This situation has become even worse during the past few years as the newly established Iraqi police have frequently been targeted by militant resistance and itself has been infiltrated by Islamist militias.

As time has passed, it has become obvious that Iraqi civilians are caught between many different sources of anguish, suffering, and aggression. U.S. and British troops have not only failed to protect the population from escalating violence by criminal gangs, Islamist militias, and terrorist groups but have themselves been a major source of violence and lack of security inside Iraq. Occupation forces have killed thousands of innocent Iraqi civilians, including women and children, as a result of their bomb attacks and random shootings, and they have been implicated in abuse, torture, and sexual violence against Iraqi men, women, and children (Al-Ali 2007:231).

Violence by Occupation Forces

While aerial bombings of residential areas are responsible for a large number of civilian deaths, many Iraqis have lost their lives while being shot at by American or British troops. Entire families have been wiped out when they approached a checkpoint or did not recognize areas marked as prohibited. Hind G.[3] has been working for many years as a doctor in al-Kindi teaching hospital in northeast Baghdad. In 2006, while living in exile in Amman, she told me the following story, her voice full of frustration and anger.

I have seen many things while working as a doctor. But what I am seeing these days is too much. I treated children with metal fragments all over their bodies because they played with unexploded bomblets that were part of cluster bombs. I saw men, women and children with no limbs, bleeding to death because they were victims of bomb attacks. Sometimes by the Americans and sometimes by terrorists. My colleague works in the maternity ward and we get lots of complications. Many women are too afraid to come to hospital, especially when they get their labor during the night. They are afraid they and their families will be shot by soldiers or attacked by gangs. So they stay at home and often it is too late when complications happen. A few weeks ago we had a badly injured pregnant woman whose husband had died when the soldiers opened fire on the car. They had a white flag but the soldiers claim they did not see it. The husband drove a bit too fast because he was worried about his wife. She was in so much pain. (Al-Ali 2007:235–36)

Some of the worst destruction and atrocities have taken place in and around the city of Fallujah, in the province of Al-Anbar, about seventy kilometers west of Baghdad on the Euphrates River.[4] According to a detailed analysis of three hundred contemporary news reports by Iraq Body Count, at least 572 of the roughly 800 reported deaths during the first U.S. siege of Fallujah in April 2004 were civilians, over 300 of whom were women and children.[5]

U.S. forces committed major war crimes during the assault: warplanes, fighter bombers, military helicopters, and gunships were used to attack residential areas, killing many civilians. In one incident "16 children and eight women were reported to have been killed when U.S. aircraft hit four houses."[6]

After a brief period of cease-fire, Fallujah once again became the target of aerial attacks for a couple of months. On November 8, 2004, the United States—with British support—began its second major assault on Fallujah, presented and justified as counterinsurgency Operation Phantom Fury. Thousands of U.S. soldiers and hundreds of Iraqi troops engaged in a concentrated assault on Fallujah with air strikes, artillery, armor, and infantry. According to U.S. military officials, between one thousand and six thousand insurgents were hiding in the city. Although the majority of residents managed to flee before the major assault, thousands remained trapped in the city. According to a high-ranking Red Cross official, "at least 800 civilians" were killed in the first nine days of the November 2004 assault on Fallujah.[7]

Samira H. was living in Baghdad but had been going regularly to Fallujah in the aftermath of the attacks in 2004 to provide humanitarian assistance. She was clearly distressed by the images that came to mind when describing her visits to the city. She started to cry as she told me about the number of injured and killed people she saw when visiting Fallujah the first time. She gathered herself and said sadly, "You know I do not want to hate Americans. But it is difficult after having seen what happened to Fallujah" (Al-Ali 2007:237).

Half of the estimated two hundred thousand Iraqis who fled the assault have yet to return to their homes. Those who managed to return have been subjected to a draconian regime of curfews, iris scans, and check-points. The vast majority of former residents of Fallujah are living in make-shift camps in and around Baghdad under extremely difficult conditions and are only a fraction of the increasing number of internally displaced people inside Iraq.

Fallujah might have received more media attention than other places, but similar U.S. military offensives in Ramadi, Haditha, Qaim, Tal Afar, and elsewhere have killed many more civilians and created thousands more refugees. These military assaults have been justified as part of the measures taken to eliminate violent insurgents responsible for targeting not only U.S. and U.K. troops but also Iraqi civilians. Though thousands of fighters might have been killed in these military assaults, thousands of innocent civilians have indeed been killed. Those who survived the attacks have lost relatives, friends, and neighbors. They have lost their homes, their livelihoods. They have also lost any sense of trust or confidence in the American and British forces and some have even developed greater sympathy for the insurgents (Al-Ali 2007:238).

In addition to killing innocent women, men, and children, the occupa-tion forces have also engaged in other forms of violence against women. There have been numerous documented accounts of physical assaults at checkpoints and during house searches. Several women I talked to reported that they had been verbally or physically threatened and assaulted by sol-diers as they were searched at checkpoints. American forces have also ar-rested wives, sisters, and daughters of suspected insurgents to pressure them to surrender.[8] Female relatives have been taken hostage by U.S. forces and used as bargaining chips. In addition to the violence related to the arrests themselves, women who were detained by the troops might suffer from the sense of shame associated with such a detention. As there has been mount-ing evidence not just of physical assaults and torture but also of rape, women who have been detained might even become victims of so-called honor crimes.

According to Amal Kadhim Swadi, an Iraqi lawyer representing women detainees at Abu Ghraib, abuse, sexual violence, rape, and torture of Iraqi women by occupation forces have been happening all over Iraq. Several documents released on March 7, 2005, by the American Civil Liber-ties Union (ACLU) indicate thirteen cases of rape and abuse of female de-tainees. The documents reveal that no action was taken against any soldier or civilian official as a result.[9] The most well-known case of rape and murder—that of Abeer Qassim al-Janaby, a fourteen-year-old girl from

Mahmudiyaha—was reported widely in the Western media. But as River-bend, the famous girl blogger from Baghdad, reflects in her blog, there are many more unreported cases of rape (Al-Ali 2007:239):

Rape. The latest of American atrocities. Though it's not really the latest—it's just the one that's being publicized the most. The poor girl Abeer was neither the first to be raped by American troops, nor will she be the last. The only reason this rape was brought to light and publicized is that her whole immediate family were killed along with her. Rape is a taboo subject in Iraq. Families don't report rapes here, they avenge them. We've been hearing whisperings about rapes in American-controlled prisons and during sieges of towns like Haditha and Samarra for the last three years. The naiveté of Americans who can't believe their "heroes" are commit-ting such atrocities is ridiculous. Who ever heard of an occupying army committing rape??? You raped the country, why not the people? In the news they're estimating her age to be around 24, but Iraqis from the area say she was only 14. Fourteen. Imagine your 14-year-old sister or your 14-year-old daughter. Imagine her being gang-raped by a group of psychopaths and then the girl was killed and her body burned to cover up the rape. Finally, her parents and her five-year-old sister were also killed. Hail the American heroes. . . . Raise your heads high supporters of the "liberation"—your troops have made you proud today. . . .
   It fills me with rage to hear about it and read about it. The pity I once had for foreign troops in Iraq is gone. It's been eradicated by the atrocities in Abu Ghraib, the deaths in Haditha and the latest news of rapes and killings. I look at them in their armored vehicles and to be honest—I can't bring myself to care whether they are 19 or 39. I can't bring myself to care if they make it back home alive. I can't bring myself to care anymore about the wife or parents or children they left behind. I can't bring myself to care because it's difficult to see beyond the horrors. I look at them and wonder just how many innocents they killed and how many more they'll kill before they go home. How many more young Iraqi girls will they rape?[10]

Violence by Islamist Militants

Islamist militants and terrorist groups pose a particular danger to Iraqi women as well. Many women's organizations and activists inside Iraq have documented the increasing Islamist threats to women, the pressure to con-form to certain dress codes, the restrictions on movement and behavior, incidents of acid thrown into women's faces, and even targeted killings. Early in 2003 many women in Basra, for example, reported that they were forced to wear a headscarf or restrict their movements out of fear of being harassed by men. Female students at the University of Basra reported that when the war ended groups of men began stopping them at the university gates, shouting at them if their heads were not covered (Al-Ali 2007:240).[11]

In 2004 reports from several cities around Iraq stated that Islamist extremists were targeting universities by threatening and even attacking female students who were wearing Western-style fashions, setting off bombs on campuses, and demanding that classes be segregated by gender. Thousands of female students decided to postpone their studies after bombs exploded in several universities. According to several women I talked to, pamphlets found on several campuses declared: "If the boy students don't separate from the girl students, we will explode the college. Any girl student who does not wear a veil, we will burn her face with chemicals." Female students have been abducted leaving campus, their captors threatening that they will be killed if they do not wear "Islamic dress" and continue to mingle with male students. Even non-Muslim women, who are not normally expected to cover their heads, do not escape the threats, students said.[12]

Not only students but women of all ages and walks of life are now forced to comply with certain dress codes and well as restrict their movement. Suad F., a former accountant and mother of four children who lives in a neighborhood in Baghdad that used to be relatively mixed before the sectarian killings in 2005 and 2006, told me the following in Amman in 2006:

> I resisted for a long time, but last year also started wearing *hijab*, after I was threatened by several Islamist militants in front of my house. They are terrorizing the whole neighborhood, behaving as if they were in charge. And they are actually controlling the area. No one dares to challenge them. A few months ago they distributed leaflets around the area warning people to obey them and demanding that women should stay at home. I have been trying not to take them so seriously, but when they threatened to kill me in front of my house I got really worried. I stopped working as an accountant after the invasion because of the lack of security, but I have been helping out in the women's NGO in the neighborhood. We are providing some basic training and humanitarian assistance to extremely poor women. I need to go out. What am I supposed to do now? (Al-Ali 2007:241)

By 2006 the threat posed by Islamist militias as well as the mushrooming Islamist extremist groups went far beyond imposed dress codes and called for gender segregation at university. In the British-occupied south, where Muqtada al-Sadr's Mahdi army retains a stranglehold, the situation has been extremely critical since 2004 as women have been systematically pushed back into their homes. One Basra woman, known as Dr. Kefaya, was working in the women's and children's hospital unit at Basra university when she started receiving threats from extremists. She defied them. Then, one day a man walked into the building and murdered her (Judd 2006).

Many other professional women have been shot in Basra since the invasion. However, by 2006, the same pressures and threats applied to women throughout Iraq except for the Kurdish-controlled areas in the north (Al-Ali 2007:242).

Aside from Shi'i Islamist militias, such as the Mahdi army linked to al-Sadr and the Badr Brigade linked to the Supreme Islamic Iraqi Council (SIIC, formerly known as Supreme Council for the Islamic Revolution in Iraq, or SCIRI), there are numerous extremist Sunni Islamist groups that have been mushrooming since the invasion. Whether Sunni or Shi'i, leaders of both militia and insurgent groups have severely curtailed women's mobility and participation in public life. They randomly issue *fatawa* (singular *fatwa*: legal pronouncements in Islam) banning women from leaving their homes, from driving, and from working. According to several women's rights activists I spoke to in Amman in 2006, the number of women who have been killed on the streets has risen since the invasion and has become a noticeable and extremely worrying pattern. "Even veiled women who are seen to be out alone or driving a car started to be targeted," Zeinab G. told me. She continued:

Women are being assassinated, just because they are women. And we don't even know whom to turn to. The police is scared itself by the militia and many units are actually infiltrated by the Mahdi army or Badr Brigade. Others would like to help but are not in a position to do so because they are just not enough and they are ill equipped. The Islamists are targeting women who have a public profile even more, but they have started to even kill women who are not in any way politically active or work in an NGO. Those of us who do, live in constant fear. Several of my colleagues have already been shot, and I have received several death threats.

In addition to the violence aimed at women who are perceived to diverge from the Islamists' specific narrow interpretations of Islam—and this holds true for both Shi'i and Sunni extremists—women are also victims of the escalating sectarian violence that has increasingly taken hold of Iraq. The main perpetrators of sectarian violence and killings are also militias and armed Islamist groups. Both the Badr Brigade and the Mahdi army have taken over several ministries and infiltrated the security and police apparatus, and they have used their positions to target, attack, and kill Sunni Iraqis. Sunni Islamist groups, on the other hand, have been involved in the targeted killing of Shi'i. By 2006 whole neighborhoods were "ethnically cleansed" as militias and militant groups took over particular areas. Although sectarian violence has thus far largely been limited to extremist groups, sectarian sentiments have spilled over into the general population as the tit-for-tat killings have increased and hatred has started to grow. Neighbors and friends are turning against each other, and ordinary civilians are perpetrating acts of violence against each other.

Women's Shrinking Rights

Targeted assassination as well as reports about Islamist groups and activists restricting women's mobility, dress code, and public spaces are symptomatic of wider conservative trends and the various ways in which women are being used in Iraq—as in many other conflict-ridden societies—to demarcate boundaries between "us" and "them." Everywhere in the world women are used to mark difference between people, between cultures, between religious groups, and so forth. Both Muslim and Western societies use statements such as "Your women dress this way and are not properly behaving" to discredit another community, nation, or culture. A shift to more conservative and restricted gender ideologies and relations framed as Islamization fulfills two objectives in the context of Iraq: first, a break with the largely secular regime of Saddam Hussein; and second, resistance to the occupying forces. Unfortunately women are being squeezed between the attempt to start a new Iraq that diverges from the policies of the previous regime and the attempt to challenge the imposition of Western cultural norms and morals generally, as well as, more specifically, U.S. and U.K. occupation.

More conservative norms and ideas about men and women and their respective roles and relations became obvious during the period of economic sanctions (see Al-Ali 2007:171–213). In the context of an economic crisis, high unemployment rates, an increase in religiosity among the Iraqi population, and an opportunistic religious campaign by Saddam Hussein in the early 1990s, Iraqi women started to experience setbacks in terms of education, labor force participation, and social freedoms and mobility. This took place against the background of a state feminism in the 1970s that pushed women into the education sector and all professions. During the Iran-Iraq war of 1980–88, when hundreds of thousands of Iraqi men were forced to fight, Iraqi women were challenged to become "super-women." They were not only the main breadwinners, filling in jobs and positions in the absence of men, but were also pushed to have numerous children to make up for the loss of lives during the long and bloody war. It was during the thirteen years of the most comprehensive sanctions regime ever imposed on a country (1990–2003) that Iraqi women started to lose some of the ground they had gained over the previous decades.

In the current climate of fear and violence there has been an even greater push toward conservative social norms, partly as a response to threats and risks, and partly a result of changing social values. Processes related to Islamization of society and Islamist politics are not only leading to increasing conservatism in gender relations but also dominating Iraqi political power struggles in the post–Saddam Hussein era. One early example of the growing impact of Islamist tendencies was the attempt in December 2003 to scrap the personal status code (family laws) in favor of sharia-based jurisdiction by the Iraqi Governing Council under then chair Abdel Aziz al-Hakim, head of the SIIC. The unified code was once considered the most progressive in the Middle East, making polygamy difficult and guaranteeing women's custody rights in the case of divorce.

There had been a unified family law in Iraq since the formulation of a new constitution in 1959 following the revolution against the monarchy and British meddling in 1958. The personal status code enshrined in the 1959 constitution was based on a relatively liberal reading of Islamic law. It codified all laws and regulations related to marriage, divorce, child custody, and inheritance. This set of laws combined Sunni and Shi'i regulations and applies to all Iraqis, contributing to a sense of unity. It facilitated mixed marriages between Sunni and Shi'i Iraqis as well as between Arabs and Kurds. Amendments to the family laws were made under the Ba'th regime in 1978. The amended personal status code widened the conditions under which a woman could seek divorce, outlawed forced marriages, required the permission of a judge for a man to have a second wife, and prescribed punishment for marriages contracted outside the court.

Although unsuccessful at the time, the attempt to change the law and the discussion around it revealed the current climate and the dangers lying ahead. The debate about the personal status laws in particular and Islamic law in general emerged again in the context of the constitution. While not the only source of legislation, Islam is the official religion and a basic source of legislation. Moreover, no law can be passed that contradicts the "undisputed rules" of Islam.[13] Neither the previous transitional administrative law (TAL) nor the current constitution explicitly mentions women's rights in the context of marriage, divorce, child custody, and inheritance. Instead, Article 41 states that "Iraqis are free in their adherence to their personal status according to their own religion, sect, belief and choice, and that will be organized by law."

In other words, Article 41 of the new Iraqi constitution stipulates that the existing family laws that apply equally to all members of society will be replaced by family laws pertaining to specific religious and ethnic communities. This would give authority to conservative religious leaders to define laws according to their beliefs and particular interpretation. It provides no safeguards against extremely regressive and discriminatory interpretations of Islamic law, such as under the Taliban in Afghanistan. And, Article 41 not only potentially means the erosion of women's rights but it also potentially increases sectarianism inside the country. It will make new mixed marriages virtually impossible and will threaten already existing ones. Most significantly, it will further a sense of communalism as opposed to unified citizenship applied equally, and might even fuel sectarian violence.

Because of several unresolved issues related to the constitution, such as the issue of federalism, the status of Kirkuk, and the opposition to Article 41, it was agreed that there would be a three-month window of opportunity to amend the proposed new clauses once the new government was formed. As of the winter of 2007, the constitutional review committee had still not come to any decision regarding Article 41 or any of the other outstanding issues.

Increasing Poverty and Humanitarian Crisis

Most Iraqi women are oblivious to the debates related to the constitution or the personal status law. Everyday survival is a priority in a context where lack of security goes hand in hand with incredibly difficult living conditions. The Iraqi infrastructure, which was already severely debilitated as a result of economic sanctions and a series of wars, has deteriorated even further since 2003. Electricity shortages, lack of access to potable water, malfunctioning sanitation systems, and a deteriorating health system are part of everyday life in post-2003 Iraq. Intisar K., who works as a doctor in a teaching hospital in Baghdad, complained about the extremely difficult working conditions in the hospitals: "It is worse now than during the most difficult times under economic sanctions." Ninety percent of the 180 hospitals in Iraq do not have key resources such as basic medical and surgical supplies. Over 12,000 of 34,000 doctors have left Iraq since 2003, 250 have been kidnapped and 2,000 have been killed since the invasion (UNAMI 2007:2).

Intisar went on to sum up what has also been documented in several UN-related documents: "We only have electricity for three to a maximum of five hours a day. There is not enough clean drinking water. Lack of sanitation is a big problem and continues to be one of the main causes of malnutrition, dysentery and death amongst young children" (Al-Ali 2007:247). It is not only lack of electricity, clean water, and petrol that affects the everyday lives of Iraqi civilians. According to recent reports published by the United Nations Children's Fund (UNICEF) and the British-based charity organization Medact, the 2003 invasion and ongoing occupation have led to the deterioration of health conditions, including malnutrition and a rise in vaccine-preventable diseases and mortality rates for children under the age of five. Iraq's mortality rate for children under five rose from 5 percent in 1990 to 12.5 percent in 2004.[14] One in three Iraqi children is malnourished and underweight, according to a UNICEF report published in Amman on May 2, 2006. Another, earlier study states that about a quarter of Iraqi children between six months and five years old suffer from either acute or chronic malnutrition.[15] The report shows that about four hundred thousand Iraqi children are suffering from "wasting" and "emaciation" as a result of chronic diarrhea and protein deficiency.[16] The survey also records the growing dropout rate of 25 percent among pupils under fifteen years of age who live primarily in rural areas and were identified as extremely poor. The main reasons given for the dropout rate are families' inability to pay for the schooling and the fact that the schools are located too far away.[17]

According to Oxfam, "eight million people are in urgent need of emergency aid; that figure includes over two million who are displaced within the country, and more than two million refugees. Many more are living in poverty, without basic services, and increasingly threatened by disease and malnutrition" (2007:3). Poverty has become extremely widespread and endemic, with 54 percent of Iraqis living on less than US$1 per day. Seventy percent of Iraqis have to survive without an adequate water supply, and 80 percent lack effective sanitation (Oxfam 2007:11). Water is frequently contaminated because of the poor sewage systems and the discharge of untreated sewage into rivers. The increase in diarrheal diseases has affected children most of all and is one of the main factors in the increased mortality rates for children (Al-Ali and Pratt 2009).

Despite incredibly difficult circumstances, since 2003 Iraqi women have been at the forefront of trying to cope with and improve their living conditions and to confront the humanitarian crisis. Locally based women's initiatives and groups, mainly revolving around practical needs related to widespread poverty, lack of adequate health care, lack of housing, and lack of proper social services provided by the state, have flourished. Women have also pooled their resources to help address the need for education and training, such as computer classes, as well as for income-generating projects. Many of the initiatives filling the gap in terms of state provisions where welfare and health are concerned are affiliated with political parties and religiously motivated organizations and groups. However, independent nonpartisan professional women have also been mobilizing to help.

In the early days after the invasion, initiatives were mainly directed toward the most immediate needs. Ameena R. and other women in her social circle and neighborhood organized themselves to feed patients left in a local hospital with no care after the violence and looting had scared away most doctors and nurses.

We started to get organized after the invasion. We went to a hospital where there were fifty people and no one was taking care of them. We took turns to cook for the patients. We organized the cleanup of our local schools. When I went with a group of women to clean up a school in our neighborhood, there was an American soldier and he tried to prevent us, but we managed to clean the school anyway. We were still afraid to send our children to school though.(Al-Ali, 2007:250)

A few months after the invasion, women got together to not only address humanitarian needs but also play an active role in education and income-generating projects. Hala G. told me during one of my visits to Amman how she and a number of her friends and colleagues started a charity for extremely poor women, widows, and orphans in Baghdad.

Bremer started to speak about civil society being open to all people. At that moment, we decided to start something, to start an organization. In the beginning, we wanted to help women. It was difficult for women to get outside their houses. We gathered women in our neighborhood and told them about our idea. We started with the project in May 2003. By July everything was settled. We knew what we wanted to do. We looked for a place. We wanted to help poor women in different ways: help them to learn something, to be skilled, help those who lost their husbands, help women to get some work. We rented a big house for three years. The owner was a doctor living outside Iraq. We used the money from our own savings and individual contributions. We only had money for two computers. Some people helped with their own means. We opened a small clinic and a small computer centre. We brought some young women who were educated in computers and they started computer classes for girls. The centre is in the middle of a residential area.

We recognized those who were extremely poor. We asked women to show us their documents to prove that they are widows. (Al-Ali 2007:250–51)

Although few reliable statistics are available on the total number of widows in Iraq, the Ministry of Women's Affairs reports that there are at least three hundred thousand in Baghdad alone and hundreds of thousands more throughout the country (UN Office for the Coordination of Human Affairs, April 2006), and estimates put the number of Iraqi widows currently registered with the ministry at over one million. Saddam Hussein was responsible for the killings of thousands of men during his repressive dictatorship: political repression and a series of wars caused a demographic imbalance such that the female population now makes up about 55–65 percent of the overall population of twenty-four million Iraqis. The situation has become much more critical since the U.S.-led invasion in 2003, as the daily violence and killings of innocent civilians go hand in hand with an ineffective government that fails to provide the necessary financial and social support for the growing number of widows. At least one million Iraqi widows are estimated to be struggling with poverty in present-day Iraq. Left with virtually no government support, no income as a result of the economic crisis and high unemployment rates, collapsed family networks because of the ongoing humanitarian crisis, and lack of security, many widows have no choice but to beg on the streets or even to engage in prostitution.

Hala's charity, like several others that have emerged since the invasion, is trying desperately to fill the gap left by the lack of government provisions and welfare. It became obvious during my interviews with Iraqi women who continue to live inside Iraq that women have been particularly hard hit by poverty, the lack of adequate health care, malnutrition, and the lack of electricity and clean water on top of the daily violence and lack of security. However, women have also been at the forefront of trying to cope with and improve difficult living conditions, sharing their scarce resources, their expertise, and their professional skills to help those in even greater need.

Women's Political Participation

In the general context of authoritarian governments, arbitrary implementation of laws, and a restriction on civil societies, women's organizations are not always as nongovernmental as their names might suggest. While independent women's organizations did not exist under the Ba'th regime, women's groups and organizations started to mushroom after the invasion. Many of these organizations, such as the National Council of Women (NCW), the Iraqi Women's Higher Council (IWHC), the Iraqi Independent Women's Group, and the Society for Iraqi Women for the Future, were founded by either members of appointed interim governments, such as the Iraqi Governing Council (IGC), or prominent professional women with close ties to political parties. Some of the organizations were initiated by returnees, that is, Iraqi women activists who were part of the diaspora before 2003. While mainly founded and represented by elite women, some of the organizations have a broad membership and have branches throughout the country. The Iraqi Women's Network (Al-Shabaka), for example, consists of over eighty women's grassroots organizations spread throughout Iraq.

In the context of the Iraqi women's movement, the very term "activism" glosses over a variety of involvements and activities, which, if considered in isolation, are not all forms of "political activism," such as charity and welfare, research, advocacy, consciousness-raising, lobbying, and development. Certain forms of activity, such as research, might develop into more political engagements, such as advocacy or lobbying. Moreover, groups and individuals, at any given point in time, might be involved in different kinds of activities: income-generating projects; literacy campaigns; adult education and consciousness-raising; workshops and seminars; demonstrations and sit-ins; and political lobbying. However, the deteriorating security situation and extremely difficult living conditions have severely curtailed the social and political spaces for women activists since 2005.

Iraqi women's rights activists work across political differences in terms of their political party ties or lack thereof, as well as their specific attitudes vis-à-vis the occupation: while some ask for an immediate withdrawal of troops, others prefer to call for a concrete timetable of withdrawal. Some women activists prefer the U.S. and U.K. troops to remain as long as there is no security out of fear of Islamist militancy and terrorism.

The main issues that have politically mobilized women of primarily educated, middle-class backgrounds throughout Iraq are the following: (1) the attempt to replace the relatively progressive personal status law governing marriage, divorce, and child custody with a more conservative law (Article 137 in 2003, and Article 41 of the new constitution of 2005/2006); (2) the issue of a women's quota for political representation (although women were unsuccessful in their attempt to obtain a 40 percent quota in the transitional administrative law [TAL], they managed to negotiate a 25 percent quota); (3) the struggle against sectarianism and for national unity; (4) the struggle against Islamist encroachment both from political parties and from militias and terrorist organizations; (5) the debate about the Iraqi constitution, mainly with respect to the role of Islam, the personal status laws, and the demand to include an article about international conventions, such as CEDAW;[18] and (6) the targeted assassinations of professional women and women's rights activists (Al-Ali 2007:254).

Several Iraqi diaspora organizations and individual activists based in the United States and the United Kingdom were initially instrumental in facilitating and encouraging Iraqi women's political mobilization. A flurry of conferences and the establishment of several women's centers marked the early phase of post–Saddam Hussein Iraq. Diaspora women got involved in charity organizations, humanitarian assistance, training programs, advocacy around women's issues, democracy and human rights, and wider political issues both inside Iraq and in their countries of residence. However, the deteriorating security situation has seriously impeded women's activism in Iraq. As middle-class professionals as well as foreign passport holders have been key targets in both the frequent kidnappings for ransom as well as assassinations, Iraqi women returnees have been particularly vulnerable. Moreover, the lack of credibility of the large number of previously exiled Iraqi politicians who have been disproportionately represented in the various interim governments and have been holding key positions has also contributed to a growing resentment toward women returnees involved in women's organizations and political processes and reconstruction in general (Al-Ali 2007:254–55).

Political transition in the form of two elections and a referendum on the constitution has not resulted in a credible and widely accepted government. Despite the 25 percent women's quota stipulated by law, the steady exclusion of women from the public sphere that started in the 1990s during the sanctions period has accelerated under the occupation. Leila H., a women's rights activist still living inside Iraq, related the following to me while I was visiting Amman for a short respite during the hot summer months of 2005.

Initially many of us were very hopeful. We did not like foreign soldiers on our streets, but we were happy Saddam was gone. Once the general chaos and the looting settled down a bit, women were the first ones to get organized. Women doctors and lawyers started to offer free services to women. We started to discuss political issues and tried to lobby the American and British forces. But especially the Americans sent people to Iraq whose attitude was: "We don't do women." Bremer was one of them. Iraqi women managed to get a women's quota despite the Americans who opposed it. Their interpretation of women's issues was to organize big meetings and conferences and to build modern women's centers. Do you think anyone went to visit these centers? What we need is more women in all aspects of governance. But the problem is that some of the women that are appointed are actually very conservative and are against women's rights. (Al-Ali 2007:256)

There has been a debate about the benefits and problems of stipulating a women's quota, especially in light of the fact that many of the conservative Islamist political parties have obviously appointed conservative Islamist women who might not necessarily be interested in the promotion of women's rights. However, in a general political climate of social conservatism and increased patriarchal power, a quota assures at least some female presence in public life and might also allow those who are more committed to women's issues and social justice to enter government institutions. Moreover, in the case of the conservative Islamist majority, it is still important to include conservative women who might or might not add to the existing discourses and debates. It is likely that some women would challenge prevailing opinions and politics and might also develop and change in the course of being involved in politics.

Conclusion

Unfortunately any discussion about women's rights and women's inclusion in reconstruction processes remains a theoretical exercise as long as the condition on the ground does not change drastically. For the majority of women basic survival for themselves and their families overshadows all other concerns. Iraqi men and women are known to leave their houses and say good-bye to their loved ones as if they will never return. Where you live in Iraq, in which town and which part of a city like Baghdad, for example, can determine the likelihood of being killed by a U.S. sniper or missile. In other places, the risk of a suicide bomb or militant attack might be greater. For women, the lack of security often results in severely restricted mobility, as they generally must be in the company of at least one male guardian.

Despite—or even partly because of—the U.S. and British rhetoric about liberation and women's rights, women have been pushed back even more into the background and into their homes. They are suffering in terms of both an ongoing and worsening humanitarian crisis and a lack of security on the streets. Women who have a public profile, whether as doctors, academics, lawyers, NGO activists, or politicians, are systematically threatened and have become targets for assassinations. The situation has become particularly critical for women who are struggling to promote women's rights inside Iraq.

The louder President Bush shouted "women's liberation" while the United States was occupying Iraq, the greater the backlash against women's rights. Ironically, the resistance to Western imperialism tends to mirror the idea that there was something inherently Western about either human or women's rights. This is despite the fact that human and women's rights abuses have been widely documented within Western countries, including the United States, but also ignores the long history of indigenous women's rights struggles within the region since the early twentieth century.

Over the past several years, the international community, including the U.S. and British governments, has increasingly supported the idea of "gender mainstreaming" in post-conflict reconstruction and peace-building as stated in UN Resolution 1325/2000. However, a stated commitment to promoting women's participation does not guarantee that women are empowered to participate. Indeed, the case of Iraq demonstrates that gender concerns may be sacrificed to "greater priorities"—namely, security and the political agendas of different actors (Pratt 2005). It is necessary to examine how and when gender-sensitive policies are pursued in post-conflict situations and with what results for women and for men.

Most significant in the context of post-9/11 interventions—the so-called war on terror—is the way women's and human rights are being severely compromised by foreign military interventions, the "internationalization" of reconstruction and state building, as well as the instrumentalization of development and humanitarian aid as tools of global security. Feminist activism within the UN framework has been discredited by the inability of the UN to uphold international law and in some instances even rubber-stamp illegal operations. Women's rights and gender mainstreaming have become part of transferable packages driven not only by women's rights agendas but by neoliberal international organizations, institutions, and government agendas. Moreover, as Deniz Kandiyoti convincingly argues,

donor-led institution building may create entities with juridical sovereignty (and international recognition) but with little *de facto* power and empirical capacity to effectively administer national territories and provide law and security. This poses serious dilemmas of legitimacy and calls for the management of multiple tensions between global and local players and political factions with different degrees of commitment to state-building. (2007:508)

As is evident in both Iraq and Afghanistan, "post-conflict" political processes and reconstruction are severely curtailed by escalating violence and increasing sectarian and ethnic conflicts. Because of the very nature of intervention in both places, Islam has become one of the main markers of "authentic identity" and resistance to foreign occupation. Similarly, women and women's rights have taken center stage. Democracy imposed from outside and above inadvertently consolidates and possibly even legitimizes social forces that oppose women's equal rights and participation in public life.

Notes

This chapter is based on material in Al-Ali 2007.

1. Nicola Pratt and I have engaged in an in-depth study of the gap between the rhetoric on women's liberation and the actual policies on Iraq (Al-Ali and Pratt 2009).

2. See also Save the Children, "Assessment in Three Schools," Baghdad, May 18, 2003.

3. All names have been changed to protect the anonymity of respondents.

4. For details about the events at Fallujah, see http://iraqbodycount.org/analysis/reference/falluja-april (accessed April 14, 2009). For an analysis, see Rai 2005.

5. For further details, see http://www.rememberfallujah.org/why.htm (accessed April 14, 2009) and http://www.iraqbodycount.org/analysis/reference/press-releases/9 (accessed April 14, 2009).

6. Patrick Cockburn, "A Guided Missile, A Misguided War," *The Independent*, April 8, 2004.

7. Inter Press Service, November 16, 2004.

8. Those suspected of being involved in resistance or terrorist activities are regularly detained and their families are not notified about their whereabouts and their well-being. Disappearances, random arrests, and torture and abuse in prisons are, ironically, common phenomena in post-Saddam Iraq.

9. Ghali Hassan, "Iraqi Women Under Occupation," May 9, 2005, http://www.countercurrents.org/iraq-hassan090505.html (accessed July 21, 2006).

10. July 11, 2006, http://riverbendblog.blogspot.com/.

11. "Iraq: Female Harassment from Religious Conservatives," April 14, 2004, http://www.IRINNews.org.

12. "Iraq: Women Fleeing College Under Islamist Threats," *Washington Times*, October 17, 2004, http://washingtontimes.com/world/20041017-013506-9889r.html.

13. Article 2. Nathan Brown (2005:2) translates "undisputed rules" as "the fixed elements of the ruling of Islam."

14. See http://www.unicef.org/infobycountry/iraq_statistics.html and http://www.medact.org/content/wmd_and_conflict/Medact%20Iraq%202004.pdf.

15. The study, *Iraq Living Conditions Survey 2004* (ILCS), was organized by the UN Development Programme (UNDP) in collaboration with the Iraqi Ministry of Planning and Development Cooperation and conducted by a Norwegian-trained team from the Central Organisation for Statistics and Information Technology in Baghdad. It drew its conclusions from interviews carried out in April–August 2004 with members of 21,688 households in Iraq's eighteen provinces.

16. Ibid.

17. See UN World Food Programme/Government of Iraq, "Food Security and Vulnerability Analysis in Iraq," survey of May 2006 with the support of UNICEF. http://www.uniraq.org/documents/Iraq_CFSVA_Flyer_EN.pdf (accessed April 14, 2009).

18. The Convention on the Elimination of All Forms of Discrimination Against Women (CEDAW); see, for example, http://www.un.org/womenwatch/daw/cedaw/.

Bibliography

Al-Ali, Nadje. 2003. Gender and Civil Society in the Middle East. *International Feminist Journal of Politics* 5 (2):216–32.
————. 2007. *Iraqi Women: Untold Stories from 1948 to the Present.* London: Zed Books.
Al-Ali, Nadje, and Nicola Pratt. 2009. *What Kind of Liberation? Women and the Occupation of Iraq.* Berkeley: University of California Press.
Bennett, Brian. 2006. Stolen Away. *Time Magazine,* May 1. http://205.188.238.109/time/archive/preview/0,10987,1186558,00.html (accessed July 12, 2006).
Brown, Nathan. 2005. The Final Draft of the Iraqi Constitution: Analysis and Commentary. *Carnegie Endowment for International Peace.* August.
Herring, Eric, and Glen Rangwala. 2006. *Iraq in Fragments: The Occupation and Its Legacy.* Ithaca, N.Y.: Cornell University Press.
Human Rights Watch. 2003. Climate of Fear: Sexual Violence and Abduction of Women and Girls in Baghdad. 15 (7[E]). http://www.hrw.org/reports/2003/iraq0703/iraq0703pdf (accessed April 14, 2009).
Judd, Tony. 2006. For the Women of Iraq, the War Is Just Beginning. *The Independent,* June 8.
Kandiyoti, Deniz. 2007. Between the Hammer and the Anvil: Post-Conflict Reconstruction, Islam and Women's Rights. *Third World Quarterly* 28 (3):503–17.
Oxfam. 2007. Rising to the Humanitarian Challenge in Iraq. Briefing Paper 105. July 30. http://www.oxfam.org/en/policy/briefingpapers/bp105_humanitarian_challenge_in_iraq_0707 (accessed October 12, 2007).
Pratt, Nicola. 2005. Reconstructing Citizenship in Post-Invasion Iraq: The Battle over Women's Rights. Unpublished conference paper, MESA, Washington D.C.
Rai, Milan. 2005. Turning Point Fallujah: How U.S. Atrocities Sparked the Iraqi Resistance. *Electronic Iraq,* May 4. http://electroniciraq.net/news/newsanalysis/

Turning_Point_Fallujah_How_US_Atrocities_Sparked_T_1947–1947.shtml (accessed April 14, 2009).

UNAMI. 2007. Humanitarian Briefing on the Crisis in Iraq. May 2. http://www.uni raq.org/documents/UN-Iraq%20Humanitarian%20Briefing%20Fact%20Sheet %20May%2007.pdf (accessed April 14, 2009).

Chapter 3
The War on Terror, Dismantling, and the Construction of Place: An Ethnographic Perspective from Palestine

Julie Peteet

By the summer of 2006, Iraq, Afghanistan, Palestine, and Lebanon were sites of intense conflict. With the Israeli invasion of Lebanon, U.S. secretary of state Rice in a widely televised interview baldly stated, "these are the birth pangs of the new Middle East." Viewing the larger "war on terror" from a spatial and experiential perspective in Palestine provides a lens through which to view the extraordinary whirlwind of violence engulfing the region. This essay advances a comparative regional approach to these birth pangs, focusing on Iraq and Palestine. For Palestinians in the West Bank and displaced Iraqis, the vision of the "new Middle East" encompasses a significant remapping and corresponding reterritorializing of people with serious consequences for demography, mobility, access to resources, and human rights.

In Palestine the impulse to reterritorialize is proceeding through the Israeli regime of closure, which includes the erection of a wall, land confiscation, checkpoints, a byzantine system of permits governing mobility, and life in confined spaces that together are dramatically relandscaping Palestine. Remapping the region is part and parcel of the war on terror and the "birth pangs." Vast areas of the West Bank are being incorporated into Israel by a concrete wall eight meters (around twenty-four feet) high that snakes deep into Palestinian territory. The wall draws a unilateral border that includes large blocks of Jewish settlements on the Israeli side, prevents a territorially contiguous Palestinian state, and separates many Palestinian villages from their agricultural lands and from each other. In Israel-Palestine, land and water resources, mobility, juridical status, and human rights are allocated along ethnic-national-religious lines. Israeli Labour politician Ehud Barak's campaign slogan for his 1999 run for prime minister was "Us here, them there" (Gordon 2008:197, 282). Spatial strategies to separate Palestinians and Israelis and keep Palestinians at bay continue to multiply: refugee camps, occupied areas, seam zones, the wall, checkpoints, curfews, and permits, among others. In both Palestine and Iraq, a strategy of control exercised through extreme violence, separation, and confinement crafts spaces where a particular form of power is wielded and a vision of the ethnic, sectarian, and national composition of space is enacted.

This essay explores the war on terror through the lens of space and regional reordering to discern the continuities and connections between events in the region. It poses two interrelated sets of questions. First, what insights can an anthropological perspective offer? Second, for Palestinians and Iraqis, what does the ongoing reterritorialized Middle East look like and how is its "birth" experienced? The ethnographic focus is on Palestine but comparisons with Iraq are fleshed out. In Iraq a process of dismantling is under way that bears some resemblance to sixty years of policies and practices that have fragmented the space of Palestine and displaced the majority of the Palestinian population.

On a regional level, a new colonial cartography is taking shape in the Middle East (Khalidi 2004) in which dismantling and staggering demographic upheavals are prominent features. The twentieth century opened with the crumbling of the cosmopolitan social world of the Ottoman Empire and gave way to nation-states and political inclusion on the basis of citizenship. Many Middle Easterners have narrated the war on terror as a contemporary attempt to fragment the region's space and reorder national borders, structures of governance, and the organization of power, human mobility, and ethnic and sectarian organization and identities. Local narratives invoke comparisons to 1916 when the French and British carved the region into their respective mandates. The war on terror has been widely understood as an attempt to impose American hegemony in the Gulf—to establish "full-spectrum dominance" by establishing permanent U.S. military bases in Iraq and the Gulf area (Carapico and Toensing 2006:10), to maintain the flow of cheap oil, to impede access by others, to extinguish the idea of resistance, and eventually to impose an Israeli-Arab peace. In other words, the first decade of the twenty-first century witnessed the attempted dismembering of Iraq (and perhaps Lebanon) and the third and final push to acquire Palestinian territory and extend Israeli sovereignty, inciting in the region, wittingly or unwittingly, sectarian and ethnic violence.

Centered in once largely secular Iraq, the war on terror unleashed sectarian (Sunni and Shi'i) and ethnic (Arab, Kurds, and Turkomen) violence and dismantled the geography and notion of a unified, secular Iraq. A dismantled Iraq and its reconfiguration along imagined ethnic-sectarian lines appealed to some in the U.S. administration. Indeed, a U.S. Senate nonbinding resolution to divide Iraq into three ethnic-sectarian entities passed by a vote of 75–23 on September 26, 2007. Proposed by then Democratic senator Joseph Biden, the resolution was publicly indicative of the deep-seated desire to partition Iraq and rested on a vision of sectarian conflict as endemic and irreconcilable. A temporal dimension can be discerned here as well that resonates with Palestine: the U.S. administration imagined Iraqis as memory-less; the past and collective memory were to recede into the background. The looting of the National Museum of Iraq certainly fits this mode of thinking. Israelis have long attempted to deny Palestinians a past in the space of Palestine; Iraqis and Palestinians are to have a future, just not one of their own making. Sectarian conflict and fragmentation are best contextualized in a historical and regional framework. The colonization of Palestine intensified as the region was forming independent states, and both secular Arab nationalism and local nationalisms were prominent forms of political consciousness. Zionism, which posits ethnic and religious affiliation as the basis of political belonging and the allocation of rights, conceives of the region as an ethnic and/or sectarian mosaic. Concomitantly, Israel has consistently rejected the notion of a secular, democratic state of its citizens. In Iraq, U.S. actions also point to such a conceptualization with each ostensibly bounded group increasingly occupying its own geospatial enclave with political power and representation apportioned by sect. It has taken incredible levels of violence to force Iraqis into sectarian and ethnic enclaves.

In Israel there is a consensus that unilateral separation from the Palestinians is vital for maintaining Jewish demographic supremacy. Indeed, separation has replaced "peace" as a goal and closure is its physical manifestation. Likewise, the idea of "Greater Israel" has been superseded to a large extent by that of unilateral separation. Concerns about a potential Palestinian majority drive the impulse to separate in order to contain the implications of such a majority between the Mediterranean Sea and the Jordan River. Israeli geographer Arnon Soffer argues that separation "offers the best prospects for ensuring the continuing Jewish character of Israel"

(2002:3). Thus the impulse to territorialize—to separate, segregate, and miniaturize—is apparent in both Israel-Palestine and Iraq.

A common grievance and thus common denominator in the region among both secular and Islamist opposition movements is the Palestine question—often dubbed "the mother of all grievances." Although this is central to Muslim-Arab attitudes toward the United States and prominent in mobilizing support for militant Islamist movements, the United States has avoided addressing it seriously, which buys time for Israel to establish more facts on the ground, that is, Jewish settlements and the extension of sovereignty. A historical series of foreign occupations are another common denominator. Israel's occupation of Palestine obviously is key. Al Qaeda's roots can be traced to the installation of U.S. military bases in Saudi Arabia in the wake of the first Gulf war; U.S. occupations of Afghanistan and Iraq are providing additional fuel. Egypt's Islamists can be traced to the Muslim Brotherhood, which arose during the British occupation. Farther west, Hezbollah emerged in the wake of Israel's 1982 invasion of Lebanon and two decades of occupation in the south. The Palestinian Islamist Hamas emerged in the context of prolonged occupation (see Cole 2005). And the Taliban has its origins in the Soviet occupation of Afghanistan. The current U.S. occupation of once fairly secular Iraq has spawned extremely militant sectarian movements such as al Qaeda in Iraq.

Although a comparison of Palestine and Iraq is feasible, significant differences do exist. Although they differ in that Palestine is an instance of settler colonialism, occupation, and competing nationalisms while the U.S. invasion, occupation, and dismantling of Iraq was conceived as part of establishing a global empire, both Israel and the United States seek control over local resources. Spatial segregation, ethnic-religious sorting out, political disintegration and enclavization, and a wall, features integral to daily life in Palestine, have increasingly become facts of daily life for Iraqis as well. In both Palestine and Iraq, the occupying forces seek control of underground resources such as oil and water and above-ground spaces for military bases and settlements as well as control of the skies, borders, and waterways. In both cases massive numbers of people have been displaced.

State-sponsored violence toward civilians, with a corresponding lack of accountability, runs rampant in Iraq and Palestine where the civilian casualties far exceed those of the U.S. and Israeli militaries. Militant resistance to these occupations is defined as terrorism while state-organized violence is defined as legitimate because it is state based and people who engage in violent acts of resistance, in other words terrorists, cannot also be victims.

During the Bush years a shared discourse of the war on terror as the "war without end" and the demonization of Arabs and Islam pervaded the U.S. and Israeli administrations. In other words, as Talal Asad points out, in trying to "distinguish between morally good and morally evil ways of killing, our attempts are beset with contradictions and those contradictions remain a fragile part of our modern subjectivity" (2007:2). Finally, the role of Western and international evangelicals on the ground in Palestine and Iraq, as vocal and enthusiastic supporters of the Israeli occupation, settlements, and the war on terror, is striking and seriously understudied (see McAlister 2007).

Anthropology and the War on Terror

What particular insights can anthropology offer and, equally important, how can we make our ideas and perspective heard among the public? While anthropologists historically frame the contemporary, studying global formations has not been our strength although this is rapidly changing; our strength has rested on our exploring how global processes are interpreted and reinscribed locally and the way local events can reverberate globally. Recently Catherine Lutz has argued for ethnographies of empire to "rescue the understanding of empire from the celebratory, sensational, and antisociological" but also to "question the singular thingness that the term *empire* suggests by identifying the many fissures, contradictions, historical particularities, and shifts in the imperial process" (2006:593). The war on terror presents a moment and a space in which to pursue ethnographies of empire—not only its imagery and contradictions but also its failings.

Anthropology's concern with culture from an insider's point of view, local-global interaction, and our comparative angle, as well as our interest in memory and forgetting and resistance to domination, all hold promise. In addition, our understanding of how individuals and societies respond to conflict and prolonged stress position us to offer insights on possible responses to military assault and prolonged occupation—the stuff of empire. Anthropological understanding of the sociopolitical uses of history, of linkages, of the interrelatedness of the social, and, in this case, of regional orders and collective memories enables an understanding of how the past can illuminate the present. (The future is another issue.) To what extent does our knowledge serve as a platform for offering predictions, or at least warnings (not prophecies), of the wider implications of launching a war? Roberto

González (2004:6) suggests a particular niche for the anthropological endeavor: *preventive diplomacy*. Middle East anthropologists understood the distinct possibility of the fragmentation of Iraq's sociopolitical order along ethnic-sectarian lines and the possibility of regional conflagration, yet their voices were absent from the media and public consciousness.

A key task for a publicly minded anthropology is to inform debate—to be an integral voice in a vigorous dialogue and debate on the war on terror. We might think about the way we write and for what audiences while remaining cognizant of the constraints the academy imposes on the untenured. A public anthropological voice, exemplified by Margaret Mead, does not carry much weight today among either the public or anthropologists themselves. Anthropology can be used for purposes other than working for the military and intelligence establishment.[1] While anthropological knowledge can be put to many uses, not all of them are in the interests of the new subjects of empire. It can equally be deployed to inform the military and the defense establishment about local cultures and on counterinsurgency tactics that are deemed culturally resonant and appropriate (see Packer 2006).

A key factor that contributed to the U.S. debacle and the public's willingness to support the war in Iraq was both the public and the politico-military establishment's stunning lack of the most basic knowledge of Iraq's social history and organization—its "tribes," clans, class structure, religious sects, and ethnic composition, its regions and regional identities in all their fluidity, and their complex and not necessarily predictable intersections with political organization and identity—the stuff of anthropology. A key feature, ignored by the U.S. administration, was the concept of region—"a sentiment that brings together citizens of a given territory despite other social factors that may set them apart, like language or religious sect" (Visser and Stansfield 2008:1). That Iraq would fracture along ethnic-sectarian lines was either "willful ignorance"[2] or astute perception;[3] in either case, Iraqi leaders with narrow sectarian agendas themselves often paved the way. Ignorance of the central role of the military in the Iraq social order was absolutely stunning or incredibly perceptive. Furthermore, the Bush administration seemed to have scant awareness of the extent of the influence of Islamist movements and ideologies as a basis of opposition. They seemed unaware of extant and potential political and religious ties between Iraqi Shi'is and Iran. In other words, they were willfully ignorant of the fault lines—those subterranean fissures that run through all societies—and of any nuances to an imagined ethnic-sectarian and now "tribal" Iraq.

The war on terror is a military, political, and cultural endeavor to conquer, govern, and impose new structures of governance and transform the regional and local social order. Ideologically, the new global spatial order advanced by the Bush administration is predicated on a dualism, a "clash of civilizations," a split between us and those like us and those others—terrorists and lawless evildoers. In this simplistic scenario, little distinction was made between Osama bin Laden, al Qaeda, Saddam Hussein, the Taliban, the Palestinian Hamas and Islamic Jihad, and the Lebanese Hezbollah. Bin Laden and Saddam Hussein were even cast as having a similar ideological and regional agenda. In other words, the U.S. administration and the public could not distinguish between Islamist militants and secular nationalists or between local and regional movements and ambitions or even between Sunni and Shi'i Islam.

Anthropology can offer insights about history, memory, and resistance as well as their regional, comparative aspects and remind us of the need to think regionally about narratives of conflict and the past. In the Arab world, historical memories of past external interventions are not uncommon; I stress the word "Arab" here to draw attention to an "Arab" past. Iraqis, for example, share with other Arabs a collective memory and narrative of Iraq's immediate past, but they also share a historically deep regional memory of specific events and encounters with the West. For example, evoking an Arab-Islamic collective memory, a Palestinian Jerusalemite, whose family has lived in the city for over a thousand years, remarked in reference to increasing Jewish settlements in the city, "This city has been occupied many times. The Crusaders were here for a hundred years and Jerusalem was eventually liberated. We lived as a pluralistic and tolerant city for hundreds of years under Muslim rule." Iraqis have a collective memory of the thirteenth-century Mongol invasion and the 1914 British occupation. In Lebanon the 2006 Israeli invasion evoked those of 1978 and 1982. Palestinian narratives locate the beginnings of their exile and dispossession in the British Mandate's promises to create a homeland for Jews in Palestine. Few are unaware that the Algerians were under French control for a century. These invasions and occupations and those of the contemporary era are not disparate unconnected events; for many in the region they are part of a long historical pattern and narrative of unequal relations with the West (see Khalidi 2004). Memory and political opposition should be twined because it is memory of the past occupations and resistance, whether historically accurate or nostalgic, that nuances and gives cultural meaning to current militant resistance.

Memories also play a role in constructing moral and communal boundaries. When the Crusaders conquered Jerusalem in 1099 after a forty-day siege, a massacre of thirty thousand Arab Christians, Jews, and Muslims ensued (Maalouf 1984). After Saladin liberated the city in 1187, Christians and Jews were able to practice their religions and synagogues were rebuilt. For nearly eight hundred years under Muslim rule Jerusalem was a site of religious pluralism and tolerance. With the 1967 occupation of the city, Israel launched a sustained policy of a demographic and cultural Judaization. To de-Palestinianize the city, Palestinian property was confiscated and legal obstacles to residency were put in place, Jewish settlers were moved into the Old City and East Jerusalem, the Palestinian economic sector faced severe restrictions, and West Bank and Gaza Palestinians had their access to the city severely restricted, transforming Jerusalem into a space of intolerance and marginality for non-Jews.

Historically, resistance to foreign domination has been fairly consistent across the region. From the battles against the Crusaders to Afghan mobilization against the British and later the Russians, to Algeria's long resistance to French settler colonialism, to Iraqi resistance to the British (Khalidi 2004) and over sixty years of Palestinian attempts to confront Israeli occupation, it is stunning that U.S. policymakers did not foresee an Iraqi insurgency. In other words, there was a "willful ignorance" of the likelihood of a militant Iraqi response. If we take a historically embedded anthropological perspective, resistance to foreign invasions and domination is hardly a rarity. Indeed, it is a fairly predictable response to conquest, one that an anthropologically informed perspective could have explicated. Not only was the possibility of resistance not on the radar screen of those planning and executing the war, Israel with a green light from the United States invaded Lebanon with similar results—chaos, large-scale loss of lives, and destruction of state infrastructure. Among Middle East academics posing the question of what compelled the 2006 Israeli invasion of Lebanon, a common answer was that it aimed to crush the idea of resistance and reassert Israel's deterrent force status in the region in addition to testing the regional waters for a possible future attack on Iran.

Attempts to dismember or cripple state and governing infrastructures have been integral tactics in the war on terror and the reordering of the Middle East. Iraq's infrastructure—its military, water, health, education, sanitation, and electricity systems—has been systematically dismantled. Israel's 2006 war on Lebanon targeted its infrastructure as well; roads, bridges, and water, electricity, and sanitation facilities were military targets; and vast swaths of housing were destroyed in the massive air campaign. These tactics coincided with the action of the United States and some EU members to cut off aid to the Palestinian Authority in the wake of the assumption of power by the democratically elected Hamas, crippling its ability to govern. The policy of economic strangulation meant salaries to over 130,000 government officials and security staff were not paid and public services were barely functioning (Eldar 2006). Journalist Akiva Eldar writes that during the initial years of the second intifada, Israelis believed that "constructive destruction" would force Palestinians to abandon resistance. Projects of dismemberment in the region are attempts to rewrite local and regional geographies, to craft ethnic-sectarian spaces, to impose external dominance, and to crush the ideas of resistance. Each has its local variant and particular form of violence.

Spaces of Exception

A state of exception prevails in Iraq, Afghanistan, Lebanon, and Palestine. Both the United States and Israel consider their presence in these arenas as exempt from the rules of international law (see Agamben 2005). The mantra of "security" has shrouded their actions with impunity. The war on terror spawned a siege mentality that underwrote the flagrant violation of human rights and international humanitarian law. The lack of concern with Iraqi or Palestinian civilian casualties remains disturbing at best. Most significantly, the temporal aspect is striking; each is part of a war without end.

One of most significant ways anthropologists can provide perspective on the war on terror is through notions of imagined geographies, the imputation of difference, and the assigning of human rights. Global space is being partitioned into, on the one hand, zones of rights and recognition and, on the other, zones of indistinction and lack of rights and recognition. Ominously, a discourse of monstrosity pervades contemporary America's war on terror. Conflict usually engenders a process of differentiation between one's own culture and that of the enemy. In Iraq this has become so extreme that soldiers and private security personnel willfully kill civilians with near impunity; in the West Bank, armed settlers perpetrate acts of violence on a daily basis against Palestinians with similar impunity.

The actions of U.S. forces in Afghanistan and Iraq closely parallel those Israel has used to quell Palestinian resistance. As polities in a state of exception, both the United States and Israel are self-positioned as sacred and inviolable places where attacks such as September 11 and militant resistance to Israeli occupation call for disproportionate military responses that are then, in part because of an ill-defined and endless war on terror, exempt from international law and the targets are exempt from its protections.

The discourse accompanying the war on terror occurs at the intersection of subterfuge and imaginative geographies. The Israeli and U.S. discourse is almost indistinguishable, and indeed Israel regularly announces that they are "on the same page" as they pursue "terrorists." Now, "terrorology" has its own institutions and spokespersons—instant experts, think tanks, ideologically driven policymakers, and university courses on "terrorism." The now emotionally charged and coded term "security" frames any discussion of the war on terror, the wall, and closure, linking U.S. and Israeli interests in fighting Muslim "terrorists." With its sheer, predictable repetitiveness, it resembles a mantra with all its qualities of mystification. Its status as a shibboleth verges on the sacred. Security is unevenly apportioned, the preserve of some and not others. The key issue, however, is whether security comes from walls, occupations, extrajudicial detention centers, and the practice of torture.

The mantra of security and terrorism has dangerously crowded out and silenced anything that might suggest alternative ways of thinking. Terrorology includes what geographer Derek Gregory (2004:249) calls the "language of the monstrous" to characterize a broad array of enemies such as Palestinians, Afghans, Iraqis, Lebanese Shi'is, and Islamists. In both the war on terror and the war on Palestine, coordinated projects to silence critique or dissent are evident, ranging from then attorney general John Ashcroft's linking criticism of U.S. policy with aid to terrorists, to Campus Watch's close monitoring of any critique or dissent from U.S. or Israeli policies and practices.

Palestine offers an intriguing perspective from which to view the war on terror. Until the occupation of Iraq, Palestine was the barometer of colonialism in the region, the common thread of grievance. It has now been joined by Iraq.

Ethnography of Closure: "Permission to Breathe"

> *The habits of violence are indeed various—the point of a knife, the*
> *end of a stick, the velocity of a bullet, the push of a button—but*

> violence encompasses more insidious means as well: the practice of
> exclusion, misrepresentation, dispossession, oblivion.
> —Ammiel Alcalay (1993)

What is now known as "closure" began in 1991 when Israeli checkpoints suddenly mushroomed around Jerusalem to control Palestinian access to the city. "Closure" refers to Israeli restrictions on the movement of Palestinian goods, labor, and people into Jerusalem, within and between the Gaza Strip and the West Bank, and between them and Israel. Illegal Israeli settlements and closure, with its wall, bypass roads, the permit and visa system, and checkpoints—around five hundred checkpoints dot the landscape of the West Bank—form an interlocking set of architectural and bureaucratic controls over Palestinian mobility. These spatial features, architectural forms, and bureaucratic rules facilitate the continuing acquisition of Palestinian land and natural resources, impose economic crisis, and incorporate significant tracts of the West Bank into Israel. Complaining about multiple checkpoints on her way to work, Lina, an administrator in a local NGO, said in exasperation, "Soon we will need permission to breathe," capturing Israel's overwhelming control over the Palestinian body, individually and collectively. Closure fixes the Palestinian body in delimited spaces and spatially allocates rights to, access to, and sovereignty over resources along ethnic-religious-national lines.

Our sense of distance is socially produced and often violently so, especially in Palestine. With closure, once short distances have become monumental exercises in mobility, fraught with anxiety and danger. Spatial tactics are the use of space as a means to achieve power and assert social control (Low and Lawrence-Zúñiga 2003:30). Spatial tactics that limit Palestinian mobility encapsulate and thus clarify and make visible and tactile the social hierarchy.

Current Israeli spatial practices in the West Bank are components of a continuing policy to dilute an Arab presence in historic Palestine. Palestinian refugee camps are spaces where those excised from the new Jewish state in 1948 were relegated and managed as a population (Peteet 2005b). Former prime minister Ariel Sharon's declaration that the current period is the second half of 1948, when Palestinians fled or were expelled and then denied the right of return, has not fallen on deaf ears. Closure to effect demographic transformation has been Israeli policy; its goal is to *remove the land* from them and reduce their numbers—to make Palestinian places into empty space which, through Jewish settlement and the extension of sovereignty, can then be reconfigured as exclusively Jewish places. In other words, once a settlement is established the land is now Israeli. This project to ensure a Jewish majority from the Jordan River to the Mediterranean is driven by "demographic panic" (Honig-Parnass 2003:68) over the high growth rates of Palestinians in Israel and the Occupied Territories. Structural violence such as draconian controls over the economy and mobility as well as pervasive settler and military violence proceed apace and are intended to encourage emigration, also known as slow-motion ethnic cleansing. However, Palestinian resistance, international opprobrium, and Jordan's determination not to accept more displaced Palestinians makes sweeping transfer, as occurred in 1948, less likely. Thus Palestinian population movements as a result of closure may be less to destinations abroad and more internal to local cities such as Ramallah. Land expropriation, severe restrictions on mobility and the economy, and fragmentation of the West Bank into multiple noncontiguous sections suggest the intent is to render unfeasible a two-state solution. Ultimately the goal seems to be to generate migrants rather than refugees who have a legal status and a presence in the international arena.

Closure: Chaos and Transforming the Landscape

In a number of public talks, Israeli journalist Amira Hass has referred to settlements, checkpoints, road barriers, and the wall as "the violence of cement." Landscape is the meaning imputed to the environment and its inscription with meaning, and refers to the way people narrate space. Israeli settlements, checkpoints, military installations, blocks of cement obstructing roads, barbed wire, trenches, and bypass roads, starkly etched into the rural topography, scar the landscape of Palestine. The wall's rough cement slabs speak to the raw power to immiserate. Jewish settlements, illegal according to international law, now house 430,000 Jewish settlers. This may be the single most diagnostic feature of Israeli policy since the Oslo process; at a time when there was to be a freeze on settlements, their numbers doubled. Palestinians received the message with little ambiguity.

Though the settlements were once claimed essential for security, journalist Aluf Been writes, "The general view in the defense establishment is that settlements do not contribute directly to security and also force the IDF to deploy troops for their defense. Moreover, there is no particular settlement . . . critical to security" (quoted in Aronson 2006:133). Israeli prime minister Olmert's "convergence" plan or unilateral drawing of a border with the West Bank is said to involve the relocation of about sixty thousand settlers from around seventy small isolated settlements to the larger settlements of Ma'ale Adumim, Ariel, and Gush Etzion.

Closure's most immediate effect has been to obstruct Palestinian mobility. In trying to grasp daily life ethnographically, I came up with the phrase "calibrated chaos." An acquaintance working with an NGO said, "The soldiers have told us chaos is their policy." Control through the imposition of calibrated chaos, the conscious policy of changing rules and regulations at will with no warning or explanation, is accomplished through a rich variety of techniques to inhibit mobility and induce anxiety: checkpoints, the wall, metal gates, earth mounds, trenches, and concrete slabs that block access to villages, and the permit system. Intermittent and prolonged curfews punctuate these measures. Unpredictability is now the norm; it shatters trust in the routines of daily life that are essential for the smooth functioning of society and for people's sense of well-being and normalcy. Even more damaging, Palestinian access to health care, educational facilities, places of employment, and social, familial, and religious sites has been severely curtailed.

An international NGO described closure as the "primary cause of poverty and humanitarian crisis in the territories" (IDMC 2006:12). Access to health care has been hindered; 97 primary health clinics and 11 hospitals are isolated from the populations they once served. There are nearly 100 documented cases of denial of access to medical care at checkpoints leading to death, including infants. If the wall divides a town, and the hospital is on other side, Palestinians may have to drive for hours, through multiple checkpoints, to reach a hospital that is just a few miles away. Ambulances are routinely obstructed at checkpoints. Soldiers step into them and check the wounded, often causing delays; sometimes they compel patients to walk or be carried through the checkpoint to take another ambulance on the other side. Closure has produced mass impoverishment because of the lack of work and lack of access to markets in Israel. Seventy-five percent of Palestinians live below the poverty line, a figure that has tripled since 2000. Half a million people now rely on international food aid, and food insecurity has now reached fifty-six percent of Gazan households (World Bank 2009). The Israeli army has killed 4,876 Palestinians since September 2000 (1,162 Israelis have been killed). Six hundred Palestinian children have been killed.[4] By 2005 over 250 extrajudicial executions by Israeli forces had killed an additional 186 Palestinian bystanders.

With closure, Palestinians say they feel as though time has stopped—one can only act in the moment. Undertaking the smallest task such as a family visit or visit to the doctor engenders a constant state of alert and heightened anxiety. In short, Palestinians are suffering a collective and individual loss of control over the most basic elements of daily life. What makes the situation so anxiety producing is not just its unpredictability (will one arrive at a chosen destination?) but that the rules change almost daily with no explanation or logic. Without warning, a checkpoint can close and simply turn back people; questions about what is going on are usually met with a gruff "shut up" or a shrug of the shoulders. Chaos and unpredictability foster disorientation. A state of generalized anxiety, nervousness, and depression is pervasive. Pharmacists report they are filling more prescriptions for antidepressants and anti-anxiety medications than ever before.

Mobility, Checkpoints, and Permission to Move

Like many facets of globalization, mobility is strikingly uneven. Zygmunt Bauman dubs this "most powerful and coveted stratifying factor" an "unequally distributed commodity" (1998:9, 2). As a pervasive feature of daily life, checkpoints fragment territory, divide people, and severely obstruct mobility. Invariably, they signal an unmediated sense of immobility, highlighting in stark physical form the inaccessibility of spaces once known and accessible. Palestinian mobility is a scarce commodity, almost completely under Israeli control, a tangible thing that Israelis have and Palestinians are denied.

Spatial difference is arbitrarily imposed on contiguous spaces and is activated by barriers that control mobility. In the West Bank, physical obstacles to mobility in 2005, for example, increased by 25 percent, from 376 to 535, ranging from checkpoints to earthen mounds blocking road access to villages (Shearer 2006:22). Checkpoints are spaces where the body is forced to undergo a disciplinary regime of coercive and subordinating power. Israeli power is displayed and strutted in this highly performative encounter between two vastly unequal sides. The participants know the script well; there is little ambiguity in this encounter. Enacting the script reaffirms and reproduces Palestinian subordination and Israeli rule. The sectarian and ethnic basis to mobility is part and parcel of a regional remapping and the differential allocation of access to space and mobility. It is similar to that which now exists in Iraq, where mobility is determined by sectarian identity, which can be a ticket to mobility or a death sentence.

Checkpoints range from small posts manned by two or three soldiers to large sites like Kalandia (just outside Jerusalem), which resembles an international border through which thousands of people are processed everyday. Only those with Jerusalem identity cards or a permit to enter the city are allowed to enter the Jerusalem side. Long lines at checkpoints are standard; metal turnstiles force the body into an assembly line procedure of mobility. Some checkpoints can be driven across; at many one must leave public transportation, walk across the checkpoint, and then pick up another bus or taxi on the other side. This long, drawn-out process adds hours and extra fares to a daily commute.

Ethnographic observations suggest that the rules of opening and closing checkpoints are quite arbitrary; one can wait hours or minutes regardless of how many cars are there or how many soldiers. The soldiers take everyone's papers and often disappear, usually without a word, and return them, sometimes quickly and sometimes hours later. On many occasions they simply put them in their pockets and return them an hour or two later. People are forced to wait in cars in the heat or cold; this can be quite difficult for the elderly and those with small children. Oddly enough, they often do not check the cars themselves. Given that security can be quite lax, it seems that waiting is the issue (Peteet 2008). Indeed, the Palestinian, invariably male, waiting at a checkpoint has become an iconic figure. Again the security angle must be questioned in that bribery is not uncommon; young men often offer the soldiers cartons of cigarettes for passage.

Palestinians watch bitterly as Israeli cars whiz through checkpoints with a friendly wave of the hand and a smile while Palestinian cars wait for permission to pass. As buses or small passenger vans approach a checkpoint, conversation tends to stop. The nervous system springs into action as people tense up and wait in anticipation. In dead silence, people automatically hold up their identity cards, always ready for quick inspection.

Palestinians talk of suffocating, of wanting to lead normal lives. "We want to enjoy the simple pleasures of life—to go to movies, to a café in Jerusalem, to travel, to feel safe," young people told me. Yet their sense of humor is evident in jokes such as this: Palestinians need cars with only first and second gears since there is not enough distance between checkpoints to go into third, let alone fourth, gear. Their small enclaves have become spaces of withdrawal that some have not left for years.

With the wall and checkpoints dividing the West Bank into noncontiguous areas, to go anywhere requires traveling long distances. For example, if a family lives on a side of the wall that cuts them off from their local clinic or schools, they may have to drive for hours and go through multiple checkpoints to reach the other side of their own town. In a society where visiting family and friends is the cement holding the social order together, closure has had a serious and observable impact on family relations.

In expansionist settler-colonial projects, the familiar landscape rapidly becomes the strange and unknown. Dramatic changes, such as new settlements, checkpoints, and flying checkpoints, and new signage in a foreign language are disorienting to those who know the terrain through a lifetime of intimate use. Palestinians now have a new lexicon of topographic names and spatial locators, which continue to expand as new spatial tactics are devised: flying checkpoints, terminals, underground passages, gates, areas A, B, and C, and bypass roads. This new geography of the homeland and its lexicon are embodied as well. The Palestinian collective is being fragmented by multiple kinds of identity cards and permits endowing each individual holder with varying degrees of mobility and differential access to space and thus different privileges. The Palestinian body is perceived as transgressive and thus subject to extensive regulation; it is punished for the least infraction and sometimes for none at all. Beatings, arrests, confiscations of the identity card, forced waiting, and shootings face the Palestinian body that transgresses Israeli rules of access to space.

Checkpoints and experiences at them are frequent topics of conversation. Palestinians routinely discuss how they reached their destination and the obstacles they faced. Twenty-year-old Ziad's attempt to visit his family offers a glimpse into Palestinian mobility. A student at Bir Zeit University, he works part-time in a local NGO. He grew up in Jenin refugee camp where his father was killed by a sniper during the 2002 Israeli assault. As the eldest of six brothers, Ziad gives money from his small salary to his mother and tries to visit every week. Ziad describes what should have been a two-hour trip from Ramallah to Jenin:

On Friday, I left Ramallah around 7:30 A.M. I was stopped at the Zaatari checkpoint and was told to go back. I asked, "Why?" The soldier said, "There is a curfew in Jenin and since you are from Jenin, you are under curfew wherever you may be." I tried waiting at the checkpoint to find a taxi to take me to Nablus. The solider yelled at me, "Emshee!" [Go away!] I finally got a taxi to Nablus and I had to go through a checkpoint I had already passed going the other way. The soldiers saw me returning and laughed at me. They knew I would be turned back at that checkpoint. I was so angry! I went to Nablus but could not find a taxi to Jenin. People told me to go to Beit Iba checkpoint in the north. There, people were lined up single file to cross through the electrically controlled metal turnstile. I was stuck in there for five minutes. The soldiers control it with a button and sometimes they lock people in for the fun of it. When I exited, the soldier smiled and said, "Shalom." He took my identity card and put it in a tray and pushed it toward me and said, "Take it." He did not want to hand it to me. After Beit Iba, I failed to find a taxi to Jenin. I didn't want to return to Nablus and I didn't want to go through the Beit Iba checkpoint again so I found a taxi to take me back to Ramallah. We went through the Ainab Gate. It is a big metal gate that closes the road. The driver stops and goes to the military office. We had to get out of the taxi, walk across, and then get another taxi. Then we came to a flying checkpoint. We got down from the taxi and the soldier said, "Where are you from?" to each of us. He asks each person like it was a game. He would come back and ask the same question again and again. Finally, the driver said, "Why do you keep asking the same thing? You have the identity cards and their answers." One more checkpoint—the soldier said I can't go to Ramallah because I am from Jenin. I told him I work there and he finally let me go. I got back to Ramallah around midnight.

Ziad's convoluted tale of mobility restrained and mocked is not unusual. Humiliation fosters a simmering anger when people are treated as foreigners in their own country, particularly at checkpoints run by eighteen- to twenty-year-old soldiers who spend much time chatting, flirting, and making fun of people waiting. They often take identity cards and then sit and chat for ten minutes or more, drinking tea, while you wait.

Access to the road system in the West Bank is organized according to ethnic and national affiliations. Only cars with Israeli plates can drive on the well-paved bypass roads; these crosscut the West Bank and connect settlements to Israel. They allow settlers direct access to Israel without having to drive through Palestinian areas. Cars have color-coded license plates so that their drivers can be easily identified. Bypass roads and the wall now prevent line of sight. In other words, Israeli settlers do not have to see the indigenous population. Their line of vision includes colorful pastoral scenes painted on the Israeli side of the wall; the Palestinian side has eye-riveting graffiti graphically expressing protest, anger, and solidarity.

Palestinian mobility is also subject to a highly complex and ambiguous system of permits. Since 1967 Israel has controlled the Palestinian civil registry and the issuance of identity cards, permits, and visas to foreigners. In many areas a permit is needed to live in one's own village or town. To enter other towns or areas, particularly Jerusalem, a permit is necessary. The granting of permits is a mysterious and time-consuming process whose criteria are highly unpredictable and hard to discern.

The permit system is an example of the imposition of chaos and uncertainty. Any Palestinian who wants to enter Jerusalem for business, education, medical care, family visits, or simply to visit the city must have a
permit. One may wait for days or weeks before being called to pick up the
permit. A typical example of the unpredictability and arbitrariness sur-
rounding the permit system is that of Abed, a sixty-two-year-old business-
man. He applied for a permit to enter Jerusalem for a business meeting
weeks in advance. The morning of the meeting, he was called and told to
pick up his permit. Upon arriving at the registry he was told to wait, which
he did for several hours without any explanation. By the time the permit
was issued the meeting was over. The clerk handed him his permit with a
smirk. Delays are the norm and the lack of explanation is standard. A professor at Al-Quds University, now isolated from Jerusalem by the wall, was
invited to give a lecture in Jerusalem. Cut off by the wall, she needed a permit to enter the city. The Israeli authorities told her to go get her permit at
9:00 A.M.. Arriving at the appointed time, she waited until noon to receive
her permit. The lecture was at 11:00. Palestinians see these arbitrary controls
as designed or calibrated to impose chaos and unpredictability and make
life so difficult that people will emigrate.

In Palestine mobility is a function of ethnic-national-religious identities. The permit system permeates the minutest details of everyday life and
has an indelible impact on family relations. For example, Selma has a Palestinian West Bank identity but is married to a Palestinian with a Jerusalem
identity. Palestinians who do not possess an Israeli-issued Jerusalem identity card are not allowed in the city without a permit even if they are married to a Jerusalem identity card holder. Selma describes what this means
for her daily life, mobility, family relations, and marriage. Her story encapsulates how the policy of closure, identity cards, and permits determines
Palestinian mobility, enhances chaos, and generates uncertainty and anxiety.

If I had known it would be like this I wouldn't have married him! I have a
baby girl. We are living in Beit Hanina, very close to Jerusalem and Ramallah where
I work. We live on the Jerusalem side of the wall so I have to pass checkpoints to
go home. My daughter is registered with her father. She cannot travel with me because she is registered with him. If I try to give her a Palestinian identity and passport, she will lose the Jerusalem identity.

When I gave birth my husband managed to bring my mother. The closure
wasn't so bad then. To avoid the checkpoints they drove her among the houses and
then another car came and took her. I remember once she was supposed to come to

the hospital but no taxi would take her—they asked her, "Do you have a Jerusalem identity?" She told them, "No I have a West Bank identity." And they said, "Sorry we can't." So no taxi would take her—they don't want to be imprisoned for driving someone without a Jerusalem identity card. So I spent the day alone.

Our families have never gotten together since we married. My father doesn't know where my husband's house is. We were hoping I could have a permit to stay in Jerusalem as I am married to a Jerusalemite. But now I have heard it has been canceled. I can't live here anymore! Before, it wasn't that bad if they stopped us at a checkpoint and said, "Go back." I could go to my parents' or to another check-point. I could try other ways, to go through bypass roads. It is too hard with the baby, to go up and down in the cars. It is not safe. I don't want to live in an unclear situation.

When I go through checkpoints, I always carry the marriage contract but now they just say go away. Now, if I am in Jerusalem with my husband and we get caught by the Israelis we have to pay around $1,000; they will take his card for one month and then he has to sign a paper that he is not supposed to be in Jerusalem with me. It is forbidden for me to be in Jerusalem with my husband. It is illegal; he could be put in prison. It depends on the soldiers, their mood. I am just going to my house and I stay there. I can't move. And I don't want anyone to come and take me be-cause it is not safe for them. So I can't go to my mother-in-law. I can't join in the social activities of the family. They live exactly where the wall is in Abu Dis, on the Jerusalem side.

The future—it is so dark. It is hard for us to think about the end of the day. I don't know if I will go home to sleep in my bed. It's like being captured and locked in a tower and waiting for my husband to come and take me because I can't move. It is so hard! You know, last month we had so many problems. Two or three weeks ago I went to my family and said, "Helas! I want a divorce." My husband is always worried because of the situation and thus he is always so upset and angry. And me, I am the same way.

The Wall

In 1994 Rabin declared, "We have to decide on separation as a philosophy" (Makovsky 2004:52). By 1995 a commission was discussing a barrier to sepa-rate Palestinians and Israelis. The idea lay dormant until Prime Minister Barak decided to start building in 2002. Israelis call it a "fence," "the secur-ity fence," or "the separation barrier." Palestinians call it "the wall" (al-jidar), the "apartheid wall," and, more bitterly, "a prison without a roof." Israelis argue, particularly for Western audiences, that separation is neces-sary for security: to prevent Palestinians from entering Israel and carrying out militant attacks. Yet the mantra of security is challenged by, on the one hand, an open discussion of the "demographic" issues it helps resolve and, on the other, long-range military weapons and Israeli regional dominance of the skies. Palestinian militants in Gaza, surrounded by an electronic fence that provides extensive, well-calibrated control over the mobility of people and goods, are able to launch homemade rockets into Israel.

An age-old technique of controlling population movements, defending territory, and quelling resistance, walls are hardly a historical novelty. Indeed, the Great Wall of China and Hadrian's Wall in England, built to prevent "barbarian" incursions, are UNESCO World Heritage sites. The wall is also thought to indicate the drawing of a unilateral border. It could incorporate into Israel as much as 53 percent of the West Bank or as little as 10 percent.

The stark slabs of upright concrete form a cement wall that snakes through populated areas, punctuated by watchtowers and firing posts every three hundred meters or so. In some areas it is composed of razor-wire fence. Accompanying the wall is a one-hundred- to three-hundred-foot-wide buffer zone that often includes trenches, electric fencing, remote sensors, a parallel road for military patrols, and cameras. At nearly twenty-five feet high (eight meters—about three times the height of the Berlin Wall) and an estimated four hundred miles (seven hundred kilometers) in length, it is significantly longer than the twelve-kilometer Berlin Wall.

Palestinians argue that if security were the issue, it could have been built on the Green Line. Yet tellingly, it is deep in Palestinian territory. In some places it extends up to fourteen miles into Palestinian territory and indeed cuts the West Bank into three parts, making the territorial contiguity of a Palestinian state dubious. The wall erases the 1967 border and isolates Jerusalem. By including blocks of settlements on the Israeli side, the wall could end up annexing 50–55 percent of the West Bank (Makovsky 2004). If the Jerusalem settlements are included, up to three-quarters of all the settlers will be spatially incorporated into Israel (Morris 2006). To construct the wall and its buffer zone has meant large-scale house demolition; thousands of acres of agricultural land have been confiscated and thousands of trees have been uprooted.

Some small towns and villages are completely surrounded by the wall with only one point of entry and exit controlled by the Israelis. In addition, the wall has crafted a "seam zone," a wedge between the wall and the 1967 Green Line. Figures vary, but it is generally acknowledged that around sixty-five thousand Palestinians live in the seam zone (Morris 2006). Entry and exit are controlled by checkpoints and gates that can only be opened by soldiers who are supposed to open them in the morning and close them at 4:00. Sometimes they do not open for days. Residents must have a permit to live in their homes and another permit to farm their land in the seam. Since almost no permits were issued for 2004 and 2005, thousands of olive trees went unharvested.

Palestinian farmers face difficulty marketing produce because the gates are not always opened and checkpoints delay deliveries. Economic insecurity and the arbitrariness of mobility contribute to high levels of anxiety and anger. The only people who can freely travel through closed zones are Israeli citizens and residents.

How do people respond to, make sense of, and narrate closure? Their reactions range from accommodation to petty resistance and from peaceful protests to overt resistance. Palestinians are accommodating new spatial realities, however, within a very narrow margin of action. For example, at checkpoints vibrant markets have sprung up that sell everything from juice and coffee to socks and clocks as Palestinians accommodate restrictions and yet try to resist economic strangulation (see Hammami 2004). Behavior at checkpoints is illustrative of both resistance and accommodation: people try to sneak or bribe their way through and engage in various forms of subterfuge. At Kalandia checkpoint, I once observed young boys throw paint and fire torches at a watchtower. On occasion, women try to sneak across by pretending to be invisible, particularly elderly women and young mothers.

Weekly protests in some villages are highly organized, peaceful affairs where mixed groups of Palestinians, Israelis, and foreigners resort to nonviolent techniques to try to halt the wall. For example, the wall was enclosing Zawiyya and three other villages into a sealed zone with village lands on the other side of the wall. Bulldozers, well guarded by Israeli military forces, uprooted thousands of olive trees, destroying the villagers' livelihood. In the summer of 2005, villagers were panicked over how they would survive. At a large protest among the bulldozed fields of olive trees, village women publicly wept and lamented, "They can come from Poland, and Holland, and Ethiopia and Russia but this is my land. It was planted by my father, and his father, and so on back hundreds of years. Why should I be afraid now? We are already dead. Everything I cook and feed my children is from these olives. From where will I bring food to feed my children?" In these narratives, historical continuity is threaded between 1948, 1967, and the present.

A state's protection of its citizens must be within the bounds of international humanitarian law; that means the response to perceived security risks must be proportionate. In July 2004 the International Court of Justice (ICJ) deemed the wall a form of collective punishment and an acquisition of land by force, and ruled 14–1 that it constitutes a violation of international humanitarian law and human rights law.

The New Cartography in the Middle East

Spatial fracturing and divisions that separate and transform landscape and place are crucial to maintaining and reproducing a hierarchy of access to natural resources, sovereignty, and human rights. Palestinian/Israeli difference is cast as one between spaces of law, civilization, and democracy and spaces of terror, lawlessness, and militant Islam. As such, the latter can be attacked without recourse to the conventions governing international conflict; Afghanistan, Palestine, Lebanon, and Iraq are all currently such spaces.

Many of the same practices engaged in by the Israelis have emerged in Iraq, particularly Baghdad. Brutal campaigns of sectarian violence have drawn deadly boundaries across Baghdad. Checkpoints control movement in Baghdad and concrete walls now carve out sectarian enclaves, which, along with violent sectarian cleansings, are transforming once "mixed neighborhoods" into exclusionary sectarian compartments.[5] Akin to Lebanon during its long civil war, the identity card can become either a pass to mobility or a death sentence at checkpoints. Uncertainty, fear, and chaos pervade everyday life. Iraq's once subterranean sectarian tensions have now exploded as sectarian violence and that of the occupation forces have propelled millions of people to flee their homes and seek shelter abroad or in other parts of Iraq. By mid-2007 about one in six Iraqis, or about 15 percent of the population, were either refugees or internally displaced persons (IDPs). Nearly 4.5 million Iraqis have been displaced; around two million are IDPs while Jordan is host to over half a million and Syria to over one million. Hundreds of thousands of refugees are scattered in Egypt, Lebanon, Turkey, and Iran.

Colonial and occupying regimes classify and partition space discursively and on the ground in such a way that eventually their meaning will become part of the taken-for-granted, routine aspects of daily life. The politics of space, enclosure, and displacement deprive those excluded from familiar places. Memories of past spatial formations may gradually fade as new memories are created in their place. At a time of a now tempered although in some instances still celebratory attitude toward transnational space and mobility, Israel has put Palestinians behind a wall to achieve demographic exclusion and national homogeneity, and Iraq has been effectively dismembered and a significant proportion of its population has been displaced.

With spatial tactics by occupiers impeding Palestinian and Iraqi access to resources and mobility, their ability to construct and reproduce place is severely hindered. Closure and settlements reorganize space and assign access and mobility according to ethnic, national, and religious affiliation while signage and naming serve to erase memories of place and create new ones (Peteet 2005b). Ultimately, the goal is to make the once taken-for-granted unfamiliar. In Iraq, spaces that were once accessible and familiar have become distant and increasingly unknowable precisely because of restrictions on mobility imposed through an ethnic, national, and sectarian definition of space accompanied by acts of violence in the face of spatial transgressions (see al-Mufti 2006).

The colonial cartography being inscribed in the West Bank and Iraq is dramatically recrafting ethnic and sect spaces, the space of human rights, and national landscapes. In Palestine the new spatial ordering allocates space, mobility, and rights according to ethnic-religious-national belonging. In this form of modern colonialism, spaces are hierarchized along a scale of premodern to modern coinciding with ethnicity and allocating rights and privileges accordingly.

The war on terror provided a boon for further Israeli acquisitions of Palestinian territory and a unilateral approach to addressing the conflict. The use of the "we" by Israeli politicians as in "we are fighting the same enemy" has given legitimacy to Israeli actions as has the conflation of political violence with terrorism. Place is where memories form. New inscriptions of place, with violent signs of an expansionist and excluding presence, may eventually color memories and dilute previous memories. The question is will, and to what extent, Palestinian and Iraqi memories eventually incorporate a dominant foreign presence in the landscape. If place acquires definition and meaning through the social activities people engage in and the social relationships they craft and pursue in them, then Palestinians and Iraqis are increasingly constrained in their capacity to make and define place. They can only craft and give meaning to place in very delimited areas and through acts of memory and resistance.

In summarizing the comparison between Iraq and Palestine, the lesson to be culled is that U.S. policy toward the region has been consistent for the past sixty years: unfettered access to cheap oil, support for Israel and its expansionist practices, support for repressive Arab regimes, and the violent crushing of resistance. In pursuit of this policy, fragmentation of the region, the breakup of states along ethnic-sectarian lines, conforming to an Orientalist imagery of the region as a mosaic of "peoples and cultures," is materializing through invasions and prolonged occupations. The human cost has been continuing humanitarian crises and massive numbers of displaced. The most immediate lesson is that in pursuit of these policies the Arab world will not be allowed to control either its resources or its destiny. On the flip side, the level of sustained resistance by both Iraqis and Palestinians, in the face of the world's most technologically sophisticated military forces, shows little sign of abating.

Notes

1. González reminds us that anthropology's "public engagement does not always result in progressive positions or even humane politics" (2004:10). *The New Yorker* (Packer 2006) ran a feature article on the war on terror that revealed that some anthropologists do put their particular knowledge and skills at the service of the military and defense establishment. In 2004 I received a postcard from a former student. Now a civilian affairs officer in Afghanistan, he wrote to thank me "for the training." I was not sure how to interpret this; was the knowledge I imparted helping him to better "rule" the Afghans? Or did such knowledge make him more aware of his own position as an occupier? I doubt it was the latter. It reminds me of the Christian fundamentalist students who eagerly enroll in anthropology courses to better prepare themselves to convert the natives using culturally appropriate knowledge.

2. Political scientist Raymond Hinnebusch (2006) used this evocative phrase to answer the question of whether the fragmentation and chaos in Iraq were anticipated and welcomed by the U.S. war planners or if they really thought they would be able to easily usher in "regime change."

3. When the United States set up the Provisional Council, it cemented sectarianism in the emerging political system; seats and representation were allocated on the basis of sect, recalling Lebanon's allocation of political representation.

4. These numbers refer to Palestinians and Israelis killed between September 29, 2000, and October 31, 2008. See Btselem: The Israeli Information Center for Human Rights in the Occupied Territories, http://www.btselem.org (accessed January 14, 2009).

5. See al-Mufti 2006 for a critical examination of the term "mixed areas."

Bibliography

Agamben, Giorgio. 2005. *States of Exception*. Trans. Kevin Attell. Chicago: University of Chicago Press.

Alcalay, Ammiel. 1993. *After Arab and Jew: Remaking Levantine Culture.* Minneapolis: University of Minnesota Press.

Aronson, Geoffrey. 2006. Settlement Monitor. *Journal of Palestine Studies* 35 (4):131–43.

Asad, Talal. 2007. *On Suicide Bombing.* New York: Columbia University Press.

Bauman, Zygmunt. *Globalization: The Human Consequences.* New York: Columbia University Press.

Carapico, Sheila, and Chris Toensing. 2006. The Strategic Logic of the Iraq Blunder. *Middle East Report* 239 (Summer):6–11.

Cole, Juan. 2005. Don't Stop with Syria's Occupation. http://www.antiwar.com (accessed December 10, 2005).

Eldar, Akiva. 2006. Parting Shots. January 10. http://www.haaretz.com (accessed February 9, 2008).

González, Roberto J., ed. 2004. *Anthropologists in the Public Sphere: Speaking Out on War, Peace, and American Power.* Austin: University of Texas Press.

Gordon, Neve. 2008. *Israel's Occupation.* Berkeley: University of California Press.

Gregory, Derek. 2004. *The Colonial Present: Afghanistan, Palestine, Iraq.* Malden: Blackwell.

Gusterson, Hugh. 2004. *People of the Bomb: Portraits of America's Nuclear Complex.* Minnesota: University of Minnesota Press.

Hammami, Rema. 2004. On the Importance of Thugs: The Moral Economy of a Checkpoint. *Middle East Report* 231 (Summer):26–34.

Hinnebusch, Raymond. 2006. Iraq War: Hegemonic Stability. Paper presented at the symposium "War in Iraq and the Wider Conflict." Emory University, November 8–9.

Honig-Parnass, Tikva. 2003. Israel's Colonial Strategies to Destroy Palestinian Nationalism. *Race and Class* 45 (2):68–85.

International Displacement Monitoring Center (IDMC). 2006. Palestinian Territories: West Bank Wall Main Cause of New Displacement amid Worsening Humanitarian Situation: A Profile of the Internal Displacement Situation. *Norwegian Refugee Council,* June 21. http://www.internal-displacement.org (accessed January 16, 2008).

Khalidi, Rashid. 2004. *Resurrecting Empire: Western Footprints and America's Perilous Path in the Middle East.* Boston: Beacon Press.

Low, Setha M., and Denise Lawrence-Zúñiga. 2003. Locating Culture. In *The Anthropology of Space and Place: Locating Culture,* ed. Setha M. Low and Denise Lawrence-Zúñiga, 1–47. Malden: Blackwell.

Lutz, Catherine. 2006. Empire Is in the Details. *American Ethnologist* 33 (4):593–611.

Maalouf, Amin. 1984. *The Crusades Through Arab Eyes.* London: Al-Saqi Books.

Makovsky, David. 2004. The Right Fence for Israel. *Foreign Affairs* (March–April) 83 (2):50–64.

McAlister, Melani. 2007. Rethinking the "Clash of Civilizations": American Evangelicals and the Winding Road to the Iraq War. In *Race, Nation, and Empire in American History,* ed. James Campbell, Matthew Guterl, and Robert Lee, 352–74. Chapel Hill: University of North Carolina Press.

Meneley, Anne. 2008. Time in a Bottle: The Uneasy Circulation of Palestinian Olive Oil. *Middle East Report* 248:18–23.

Morris, Tim. 2006. Only a Wall? *Forced Migration Review* 26:30.

al-Mufti, Burhan. 2006. Mixed Areas: A Dangerous Term. *Middle East Report* 239 (Summer):28.

Packer, George. 2006. Knowing the Enemy: Can Social Scientists Redefine the "War on Terror"? *The New Yorker*, December 18.

Peteet, Julie. 2008. Stealing Time. *Middle East Report* 248 (Fall): 14–15.

———. 2005a. Naming in the Israeli-Palestinian Conflict. *Third World Quarterly* 26 (1):153–72.

———. 2005b. *Landscape of Hope and Despair: Palestinian Refugee Camps*. Philadelphia: University of Pennsylvania Press.

Shearer, David. 2006. Territorial Fragmentation of the West Bank. *Forced Migration Review* 26:22–23.

Soffer, Arnon. 2002. Demographics in the Israeli-Palestinian Dispute. *PolicyWatch/PeaceWatch #370*. Washington, D.C.: Washington Institute for Near East Policy.

Visser, Reidar, and Gareth Stansfield, eds. 2008. *An Iraq of Its Regions: Cornerstones of a Federal Democracy?* New York: Columbia University Press.

World Bank. 2009. Gaza Strip. Country Study. Washington, D.C.: World Bank. http://www.worldbank.org/WEBSITE/EXTERNAL/MENAEXT/Westbankgaza (accessed April 6, 2009).

Chapter 4
Losing Hearts and Minds in the "War on Terrorism"

Jeffrey A. Sluka

According to the great theorists of guerrilla warfare such as Mao Zedong, Che Guevara, Ho Chi Minh, Vo Nguyen Giap, and Tom Barry, insurgent conflicts, unlike other forms of armed conflict or war, are fundamentally *political rather than military* struggles for the *"hearts and minds"*— that is, the popular support—of the civilian population (Taber 2002). That population includes four expanding levels of popular consciousness: first, the local population in the war zones; second, the encompassing national population; third, if the situation is imperialism and the government supported or controlled by a foreign power, the population in that country; and fourth, the international audience or world population as a whole. Here, I argue that, based on "lessons learned" in my research on popular support for the Irish Republican Army (IRA) and Irish National Liberation Army (INLA) in Northern Ireland, by the end of 2006 the United States and its allies had already lost the war on terrorism because by then they had lost the battle for hearts and minds or public support on all four of these levels.

In 1981–82 I conducted my first period of fieldwork in Northern Ireland in Divis Flats, an impoverished inner-city ghetto on the Catholic-Nationalist Falls Road in Belfast. The high-rise state housing project was one of the main battlegrounds of the war, and the residents had, for over eighteen years since 1969, lived under British military occupation and been caught in the crossfire between the Republican guerrillas, the state security forces, and Loyalist death squads. The community was reputed to be an IRA fortress and INLA stronghold, and was the scene of some of the worst political violence of the "troubles," as the war was euphemistically referred to. Frequent patrols of heavily armed, combat-ready British troops and militarized police passed through on foot and in armored Land Rovers, and the entire complex was under constant surveillance from an army observation post located on top of the tallest building—Divis Tower—and from helicopters continuously hovering overhead. While trying to live normal lives in one of the central "killing fields" of the conflict, the people of Divis Flats had been assassinated by Loyalist death squads and attacked by Protestant mobs; killed and injured by rubber and plastic bullets fired during frequent riots and periods of civil disorder; harassed, intimidated, arrested, interned, interrogated, tortured, and generally brutalized by policemen and British soldiers on their streets; and some had been beaten up or "kneecapped" by the IRA or INLA for engaging in antisocial or criminal activities.

In the book that emerged from my fieldwork in Divis Flats (Sluka 1989), I describe in detail the role played by state repression—particularly the military and judicial counterinsurgency apparatus—in the formation of community or popular support for the IRA and INLA. In my analysis of the relationship between the guerrillas and the local community that supported them, I applied the now classic hearts and minds model that guerrilla warfare represents a form of politico-military struggle aimed not at winning territory and battles, the focus of conventional warfare, but rather at gaining the support or winning the hearts and minds of the people, and found that 47 percent of the community directly supported the IRA and/or INLA. This was enough support to sustain a successful armed campaign for twenty-five years from 1969 to 1994, and the guerrillas were never defeated. By the end of 2006, more than 60 percent of Iraqis supported insurgent attacks.[1] This is a significantly higher degree of support than the IRA and INLA had in Northern Ireland, and they proved to be fundamentally undefeatable. When the battle for hearts and minds was lost, the wars in Iraq and Afghanistan became unwinnable, certainly as long as a majority of the people in these countries support insurgent attacks on what they see as occupying foreign forces.

The most fundamental lesson of my research on popular support for the IRA and INLA was that they enjoyed a high level of support among the Catholic community as a direct result of the repressive counterinsurgency tactics employed by the British army and police. I, and other researchers, found that the oppression that resulted from military occupation and aggressive counterinsurgency tactics against civilians was the primary factor that generated support and "volunteers" for the IRA and INLA (Sluka 1989, 1995; Feldman 1991; White 1989). The British government and security forces made the commonly fatal counterinsurgency mistake; because it was difficult for them to come to grips with the guerrillas themselves, they put the Catholic ghettos under military occupation and applied force and judicial repression—that is, state terror—in a highly indiscriminate manner against the population they believed supported the guerrillas. In direct opposition to the intended result of pacification, this served only to alienate them, and this catalyst served to create and continuously reinforce popular support for the IRA and INLA. This became a vicious cycle of state repression and popular resistance, because as support for the guerrillas grew as a direct result of the counterinsurgency "dirty war," the security forces and Loyalist death squads increasingly treated the Catholic population as guerrilla supporters who deserved to be repressed. The result was a failed counterinsurgency campaign and a quarter-century of guerrilla warfare in Northern Ireland.

The problem was that the security forces engaged in too many actions in which entirely innocent people suffered. Too many innocent people were hurt by tear gas or injured or killed by plastic or real bullets fired by the security forces; too many innocent people had their homes ransacked in searches, were stopped, questioned, and searched in the streets, and harassed and abused by policemen and British soldiers; and too many innocent people were subjected to judicial repression under draconian "antiterrorism" legislation that made a mockery of human rights in Northern Ireland. The result was that many people became convinced that violence against the state was politically and morally justified, and support for the IRA and INLA flowed directly from this popular conviction. In particular, I found that popular support for the guerrillas was based not only on rational political considerations but also on *moral* evaluations: to many, if not most, it was the guerrillas—or *terrorists*, from the British perspective—who held the moral high ground.

In my research in Northern Ireland (and this has been confirmed by anthropologists who have worked in other zones of insurgency, e.g., Zulaika 1988, Feldman 1991, and Mahmood 1996), I found four main things that alienated popular support from the government and lost the hearts and minds of the civilian population:

1. civilian casualties;
2. political murder ("extrajudicial" killings);
3. judicial repression (draconian "antiterrorism" laws, arbitrary and in-

definite detention in special prisons, and harsh methods of interrogation including torture);

4. everyday human rights abuses under military occupation (body, home, and vehicle searches, abuse by soldiers on patrol and at checkpoints, etc.).

On the evidence we now have, all of these have been central to the conduct of the U.S.-led "war on terrorism." According to Amnesty International, the main forms of state terrorism are arbitrary detention, unfair trial, torture, and political murder or extrajudicial execution. By resorting to large-scale state terrorism in the "war against terrorism," the Bush administration lost the moral high ground. During 2006, virtually the entire world came to this conclusion, and that was the moment when and the most fundamental reason why the battle for hearts and minds was lost. In September of that year, a fateful month in the war on terrorism, former secretary of state Colin Powell hit the nail on the head when he warned, "The world is beginning to doubt the moral basis of our fight against terrorism" (Harper 2006).

By the end of 2006, the United States and its Coalition allies were bogged down in two escalating counterinsurgency wars they were woefully unprepared for. The Bush administration believed there would be no protracted guerrilla war in Iraq because the people would welcome the invaders as liberators and that a few hundred Special Forces could defeat the Taliban in Afghanistan. Because the military did not anticipate and did not intend to fight an insurgency in either country, they did not plan or prepare for it and were thus caught on the back foot with having to cope with this reality—namely, large and growing guerrilla wars in both countries.

In Iraq the combined forces of the U.S.-led Coalition and Iraqi government numbered more than four hundred thousand, but the country remained an increasingly lawless jungle with an expanding insurgency. By November 2006, the military claimed they were killing or capturing more than five hundred insurgents a month, but car bombings, armed attacks, and civilian deaths were rising dramatically, and the estimated ranks of the Sunni-backed insurgency had swelled to twenty thousand plus and rising. As mentioned above, according to an ABC News poll in September 2006, 60 percent of Iraqis approved of insurgent attacks on U.S.-led forces.

At the same time, Afghanistan also experienced the worst surge in violence since the U.S.-led invasion in 2001 to remove the former Taliban regime from power. The Taliban made a dramatic resurgence in the south

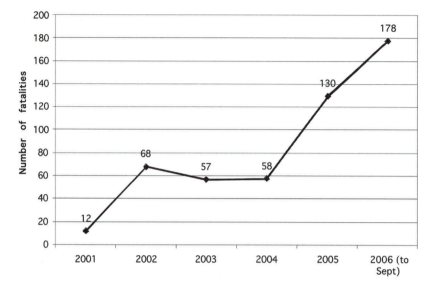

Figure 1. Afghanistan: U.S. and Coalition military fatalities. Source: http://iCasualties.org/oef/.

and east, large swaths of the country were again under their control, and the government clung to the cities in the south while NATO forces in Kandahar and Halmand were now locked in an all-out war. While "only" 139 U.S. and Coalition troops died in Afghanistan in 2005, the ratio of casualties to overall troop levels made Afghanistan as dangerous as Iraq. While President Bush touted Afghanistan as a success, the security situation there was, in fact, seriously deteriorating. Taliban attacks were up and had become more aggressive, including increasing use of suicide bombs, casualties were increasing dramatically, and military commanders expected the violence to get worse.

Nearly five years after the U.S. military deposed the Taliban there were about twenty-two thousand Coalition troops in Afghanistan, but this was not nearly enough to defeat the growing resistance and resurgence of the Taliban and al Qaeda in the countryside and mountains, and victory was as distant and remote as the long-embattled nation itself.

Today, we live in times of war and are confronted daily with the extraordinary—some would say hegemonic—power of the U.S. spin machine, even involving apparently reputable journalists, scholars, intellectuals, and politicians, with the hidden agenda of what Chomsky terms "man-

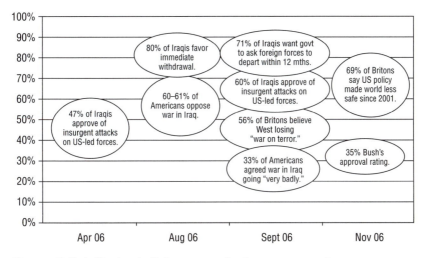

Figure 2. Polls indicating declining support for the war on terrorism.

ufacturing consent"—or popular support—for the Bush administration's policies. The so-called war on terrorism *is being waged in our heads*: multiple opinion polls over the past few years have shown that popular support for the wars in Afghanistan and Iraq has declined at all levels—among Iraqis and Afghanis in the war zones, among Americans at home, and among the world community—and there is growing evidence that even within the military, among both the officers and the troops, support for the war, the battle for *their* hearts and minds, is being lost.[2]

Iraq and Afghanistan "Body Count," 2001–6

Casualties—civilian and military—are the single main factor that causes people to turn against a war. Up to November 2006, since Operation Enduring Freedom began in Afghanistan in October 2001, an unknown number of civilians had been killed and wounded. Incredibly, no figures for civilian casualties had been reported since 2004, at which time some 3,500 deaths and 6,300 wounded had been reported. Since then the war had intensified significantly, and the civilian toll had undoubtedly been high and growing, but not reported. I would estimate that at least 10,000 civilians had been killed. Since 2001, 500 U.S. and Coalition troops had been killed and 1,500 wounded and, hardly ever mentioned, approximately 12,000 Afghan troops had been killed and 32,000 wounded.

According to Iraq Body Count, since Operation Iraqi Freedom began in March 2003, around 50,000 civilians had been killed outright and 1,180,000 wounded; 3,050 U.S. and Coalition troops had been killed and about 25,000 wounded; and, once again, hardly ever mentioned, approximately 32,000 Iraqi troops had been killed and 100,000 wounded. However, a *Lancet* survey published in October 2006 of mortality since the 2003 invasion concluded that up to July of that year there had been 655,000 "excess deaths"—including 7,250 insurgents and 863 suicide bombers but the vast majority of them noncombatant civilians—as a consequence of the war. These deaths resulted primarily from violence in Iraq and the near collapse of its medical infrastructure, and corresponded to 2.5 percent of the population. The Iraq Body Count figures are the most often cited but acknowledged as "conservative," while the *Lancet* figures are the most controversial because they are so high. However, the *Lancet* figures are probably the most *ethnographically* valid because they recognize as "casualties" *both the direct and indirect victims* who have suffered as a result of the conflict—for example, not only those killed in the violence but also those who have died who would not have if the infrastructure and civil society of Iraq had not been disrupted by the war.

With the exception of the *Lancet* survey, these figures are conservative because they hide the large numbers of casualties who, for various reasons, do not get counted. Several hundred "civilian contractors" (mostly mercenaries) had been killed, and up to November 2006 the U.S. military said they had suffered over fifty thousand nonfatal "casualties." These wars had left tens of thousands of soldiers and hundreds of thousands of civilians maimed, sick, or psychologically disturbed, and the casualty rates were still increasing.

Chronology of Losing Hearts and Minds

2002

The year 2002 was marked by increasing civilian casualties in Afghanistan and increasing reports of misconduct by U.S. troops there. The number of Afghan civilians killed by U.S. bombs surpassed the death toll of the 9/11 terrorist attacks in the United States. Nearly 3,800 Afghans died between October 7 and December 7.[3] In 2005 a secret U.S. Army report concluded

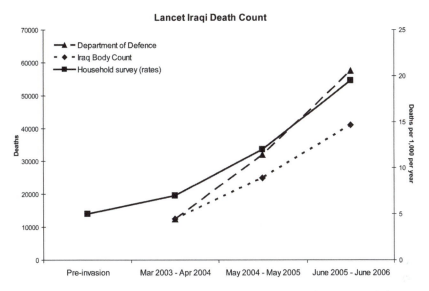

Lancet Iraqi Death Count

Figure 3. Trends in the number of deaths reported by Iraq Body Count and the MultiNational Corps-Iraq and the mortality rates found by this study. Source: Gilbert Burnham, Riyadh Lafta, Shannon Doocy, and Les Roberts, "Mortality After the 2003 Invasion of Iraq: A Cross-Sectional Cluster Sample Survey," *Lancet* 368 (9545):1421–28.

that in 2002 two detainees died and others were badly beaten or tortured while held at a detention site in Bagram. Evidence suggested that prisoner abuse by Special Forces units had been more common in Afghanistan than previously acknowledged—particularly harsh treatment (torture) and excessive detentions—and investigations revealed an extremely high level of physical abuse (torture) of detainees transferred from Special Forces field bases to the prison in Bagram (Sack and Pyes 2006).

2004

In November 2004 the U.S. military launched a massive ground and air assault to recapture the insurgent city of Fallujah, which reportedly resulted in the deaths of over 5,000 insurgents, and during which 92 U.S. Marines were killed and 500 wounded. While there are no official U.S. estimates of civilian casualties, one Iraqi NGO put the number of civilian deaths in the assault at 4,000–6,000. U.S. officials reported that more than half of Fallujah's 39,000 homes were damaged and about 10,000 destroyed. The attack was motivated by revenge for the killing of four U.S. contractors whose bodies were hung over the bridge in the center of town, but it was taken against all the civilians of Fallujah. The town was heavily shelled, bombed, and strafed, and cluster bombs and white phosphorous—both illegal weapons—were used (Foulk 2006; Project Censored 2006).

While presented in the media as a military victory, the battle was, in broader terms, a defeat because it produced mass alienation of the local population from the U.S.-led occupation and support for the insurgents. In the immediate aftermath of the offensive "calm" was restored in Fallujah, but then the number of insurgent attacks increased again. Glantz (2005) concludes that Fallujah was like the straw that broke the camel's back, and that since then the vast majority of Iraqi people have supported attacks on American troops.

In 2004 the war on terrorism also spilled over into Pakistan, where the U.S. and Pakistan militaries threatened to bomb villages that did not assist in the war against al Qaeda. Under U.S. pressure, the Pakistan army sent 70,000 troops into South Waziristan to search for al Qaeda fighters and the elusive Osama bin Laden. They sought to enlist the support of local tribes and "battled" those who did not cooperate. They bombed, burned, and bulldozed the homes and belongings of those deemed collaborators or merely uncooperative, while tribes that complied with the army were rewarded with aid and spared from bombardment (Rafiqui and Garcia 2004). The casualties in this spillover war in Pakistan are unknown but no doubt high.

December 2005

In their annual report, Human Rights Watch (2006) concluded that "In 2005 it became disturbingly clear that the abuse of detainees had become a deliberate central part of the Bush administration's strategy of interrogating terrorist suspects."

February 2006

Video footage of British troops beating young Iraqi civilians in early 2004 emerged, which the British press said provided "a propaganda gift for our enemies."[4] A UN Commission on Human Rights report found that the United States had committed acts amounting to torture at Guantánamo

Bay and called for its closure, and for the United States to revoke all "special interrogation techniques" authorized by the U.S. Defense Department.[5]

March 2006

Insurgent incidents had increased from about 150 per week to over 700 per week in Afghanistan over the previous year, and Amnesty International and other aid agencies warned that the insurgency was growing as goodwill toward U.S. troops faded. Security had not been restored, and there were signs that the goodwill widely felt toward U.S. and Coalition forces following the removal of the Taliban from power was being replaced by resentment and opposition because of serious human rights violations. During a visit to Afghanistan in December 2005, Amnesty International met some of the hundreds of people whom U.S. and allied forces had detained in mass arbitrary arrests following raids on villages and towns. These raids relied on often flawed intelligence about alleged centers of "insurgents." The soldiers' conduct in the raids humiliated and degraded local people, notably through their treatment of women and the manner of their searches. Dozens of people reported months of arbitrary detention under U.S. custody at Bagram airbase, as they were held without charge, trial, or access to legal representation (Amnesty International 2006b:1).

Amnesty International also published a report on detention and torture at Abu Ghraib that severely criticized U.S. and British forces in Iraq for detaining 14,000 people without charge or trial for long periods of time, and reported growing evidence that Iraqi security forces were torturing detainees. According to Amnesty International and Human Rights Watch, Iraqi detainees had been routinely subjected to beatings, sleep deprivation, stress positions, "water boarding," the use of dogs, exposure to hot and cold temperatures, forced exercise, and other forms of abuse—including sexual, racial, and religious abuse—by U.S. interrogators. Journalists noted that "The problem for the Pentagon is that *every new incident involving civilian deaths triggers a new wave of anti-American fervor.*"[6]

April 2006

In April 2006 six retired two-, three-, and four-star U.S. Army and Marine Corps generals scathingly criticized the secretary of defense's handling of the Iraq War and called for his resignation. Their critiques varied from the view that the war had been a series of tactical blunders to the view that it had been a strategic disaster doomed from the start. It was unprecedented in U.S. history for so many generals to speak out so strongly against the leader of an ongoing war and demand his removal: "We're not the French generals in Algeria," said Major General Paul Eaton. "But we damned well know that the Iraq War we've won militarily is being lost politically" (Whalen 2006).

May 2006

Amnesty International reported that torture and inhumane treatment were "widespread" in American-run detention centers in Afghanistan, Iraq, Cuba, and elsewhere, despite Washington's denials: "The U.S. government is not only failing to take steps to eradicate torture, it is actually creating a climate in which torture and other ill-treatment can flourish."[7]

July 2006

This was the deadliest month of the war to date for Iraqi civilians. An average of more than 110 Iraqis were killed each day, and the total number of civilian deaths that month, 3,438, was a 9 percent increase over the tally in June and nearly double the toll in January. Along with a sharp increase in sectarian attacks, the number of daily attacks against U.S., Coalition, and Iraqi security forces had also doubled since January, providing more evidence that the anti-American insurgency was growing. For example, in July U.S. forces encountered 2,625 roadside bombs, up from 1,454 six months earlier in January (Coghlan and Sengupta 2006).

July–September 2006

According to the UN, the death toll among Iraqi civilians hit a record high in the summer of 2006, with 6,599 violent deaths reported in July and August alone. Many of the deaths were attributed to rising sectarian tensions that had pushed Iraq toward civil war. In September known Iraqi deaths were running at more than 100 a day because of sectarian murders, al Qaeda and nationalist insurgent attacks, and fatalities inflicted by the multinational forces (Beaumont 2006).

August 2006

The chief of intelligence for the Marine Corps in Iraq filed an unusual secret report concluding that the situation in western Al-Anbar province was dire.

He said the prospects for securing the province were dim and that there was almost nothing the U.S. military could do to improve the situation there. An army officer summarized it as arguing that in Anbar province, "We haven't been defeated militarily but we have been defeated politically—and that's where wars are won and lost" (Ricks 2006b). Anbar is one of the most critical Iraq provinces because it is the main stronghold of Sunni resistance.

A series of polls taken during the second half of August 2006 showed that among Americans support for the war in Iraq was at an all-time low. Almost two-thirds of Americans in three major polls said that they opposed the war (Regan 2006). In Iraq, a poll done by an Iraqi firm showed that 80 percent of Iraqis favored an immediate withdrawal (Paley 2006).

Serious incidents of U.S. troop misconduct continued to emerge. Military prosecutors and investigators probed the killing of three Iraqi detainees by U.S. troops near Samarra in May and reported that the unit's commanders had created an atmosphere of excessive violence by encouraging "kill counts" and had issued an illegal order to "kill all military-age males." Witnesses described a brigade that operated under loose rules allowing wanton killing and tolerating violent, anti-Arab racism, and one said that "a culture of racism and unrestrained violence pervaded the unit" (Daragahi and Barnes 2006).

A senior Defense Department official said that in Iraq, "The insurgency has gotten worse by almost all measures, with insurgent attacks at historically high levels. The insurgency has more public support and is demonstrably more capable in numbers of people active and in its ability to direct violence than at any point in time" (Gordon, Mazzetti, and Shanker 2006).

In Afghanistan it was reported that despite, or perhaps because of, the war on terrorism there, the country was descending into chaos again. A Taliban wave was reconquering the country, and fighting was spreading through Kandahar province. The replacement of U.S. forces with NATO ones encouraged the Taliban, which issued decrees announcing that it was an Islamic duty to kill all those working with the government or foreign agencies. Security for local people had become virtually nonexistent, and "warlordism" and heroin/poppy cultivation had soared. In the capital city of Kandahar, foreigners were no longer welcome and no NATO patrols could pass through the city; the residents said that the city was lost because if the Americans left it would fall in a week (Pazira 2006; Jones 2006).

September 2006

In Afghanistan attacks grew more frequent and lethal, and civilians were increasingly paying the price; more than 2,300 people had been killed in 2006 in the "Taliban resurgence." Across the country, roadside bomb attacks were up by 30 percent and suicide bombings had doubled. Statistically, it was now nearly as dangerous to serve as an American soldier in Afghanistan as it was in Iraq. Reports indicated that U.S. and British policy had inflicted lawlessness, misery, and starvation on the Afghan people. Thousands of villagers, fleeing the fighting and an ongoing drought, had lost their livelihood and were suffering dreadful conditions in refugee camps. The country was now dominated not by the government in Kabul but by a patchwork of warlords, terrorist groups, and opium traffickers. The Taliban had regained control over the southern half of the country, and their front line was advancing daily. British lieutenant general David Richards stated that "We have greater firepower, so we tend to win, but, of course, they can take their losses while our casualties will invariably lead to concern back home. You also have to think that each time we kill one, how many more enemies we are creating. And, of course, the lack of security means hardly any reconstruction is taking place now, *so we are not exactly winning hearts and minds*" (Sengupta 2006; italics mine).

In Iraq the situation on the ground also continued to get worse. A Pentagon study indicated that attacks by insurgents increased to eight hundred per week in the second quarter of the year, double the number in the first quarter, and Iraqi casualties had increased by 51 percent (Rashid 2006). The UN special investigator on torture reported that torture in Iraq was "totally out of hand," with militias, terrorist groups, and government forces disregarding rules on the humane treatment of prisoners. He said that the situation was so bad "many people say it is worse than it has been in the times of Saddam Hussein."[8] The increasing death toll was the result of a spiral in sectarian clashes as well as the ongoing insurgency against the U.S.- and British-led occupation.

A highly classified U.S. intelligence document—*Trends in Global Terrorism: Implications for the United States*—concluded that the war in Iraq had spawned a new wave of Islamic radicalism and increased the global threat of terrorism since the 9/11 attacks in the United States. In a stark assessment of terrorism trends, the National Intelligence Estimate, the most comprehensive assessment yet of the war, based on analyses of all sixteen U.S. intelligence agencies, concluded that "The Iraq war has made the overall terrorism problem worse," and described the Iraq conflict as the primary recruiting vehicle for violent Islamic extremists. It said that Islamic radicalism, rather than being in retreat, had metastasized and spread across the globe, and cited the Iraq War as a leading reason for the diffusion of jihad ideology. In short, it concluded that the war in Iraq was creating both more terrorism and more terrorists, and had made the overall terrorism problem worse.

Five years after 9/11, a New York Times/CBS poll found that nearly two-thirds of Americans believed the war in Iraq was going either "somewhat" (28 percent) or "very" badly (33 percent). Growing public pessimism with the war was indicated by several other polls in which a majority of respondents said they believed the decision to go to war in Iraq was a mistake that had made the United States less, rather than more, safe. A BBC poll indicated that 56 percent of Britons believed their country and Western governments were losing the war on terror.

Polls by the U.S. State Department and independent researchers in Iraq indicated that a strong majority of Iraqis favored immediate U.S. military withdrawal from the country, believing their swift departure would make it more secure and decrease sectarian violence. In Baghdad nearly three-quarters of residents polled said they would feel safer if U.S. and other foreign forces left Iraq, and 65 percent favored an immediate pullout. Other polls found that 71 percent of Iraqis wanted the Iraq government to ask foreign forces to depart within a year, and about 60 percent of Iraqis approved of attacks on U.S.-led forces.[9]

The media reported that U.S. "operatives" were guilty of torturing detainees to death in Afghanistan and Iraq. Of the forty-four known deaths of detainees in U.S. custody, twenty-one were homicides and eight appeared to have been the result of torture techniques (ACLU 2006).

October 2006

Civilian casualties increased in Afghanistan, NATO and Afghan forces faced increasing attacks, security was minimal, civilians were dying, and alienation from the Kabul government was growing by the day. Human Rights Watch warned that NATO tactics were "increasingly endangering the civilians that they are supposed to be protecting, and turning the local population against them."[10] NATO's top commander in Afghanistan, British lieutenant general David Richards, said the country was at a tipping point and "70% of Afghans" were likely to switch their allegiance to resurgent Taliban militants if there was no visible improvement in people's lives in the next six months. He said that "If we do not take advantage of this, then you can pour in an additional 10,000 troops next year and we would not succeed because we would have *lost by then the consent of the people.*"[11] In Iraq the UN reported that indiscriminate killing of civilians by death squads, insurgents, and militias had reached unprecedented levels. In July and August 2006, over six thousand civilians were killed, and torture had become widespread. The surge in violence prompted President Bush to concede that the war was going badly, and the United States and Britain began looking for an exit strategy.[12] Britain's top army commander, General Sir Richard Dannatt, said that the war in Iraq was fanning Islamic militancy and that British troops should "get out some time soon because our presence exacerbates the security problems": "Whatever consent we may have had in the first place may have turned to tolerance and has largely turned to intolerance."[13] He also warned that the war in Iraq could "break" British forces if they stayed in the country for more than a few years.

November 2006

Domestically, President Bush's approval rating reached its lowest point at 35 percent (November 7), down from a high of 88 percent immediately following 9/11. While pessimism about and opposition to the increasingly unpopular wars in Iraq and Afghanistan were not the only factors in this decline, they were certainly the biggest part of it. Internationally, President Bush was now ranked with some of his bitterest enemies as a cause of global anxiety. According to a survey that revealed just how far the United States' reputation had fallen among former supporters since the invasion of Iraq, British voters saw President Bush as a greater danger to world peace than North Korean leader Kim Jong-il, Iranian president Mahmoud Ahmadinejad, and Hezbollah leader Hassan Nasrallah. A poll in Britain indicated that 69 percent believed U.S. policy had made the world less safe since 2001, and only 7 percent thought action in Iraq and Afghanistan had increased global security. This finding was mirrored in Canada and Mexico, with 62 percent of Canadians and 57 percent of Mexicans saying the world had become more dangerous as a result of U.S. policy.[14] In Britain 71 percent said the invasion of Iraq was unjustified, a view shared by 89 percent of Mexicans and 73 percent of Canadians (Glover 2006).

Analysis

The wars in Iraq and Afghanistan have effectively defeated the U.S. counter-terrorism program and have provided the conditions for demanding jihad to oppose them: an infidel power invading and occupying two Muslim countries, all of which was perceived as unprovoked, no weapons of mass destruction, and, in the case of Iraq at least, no connection with international terrorism, al Qaeda, or 9/11. Many senior Western officials noted that while Osama bin Laden could not declare a jihad, other Muslim clerics did, and the wars in Iraq and Afghanistan effectively provided the context for them to do so.

Many observers also rightly criticized American counterinsurgency methods as heavy-handed, overly focused on military means, inflexible, culturally insensitive, and badly marred by the torture and murder of prisoners at the Abu Ghraib (in Iraq) and Bagram (in Afghanistan) detention facilities (not to mention the torture at other locations such as Guantánamo Bay,[15] or by Iraqi, Afghan, and Pakistan security forces, or in prisons in other countries where detainees have been "rendered").[16] The U.S. approach to pacifying Iraq in the months after the collapse of Saddam Hussein helped spread the insurgency and made it bigger and stronger than it might have been, and when a majority of Iraqi (and Afghan) public opinion began to turn against the Americans and see them as occupiers rather than liberators, the presence of U.S. and Coalition troops became counterproductive.

Thus, at that moment, sometime in 2006, when a majority of Iraqis and Afghans no longer viewed the U.S. and Coalition forces as "liberators" and began to view them as "occupiers" and support insurgent attacks against them, the battle for their hearts and minds was lost.

This shift in popular perception was primarily a result of the large numbers of civilian casualties and the frank embrace of the techniques of "dirty war." In both Iraq and Afghanistan the people's will to resist grew ever stronger with each innocent civilian killed, injured, imprisoned, or tortured, with each village demolished, and with each massacre committed. *The simple, yet apparently still unlearned, rule is that fighting terrorism by employing terrorism (creating innocent victims) creates more terrorism.* The strategic implication is that each civilian killed or abused represents another extended network of family and friends with direct, personal reasons to hate the occupiers. As a result of the indiscriminate violence of the military occupation, the majority of insurgents and "terrorists" in Iraq and Afghanistan were locals defending their homeland, not the ideologically motivated "foreign fighters" the United States claimed they were.

With respect to "dirty war," allegations of U.S. troop misconduct in Iraq and Afghanistan mounted dramatically, and military tactics on the ground, including large-scale sweeps where all military-aged men were rounded up and questioned, as well as aggressive interrogation and torture of suspects,[17] turned local people against the U.S. and British forces. In particular, the large-scale military operations in Fallujah, Ramadi, Samarra, and Mosul alienated many—if not most—of the local populations in these key areas. The two most alienating things were the thousands of innocent people killed and wounded, and the torture and disappearance of thousands of detainees. What concerned most Iraqis about Abu Ghraib was not just the torture that went on there but also the fact that so many people had been arrested, taken there or to Camp Bucca, and simply disappeared. By the end of 2006, the U.S. military was still holding 10,000–15,000 people in prison as "security detainees." They got no trial or lawyer, had been charged with no crimes, and were never allowed to see their families, and it was reported that on the ground all over Iraq one heard stories of abuse in these detention centers (e.g., see Jamail 2005).

Thus, it appears that the United States has "flunked counterinsurgency 101," and neither the American military nor the Bush administration apparently learned even the most elementary counterinsurgency lessons from the war in Vietnam. The use of high-profile, aggressive tactics like roundups, constant patrolling, indiscriminate firepower, and the abuse of prisoners alienated civilians in Iraq just as such tactics did in South Vietnam. When American soldiers in Iraq complain, just as they did in Vietnam, that the enemy "melts" away or that they are "hiding" among civilians, it is because, on some very basic level, they and their commanders still do not "get" how a guerrilla war actually works (Ricks 2006a).

In 2006 it was reported that the Pentagon recognized that they were failing and had completed a reassessment of their tactics: "Top officers are literally rewriting the book on how to conduct counterinsurgency operations—a skill that has atrophied in the three decades since the Vietnam War but has become painfully relevant *in Iraq and Afghanistan, where winning hearts and minds has proven far more difficult than killing enemy forces*" (Bender 2006; italics mine). The Defense Department identified serious deficiencies across the board, including that U.S. troops in Iraq had often used too much force when conducting operations in civilian areas, unnecessarily alienating local populations; U.S. commanders were too slow to establish working relationships with local allies; and providing security for the Iraqi people should have been an early priority.

By 1970 a majority of Americans believed that the Vietnam War was a mistake, and by the end of 2006 a similar percentage felt the same way about the war in Iraq. Back then, the White House clung for dear life to "Vietnamization," and now the same holds true for the current plan of "Iraqification" leading to withdrawal. The Iraqification process is a self-deception; its central premise, that Iraqi forces can be trained and equipped to secure their own country, allowing the Americans to go home, is a replay of the failed Vietnamization scenario. Efforts to win the local citizens' hearts and minds and carry out reconstruction projects are also failing as extremists attack "soft" targets, such as teachers, civil servants, and police officers, decapitating the local administration and terrorizing the people.

The allusion to the Vietnam War is entirely appropriate. In addition to many of the same failed tactics, even the language—"cut and run," "stay the course"—is the same, as are references to "kill counts" and the way U.S. troops refer to the locals as "hajis"[18] the way their predecessors in Vietnam referred to "gooks." There is increasing demoralization among U.S. troops, and the battle for their hearts and minds is being lost as well. Increasing reports from within the military itself indicate that many soldiers of all ranks in the field in Iraq and Afghanistan no longer believe in the justice or efficacy of their mission.

In September 2006 a European diplomat assigned to Baghdad summarized the situation in Iraq: "If the Americans leave, it's a disaster; if they stay, it will get worse" (cited in Haski 2006). This choice between two bad "solutions" illustrates the trap into which President Bush put himself and from which he could not extricate himself. By the end of 2006, while he continued to proclaim that the United States was winning the war against terrorism, few around the world believed him, and even his own military and intelligence services asserted the opposite.

The wars in Iraq and Afghanistan have been a terrible and bloody mistake, and by the end of 2006 the situation for the United States, if not the world, was much worse than it was in September 2001. Both Iraq and Afghanistan faced a threefold failure: no peace, no democracy, and no reconstruction. By any definition, Iraq was now in a state of civil war. Indeed, the only thing standing between Iraq and a descent into Bosnia-like devastation was 140,000 U.S. troops—and even they were merely slowing the fall. The internecine conflict could easily spiral into one that threatens not only

Iraq but also its neighbors throughout the oil-rich Persian Gulf region with instability, turmoil, and war. With these wars growing less popular every day, intensifying the military effort as a strategy for winning them is futile and likely to trigger renewed protests, particularly in light of the growing sense among both national security elites and the general population that the Bush administration's decision to invade Iraq was a major mistake and that the war is unwinnable.

The invasions of Iraq and Afghanistan have exacerbated terrorism and the Bush administration squandered the moral authority the United States acquired as a consequence of the 9/11 terrorist attacks. The war on terrorism has failed, and global terrorism now has much more support. In 2001 al Qaeda launched the 9/11 terrorist attacks on America that precipitated the war on terror, particularly the U.S.-led invasions of Afghanistan and Iraq. More than five years later, far from ending terrorism, the Bush administration's tactic of using overwhelming military might—that is, state terrorism—to fight terrorism had rebounded, spawning an epidemic of global violence that has claimed hundreds of thousands of lives.

In 2001 the U.S.-led invasion swept away the Taliban regime in a matter of weeks, and did the same for Saddam Hussein's regime in 2003, but far from bringing stability and democracy to Afghanistan and Iraq, the outcome has been one of constant warfare. In Iraq the United States squandered its initial victory, allowed the nation to descend into violence and anarchy, and has gone from liberator to despised occupier. In particular, just as occurred in Northern Ireland, the abandonment of the rule of law in the war on terrorism was a grave mistake, and the United States has gone from being a country that publicly condemned torture but secretly supported it to a country that practices torture as a matter of routine.[19] The exorbitant monetary cost of the wars in Iraq and Afghanistan are also bankrupting the U.S. economy. In January 2006, it was reported that the cost of these wars was approaching half a trillion dollars—nearly the same cost as the thirteen-year-long Vietnam War—and a congressional analysis in September 2006 showed that the Iraq War alone was costing U.S. taxpayers about $2 billion a week. By February 2008 the cost of the wars in Iraq and Afghanistan had grown to a staggering three trillion dollars.[20]

The damage sheet would be bad enough if it were limited to the cost of the wars in Iraq and Afghanistan in blood and money, but it becomes frightening when one analyzes the regional and international consequences: further destabilization of the region, 4.5 million refugees, a gift to Iran in its quest for power, and a serious boost for the jihadist movement around the world. Fighters in Iraq and Afghanistan are receiving training, building networks, and becoming further radicalized, and the U.S. occupation of these Muslim countries is proving to be a dream recruiting tool for Islamic militants worldwide.

In Iraq and Afghanistan, in the United States, and around the world, there is growing public disgust and frustration with these wars, and the Bush administration's violation of international law has severely damaged the reputation of the United States in the international community. This means that the U.S. administration is losing the struggle for hearts and minds and thereby losing the war on terrorism. The debate over the U.S. and British role in Iraq is now centered on two simple questions: How soon will they withdraw, and what kind of country will they leave behind? These two wars—the central fronts in the war on terrorism—have backfired, producing more recruits for terrorism and deep divisions among the American people. They will only get much worse as long as they continue.

The war in Afghanistan has also proven to be a disaster for the struggle against Osama bin Laden and al Qaeda. Bin Laden is ill and invisible, but by 2006, five years after 9/11, his al Qaeda movement, defined by the United States and its allies as an "international terrorist network," had become the fulcrum of an expanding global Islamic resistance movement. That is, al Qaeda has evolved from being a small, isolated organization into the militant edge of a popularly supported, "globalized" political movement centered in the Islamic world.

The wars in Iraq and Afghanistan have not brought democracy and stability but have increased the number of insurgents and their supporters. As Howard Zinn (2006) has observed, "war in our time inevitably results in the indiscriminate killing of large numbers of people. To put it more bluntly, war is terrorism. That is why a 'war on terrorism' is a contradiction in terms. Wars waged by nations . . . are a hundred times more deadly for innocent people than the attacks by terrorists are."

In a replay of the Vietnam War experience, the battle for hearts and minds in the U.S.-led war on terrorism has been lost. Whatever counterinsurgency lessons were learned in that disastrous Southeast Asian war were apparently "unlearned" for the wars in Iraq and Afghanistan. Near the end of the Vietnam War, a famous antiwar poster emerged depicting a Vietnamese peasant woman with an M-16 rifle pointed at her head with the ironic caption "Winning hearts and minds in Vietnam." But in the years since then that lesson appears to have been lost. Post–Vietnam War slogans parodying the original message emerged, including "Give us your hearts and minds or we'll burn your damn village down" and "If you grab 'em by the balls, their hearts and minds will follow." Another ironic or oxymoronic Vietnam-era slogan that has made a comeback in the war on terrorism in Iraq, Afghanistan, and Pakistan is "We had to destroy the village in order to save it." It is clear that in Iraq and Afghanistan, the point—perhaps the most important lesson of the Vietnam War and of my research on popular support for the IRA and INLA in Northern Ireland—that military repression produces resistance rather than submission was "unlearned."

Anthropologists should also be aware that there is a battle for *our* hearts and minds in the war on terrorism as well, and a danger of recolonization of the discipline as an applied science of state control. During the Vietnam War, the discipline first confronted the issue of anthropology in the service of counterinsurgency. In 1968 Kathleen Gough reminded us that, historically, anthropology had served as the 'handmaiden of colonialism.' In 1970 Eric Wolf and Joseph Jorgensen publicly exposed the relationship between anthropology and counterinsurgency, which created great controversy within the discipline and ultimately led directly to the development of the first code of anthropological ethics. They observed that "the old formula for successful counter-insurgency used to be ten troops for every guerrilla. . . . Now the formula is ten anthropologists for each guerrilla" (1970:32). In 1976 June Nash warned us that in the age of decolonization, anthropologists came to be classified with the enemy. As a consequence, for the next thirty years anthropologists considered involvement in counterinsurgency and other applied military research as ethically "taboo."

However, since 9/11 there has been renewed debate within the discipline over what role anthropologists should play in the war on terrorism. On one side are those who hold fast to the taboo against counterinsurgency research, and on the other are those who believe that in times of war American anthropologists have a patriotic duty to serve their government in the war effort (as many did during World War II). The issue of anthropologists doing "counterterrorism" research (which from the government's perspective is the same as counterinsurgency research)[21] has taken on new urgency as the failure of the wars in Iraq and Afghanistan has become more apparent. By 2004 the U.S. military was already reassessing their tactics, and senior leaders in the Department of Defense (DOD) were, belatedly, calling for cultural knowledge of the adversary. The director of the Office of Force Transformation concluded that "knowledge of one's enemy and his culture and society may be more important than knowledge of his order of battle," and the Office of Naval Research and the Defense Advanced Research Projects Agency sponsored the Adversary Cultural Knowledge and National Security Conference, the first major DOD conference on the social sciences since 1962 and the infamous Project Camelot (McFate 2005). In 2005 the CIA launched the Pat Roberts Intelligence Scholars Program to sponsor trainee anthropologist-spies through American university courses (Price 2005). This development was met with anger and concern among anthropologists; John Gledhill, president of Britain's Association of Social Anthropologists, called the scholarships ethically dangerous and divisive. He warned that they could foster suspicion within universities worldwide and cause problems in the field.[22]

Even more controversial, in 2005 the U.S. Army initiated a new experimental counterinsurgency program called the Human Terrain System (HTS),[23] which began to "embed" anthropologists and other social scientists with combat brigades in Iraq and Afghanistan to help them gather intelligence (referred to as "conducting research") and understand local cultures better. The goal is to provide soldiers in the field with knowledge of the population and its culture in order to enhance operational effectiveness and reduce conflict between the military and the civilian population. The HTS system has generated great controversy among anthropologists, many of whom view it as fundamentally unethical, inherently harmful to those studied, and an attempt to "weaponize" the discipline (Price 2006). In October 2007 the American Anthropological Association published a statement denouncing HTS as unethical, a disgrace to the discipline, and a danger to both research participants and anthropologists in the field. Regardless of the small number of anthropologists involved in these programs, they have greatly exacerbated the already considerable danger, which nearly all anthropologists face in their fieldwork, of being suspected of being spies.

Conclusion: Lessons Learned and Unlearned

It is useful to review the basic lessons learned that appear to have been unlearned in the war on terrorism in Iraq and Afghanistan. These errors are not new; in fact, they represent the classic errors of counterinsurgency warfare, which, taken together, provide a virtual blueprint for how to lose a battle for hearts and minds.

The main factors that alienate popular support from the government and lose the hearts and minds of the civilian population are civilian casualties, murder or "extrajudicial killings" by state forces, judicial repression (i.e., implementation of draconian "antiterrorism" laws, lack of due process, establishment of special—that is, political—courts and prisons, arbitrary and indefinite detention, and harsh methods of interrogation including torture), and human rights abuses incidental to military occupation (e.g., abuse and brutality during body, home, and vehicle searches, and by soldiers on patrol and at checkpoints). As noted earlier, these are generally recognized as the characteristic forms of state terrorism, and, as we have seen, all have been central to the conduct of the U.S.-led war on terrorism. They undermine the legitimacy of the government and armed forces and generate popular support for the resistance. By resorting to large-scale state terrorism in the war against terrorism, the moral high ground, and the battle for hearts and minds, is lost.

Beyond these lessons learned then unlearned is the fundamental failure to comprehend or accept the basic validity of the hearts and minds model of guerrilla warfare. The U.S.-led Coalition forces still do not understand that insurgent conflicts are fundamentally *political rather than military* struggles for the popular support of the civilian population, and have relied almost entirely on a military approach. This counterproductive overreliance on military methods is viewed by guerrilla warfare theorists as the "classic" counterinsurgency error. The U.S. and Coalition governments and armed forces were not adequately prepared for the political, economic, and social conditions they would face. In particular, not enough was done to win over the populace and gain support for the new government by restoring basic security and amenities such as water, electricity, sewage, and health care, and far too little was done to minimize civilian "collateral damage" resulting from the military occupation and harsh counterinsurgency tactics employed in the field, which have been little different from those employed in the failed Vietnam War. Despite the touting of the "new" counterinsurgency doctrine identified with the celebrated General Petraeus and endorsed by the U.S. military in their new *U.S. Army/Marine Corps Counterinsurgency Field Manual* (FM 3–24 2007), despite the fact that Petraeus endorses the traditional model that insurgent wars are 80 percent political and only 20 percent military, and despite the fact that the new counterinsurgency manual states that winning requires first ensuring the security and well-being of the civilian population, *the U.S. forces are still relying on the opposite—80 percent military and 20 percent civil operations.*[24] That is, the strategy remains an overwhelmingly military one, and the damage done in the process more than defeats any civil operations the military engage in. Thus, while they were able to win the initial war against the Iraqi military, by alienating the civilian population and losing their hearts and minds, the United States and its Coalition allies lost the "peace" that followed.

Notes

This essay was originally presented at the annual meeting of the American Anthropological Association on November 15, 2006, in the session "Critical Anthropological Perspectives on the 'War on Terrorism.'"

1. "New Poll Says Majority of Iraqis Approve of Attacks on U.S. Forces," ABC News, September 27, 2006.

2. On losing "hearts and minds" in the military, see Danner 2004; Iraq Veterans Against the War and Glass 2008; Leve 2008; and Hedges and Al-Arian 2009.

3. "Afghanistan's Civilian Deaths Mount," BBC News, January 3, 2002.

4. *Dominion Post*, February 14, 2006.

5. *Dominion Post*, February 16, 2006.

6. *Dominion Post*, March 27, 2006; italics mine.

7. *Dominion Post*, May 4, 2006.

8. "Torture in Iraq Worse Now Than Under Saddam?" Associated Press, September 21, 2006.

9. "Most Iraqis Favor Immediate U.S. Pullout, Polls Show," *Washington Post*, September 26, 2006.

10. "Civilian Deaths Turn Afghans Against NATO: Report," Reuters, October 30, 2006.

11. *Dominion Post*, October 10, 2006; italics mine.

12. *Sunday Star-Times*, 22 October 22, 2006.

13. *Dominion Post*, October 14, 2006.

14. "British Believe Bush Is More Dangerous Than Kim Jong-Il," *The Guardian*, November 3, 2006.

15. By November 2006, at least 760 "detainees" had passed through the camp and about 493 remained. Most had not been accused of hostile acts, none had yet been brought to trial, and since the camp opened four years earlier only 10 prisoners had been charged. Only 8 percent were suspected fighters for terrorist groups, while another 30 percent were listed as members of terrorist organizations; the rest were said to be "associated" with terrorism (*The Week*, February 17, 2006). The U.S. government defined them as "unlawful combatants" not "prisoners of war," so they could be treated as exempt from the Geneva conventions and held for as long as the war on terrorism continues—which could, at least theoretically, be forever.

16. This is a chilling new American/CIA euphemism for the policies permitting torture. We are familiar with "collateral damage" (civilian deaths) and "terminate with extreme prejudice" (assassinate); now we have "rendition," the official term for kidnapping suspected terrorists and secretly flying them to be interrogated in countries where there are no laws against torture. Rendition is a form of forced disappearances in the war on terrorism.

17. "Suspects" and "detainees" can, of course, be entirely innocent, and in the war on terrorism it appears that many, if not most, of those so labeled have committed no criminal offense. These terms are similar to the term "internees" used for those detained under the failed "internment" policy introduced in Northern Ireland in 1971, which caused mass alienation among Catholics and generated recruits and popular support for the IRA.

18. This is a reference to Muslims who have made the hajj pilgrimage to Mecca.

19. Torture is abhorrent, self-perpetuating, and illegal, and it does not work. In fact, it has serious counterproductive consequences in that it undermines the moral authority and legitimacy of the government, stimulates resistance, and generates support and recruits for militant groups. It did not work in Northern Ireland, Algeria, Vietnam, or any other imperial or colonial conflict, and it will not work in the war against terrorism. This is another old lesson of failed counterinsurgency that has been "unlearned."

20. Joseph Stiglitz and Linda Bilmes, "The Three Trillion Dollar War," *The Times*, February 23, 2008.

21. The failure to distinguish between "insurgency" and "terrorism" and the blurring and confusion of the two is one of the central errors of the now voluminous and rapidly growing but terribly flawed literature on terrorism.

22. "Fears over CIA 'University Spies,'" BBC News, June 2, 2005.

23. In 2007 the American Dialect Society named "Human Terrain Team" the most euphemistic phrase of the year.

24. See Sarah Sewell, "He Wrote the Book: Can He Follow It?" *Washington Post*, February 25, 2007.

Bibliography

American Civil Liberties Union (ACLU). 2005. U.S. Operatives Killed Detainees During Interrogations in Afghanistan and Iraq. http://www.aclu.org/intl humanrights/gen/21236prs20051024.html (accessed September 18, 2006).

Amnesty International. 2006a. *Beyond Abu Ghraib: Detention and Torture in Iraq*. New York: Amnesty International.

———. 2006b. Afghanistan "Success" Ebbing Away. *The Wire* (Amnesty International monthly magazine), March 2006. http://web.amnesty.org/web/wire.nsf/print/March2006Afghanistan (accessed November 3, 2006).

Beaumont, Peter. 2006. Civilian Deaths Soar to Record High in Iraq. *The Guardian*, September 22.

Bender, Bryan. 2006. Pentagon Studying Its War Errors. *Boston Globe*, August 16.

Burnham, Gilbert, Riyadh Lafta, Shannon Doocy, and Les Roberts. 2006. Mortality After the 2003 Invasion of Iraq: A Cross-Sectional Cluster Sample Survey. *The Lancet*, October 11, http://en.wikipedia.org/wiki/Image:2nd_Lancet_Iraq_death_count_Figure_4.gif (accessed October 11, 2006).

Coghlan, Tom, and Kim Sengupta. 2006. The War on Terror, Five Years On: An Era of Constant Warfare. *The Independent*, September 4.

Danner, Mark. 2004. *Torture and Truth: America, Abu Ghraib, and the War on Terror*. New York: New York Review Books.

Daragahi, Borzou, and Julian Barnes. 2006. Officers Allegedly Pushed "Kill Counts." *Los Angeles Times*, August 3.

Feldman, Allen. 1991. *Formations of Violence: The Narrative of the Body and Political Terror in Northern Ireland*. Chicago: University of Chicago Press.

FM 3–24. 2007 [2006]. *The U.S. Army/Marine Corps Counterinsurgency Field Manual*. Chicago: University of Chicago Press.

Foulk, Vincent. 2006. *The Battle for Fallujah: Occupation, Resistance and Stalemate in the War in Iraq*. Jefferson, N.C.: McFarland.

Glantz, Aaron. 2005. *How America Lost Iraq*. New York: Penguin.

Glover, Julian. 2006. British Believe Bush Is More Dangerous Than Kim Jong-il. *The Guardian*, November 3.

Gordon, Michael, Mark Mazzetti, and Thom Shanker. 2006. Bombs Aimed at GIs in Iraq Are Increasing. *New York Times*, August 17.

Gough, Kathleen. 1968. World Revolution and the Science of Man. In *The Dissenting Academy*, ed. by Theodore Roszak, 125–44. New York: Random House.

Harper, Tim. 2006. Powell Wades into Detainee Dispute. *Washington Bureau*, September 15.

Haski, Pierre. 2006. Frightening Balance Sheet. *Libération*, September 28.

Hedges, Chris, and Laila Al-Arian. 2007. The Other War: Iraq Vets Bear Witness. *The Nation*, July 30.

Hedges, Chris, Laila Al-Arian, and Eugene Richards. 2009. *Collateral Damage: America's War Against Iraqi Civilians*. New York: Nation Books.

Human Rights Watch. 2006. *World Report*. New York: Seven Stories Press.

Iraq Veterans Against the War, and Aaron Glass. 2008. *Winter Soldier: Iraq and Afghanistan*. Chicago: Haymarket.

Jamail, Dahr. 2005 World Tribunal for Iraq, Culminating Session Testimony. Inter Press Service, June 25. http://dahrjamailiraq.com/world-tribunal-for-iraq-culminating-session-testimony (accessed August 27, 2005).

Jones, Ann. 2006. Why It's Not Working in Afghanistan. TomDispatch.com, August 27. http://www.truthout.org/docs_2006/082806F.shtml (accessed August 30, 2006).

Leve, Ariel. 2008. Patriot Missiles: Iraq Veterans Against the War. *The Sunday Times*, March 2.

Mahmood, Cynthia Keppley. 1996. *Fighting for Faith and Nation: Dialogues with Sikh Militants*. Philadelphia: University of Pennsylvania Press.

McFate, Montgomery. 2005. Anthropology and Counterinsurgency: The Strange Story of Their Curious Relationship. *Military Review*, March–April. http://www.army.mil/professionalwriting/volumes/volume3/august_2005/7_05_2.html (accessed November 9, 2006).

Nash, June. 1976. Ethnology in a Revolutionary Setting. In *Ethics and Anthropology: Dilemmas in Fieldwork*, ed. Michael Rynkiewich and James Spradley, 148–66. New York: Wiley and Sons.

Paley, Amit. 2006. Most Iraqis Favor Immediate U.S. Pullout, Polls Say. *Washington Post*, September 27.

Pazira, Nelofer. 2006. Return to Kandahar: The Taliban Threat. *Belfast Telegraph*, August 21.

Price, David. 2005. The CIA's Campus Spies. *Counterpunch*, March 12–13.

———. 2006. Resisting the Weaponization of Anthropology. *Counterpunch*, November 20.

Project Censored. 2006. Media Coverage Fails in Iraq: Fallujah and the Civilian Death Toll. http://www.projectcensored.org/top-stories/articles/2-media-cov erage-fails-on-iraq-fallujah-and-the-civilian-deathtoll/ (accessed September 20, 2006).

Rafiqui, Asim, and Malcolm Garcia. 2004. Frontier Justice. *Mother Jones*, September–October.

Rashid, Ahmed. 2006. Losing the War on Terror. *Washington Post*, September 11.

Regan, Tom. 2006. Polls Show Opposition to Iraq War at All-Time High. *Christian Science Monitor*, September 1.

Ricks, Thomas. 2006a. *Fiasco: The American Military Adventure in Iraq*. New York: Penguin.

———. 2006b. In Iraq, Military Forgot the Lessons of Vietnam. *Washington Post*, July 23.

Sack, Kevin, and Craig Pyes. 2006. Deaths Were a "Clue That Something's Wrong." *Los Angeles Times*, September 25.

Sengupta, Kim. 2006. Soldiers Reveal Horror of Afghan Campaign. *Independent*, September 13.

Sluka, Jeffrey A. 1989. *Hearts and Minds, Water and Fish: Support for the IRA and INLA in a Northern Irish Ghetto*. Greenwich, Conn.: JAI Press.

———. 1995. Domination, Resistance and Political Culture in Northern Ireland's Catholic-Nationalist Ghettos. *Critique of Anthropology* 15 (1):71–102.

Taber, Robert. 2002. *War of the Flea: The Classic Study of Guerrilla Warfare*. New ed. Dulles: Potomac Books.

Whalen, Richard. 2006. Revolt of the Generals. *The Nation*, September 28.

White, Robert. 1989. From Peaceful Protest to Guerrilla War: Micromobilization of the Provisional Irish Republican Army. *American Journal of Sociology* 94 (6):1277–1302.

Wolf, Eric, and Joseph Jorgensen. 1970. Anthropology on the Warpath in Thailand. *New York Review of Books*, November 19, 26–35.

Zinn, Howard. 2006. War Is Not a Solution for Terrorism. *Boston Globe*, September 2.

Zulaika, Joseba. 1988. *Basque Violence: Metaphor and Sacrament*. Reno: University of Nevada Press.

Chapter 5
Mimesis in a War Among the People: What Argentina's Dirty War Reveals About Counterinsurgency in Iraq

Antonius C. G. M. Robben

When by 2004 U.S. forces had become bogged down in the hostile Sunni Triangle, the buzzwords "shock and awe" of the March 2003 aerial bombing of Iraqi troops and infrastructure were replaced by "swarming" as a trendy term to describe what was becoming an ordinary counterinsurgency war in a high-tech jacket. Superior firepower has always been a characteristic of American warfare, and the "shock and awe" strategy seemed to surpass, at least in word and imagination, all previous campaigns. However, one year after the 2003 fall of Saddam Hussein's brutal regime, American counterinsurgency units were swarming around cities such as Baghdad, Fallujah, Samarra, Ramadi, and Khaldiya, hoping to capture an elusive insurgency resisting the presence of U.S. and Coalition troops. The multipronged attack on Samarra in March 2006 was tellingly code-named Operation Swarmer.

Swarming combines sophisticated communication technologies with small, mobile combat units. Electronically informed by computer-stacked Tactical Operations Centers about the position of friendly units, the swarming troops can react quickly to mobile enemy combatants. "The aim is to coalesce rapidly and stealthily on a target, attack it, then dissever and redisperse, immediately ready to recombine for a new pulse" (Arquilla and Ronfeldt 2003). Dispersed swarm units can merge more effectively when enemy presence is detected than can troops engaged in conventional assault operations, and retreat and reconverge more quickly on suspected insurgency units elsewhere (Edwards 2000). This swarm tactic has been employed in Iraq, next to more conventional counterinsurgency operations such as cordoning and searching entire neighborhoods for weapons and insurgents or evacuating the civilian population and then attacking the remaining combatants with massive force (Herring and Rangwala 2006:180–85). A U.S. bipartisan study group stated in November 2006, "Currently, the U.S. military rarely engages in large-scale combat operations. Instead, counterinsurgency efforts focus on a strategy of 'clear, hold, and build'—'clearing' areas of insurgents and death squads, 'holding' those areas with Iraqi security forces, and 'building' areas with quick-impact reconstruction projects." The same source admitted, however, that this strategy was unsuccessful: "Perpetrators of violence leave neighborhoods in advance of security sweeps, only to filter back later" (Baker and Hamilton 2006:12). Swarming is a much more dynamic and effective counterinsurgency tactic than is a neighborhood sweep, so claims the current military thinking, because it can trump the insurgents' own swarming capabilities and capture them unawares. The situation in Iraq showed, however, that not only the insurgents but especially the civilian population bore the brunt of this new tactic. The post-invasion situation went from bad to worse when the U.S. and Coalition forces adopted an erratic swarming tactic that further alienated the Iraqi population, whose hearts and minds had to be won.

Swarming is a tactical change that tries to attune counterinsurgency to a major paradigm shift in contemporary warfare. According to British general Rupert Smith, the "industrial war" of armies fighting one other on a physical battlefield is being replaced by a "war amongst the people . . . in which the people in the streets and houses and fields—all the people, anywhere—are the battlefield. Military engagements can take place anywhere: in the presence of civilians, against civilians, in defense of civilians. Civilians are the targets, objectives to be won, as much as an opposing force" (2005:3–4). Smith (2005:17) argues that the war among the people is not a war in the classical sense of an armed confrontation between states with a clear beginning and end, but a continuous conflict between states and non-state groups with malleable objectives that are often political and seldom military.

The dispersed swarm seems to make military sense in a war among the people fought in amorphous conflict zones instead of clear battlefields, if one accepts Smith's solution of using lethal force against insurgents instead of exploring political alternatives. However, this tactic raises serious doubts when the on-the-ground operations in Iraq are compared with similar counterinsurgency experiences in Latin America during the 1970s and

1980s. These tactics were also developed on the mimetic principle of imitating the insurgency.

A comparison of Latin American counterinsurgencies and the operations by U.S. and Iraqi troops demonstrates that swarming increased the chances of civilian casualties and human rights violations, and was a narrow operational response to a complex situation created first by a mistaken invasion and later by a misguided response to insurgent violence. The U.S. authorities have largely been trying to find military solutions to the political violence in Iraq, despite attempts to rebuild Iraq's infrastructure, create democratic institutions, and train new police and armed forces. These armed efforts failed to account for the ideological biases of the war on terror, the moral shortcomings of the military operations, the neglect of the political consequences to Iraqi society, and a disregard for the human cost to the Iraqi people. Even the much applauded 2007 U.S. troop surge was a narrow military response that lessened the violence for the time being but was not part of a comprehensive plan that could take advantage of the improved security to provide sustained political solutions and work steadily toward national reconciliation in a deeply divided country. Internecine fighting can flare up easily between former Sunni insurgents and Shi'i militias, and persuade the Iraqi security forces to enter into aggressive counterinsurgency operations that will sow fear among the entire population.

The irony of the war in Iraq is that the Iraqi people, who were supposed to reap democracy, security, and overall well-being from the overthrow of Saddam Hussein, were in fact victimized by a war that was conceived and waged without any genuine concern for their civil and human rights owing to ideological biases, self-righteousness, political disingenuity, and tactical misconceptions. The negative long-term consequences of such warfare on the affected Latin American societies are now better understood, and these insights foreshadow developments that have begun to occur in Iraq as well.

The Global War on Terror

Iraq is not Argentina, the U.S. government and military are not the Argentine dictatorship and armed forces of the 1970s, and the Cold War is not the global war on terror. The two counterinsurgency wars are inserted in different political systems and geopolitical realities, and the U.S. and Argentine military differ in the weapons systems at their disposal and the oversight mechanisms to periodically recalibrate strategies and tactics. The political checks and balances of the United States and competing views within the U.S. Armed Forces about how to fight insurgencies have prevented the Iraq War from declining into the unbridled dirty war that characterized Argentina. Still, there are several similarities in the ideology, operational practices, and treatment of captives and civilians in the counterinsurgency campaigns by Argentine and U.S. troops that advance our understanding of the Iraq War. Furthermore, the Iraqification of counterinsurgency operations may lead to dirty war practices if Sunni Arab nationalists, Sunni Islamists, Shi'i militias, and foreign mujahideen decide to take up arms again with full force.

The Argentine military regarded their so-called dirty war against the revolutionary insurgency and the political left as a struggle of good against evil, of Christian civilization against an atheist communist ideology aiming to rule the world: "The subversive war. . . . is the clash of two civilizations, ours and the Marxist, to determine which one will be dominant and thus inspire or direct the future organization of the world. More concretely, it is about discovering which scale of values will serve as the foundation of such organization."[1] President George W. Bush showed a similar conviction in his reaction on the terrorist assault on September 11, 2001: "This is not, however, just America's fight. And what is at stake is not just America's freedom. This is the world's fight. This is civilization's fight. This is the fight of all who believe in progress and pluralism, tolerance and freedom."[2] Civilization and evil are juxtaposed in a battle about human existence.

This good-versus-evil thinking also dominated the decision to attack Iraq. Saddam Hussein had to be deposed because his regime concealed weapons of mass destruction and long-range missiles that would allow the Iraqi dictator to attack Europe or pose a threat to the United States by passing chemical, biological, or radiological weapons to al Qaeda terrorists. Two days before the invasion of Iraq, President Bush declared, "In the 20th century, some chose to appease murderous dictators, whose threats were allowed to grow into genocide and global war. In this century, when evil men plot chemical, biological and nuclear terror, a policy of appeasement could bring destruction of a kind never before seen on this earth. Terrorists and terror states do not reveal these threats with fair notice, in formal declarations—and responding to such enemies only after they have struck first is not self-defense, it is suicide."[3] Prime Minister Tony Blair stated to the House of Commons on March 18, 2003, that rogue states and Islamist terrorists are "the central security threat of the 21st century. . . . The threat sows chaos. And there are two begetters of chaos. Tyrannical regimes with WMD [weapons of mass destruction] and extreme terrorist groups who profess a perverted and false view of Islam" (2005a:330, 335).

Tony Blair's foreign policy ideas were inspired by senior British diplomat Robert Cooper. Cooper divides the world into premodern or failed states, modern nation-states, and postmodern states. The premodern zone and parts of the modern zone are full of danger and chaos that threaten the postmodern zone of security. The postmodern state "needs to get used to the idea of double standards. Among themselves, the postmodern states operate on the basis of laws and open co-operative security. But when dealing with more old-fashioned kinds of state outside the postmodern limits, Europeans need to revert to the rougher methods of an earlier era—force, pre-emptive attack, deception, whatever is necessary for those who still live in the nineteenth-century world of every state for itself. In the jungle, one must use the laws of the jungle" (2004:61–62).

Such Manichaean thinking, which divides the world in zones of order and zones of contaminating chaos, pervades the counterterrorist thinking of today, as it did several decades ago in Latin America. A superior, emancipatory Western democracy feels threatened by transnational terrorist networks and is contrasted with an inferior, retrograde Eastern Islamism, very much in the way that Latin American military regimes juxtaposed the free Western, Christian civilization with an enslaving atheist communist system and its expansionist strategy of local insurgencies. A belief of moral righteousness and cultural superiority made Bush and Blair just as ready to send American and British troops to die in Iraq as to accept Iraqi civilian casualties as the price to pay for freedom. As Tony Blair (2005b:349; see also Cooper 2004:78) said in March 2004, "The best defense of our security lies in the spread of our values. But we cannot advance these values except within a framework that recognizes their universality." This view has remained unaltered throughout the Iraq War. President Bush reiterated in January 2007, "The challenge playing out across the broader Middle East is more than a military conflict. It is the decisive ideological struggle of our time. On one side are those who believe in freedom and moderation. On the other side are extremists who kill the innocent, and have declared their intention to destroy our way of life."[4]

The enemy's evilness is considered so boundless and so antithetical to the self-declared universal values of the Western world that all actions against it are believed to be intrinsically good and well intended. If others resist those values or dare to threaten them, then Western nations should take off their gloves and impose their values in pitiless ways because pre-modern people will only obey an iron hand, so the reasoning goes. However, as Susan Neiman (2004:xv) has pointed out, "Each party to such conflicts insists with great conviction that its opponents' actions are truly evil, while its own are merely expedient. It's a simple failure, but one that can cause no end of misery as long as each side is certain that the other embodies evil at its core." In Iraq lives are sacrificed in what is believed to be a just war because of the greater goods of democracy and liberty for all, as if such losses of life are an inevitable trade-off. This ideological agenda has been particularly prominent at the White House and Downing Street but does not translate one-to-one into the military strategy for Iraq. Critical voices have been raised among the highest echelons of the U.S. and British armed forces as well as by military commanders in Iraq. However, the violation of the individual rights of enemy combatants and civilians in harm's way is hard to resist when rationalized by a dehumanizing Manichaean framework and understood as the price to pay for democracy. Military expediency takes precedence over cultural sensitivity, as U.S. captain Paul Kuettner remarked: "We're not going to risk the lives of one of our soldiers to be culturally sensitive" (Shadid 2005:231). Such deterioration of counterinsurgency into human rights violations took place during the Argentine military rule in the 1970s and also became a reality during the Iraq War.

Counterinsurgency in Iraq

U.S. forces in Iraq have had a troubling record of causing civilian deaths since the early days of the occupation. In the five-month period after President Bush's end-of-the-war declaration on May 1, 2003, ninety-four civilians were killed in Baghdad alone under questionable circumstances. The victims were killed in three situations: (1) raids on homes; (2) clashes with armed assailants; and (3) checkpoints. A report documenting these killings signaled "a pattern by U.S. forces of over-aggressive tactics, indiscriminate shooting in residential areas and a quick reliance on lethal force. In some cases, U.S. forces faced a real threat, which gave them the right to respond with force. But the response was sometimes disproportionate to the threat or inadequately targeted, thereby harming civilians or putting them at risk" (Human Rights Watch 2003:4). In one case from July 2003, a U.S. task force was raiding a home in Baghdad in search of Saddam Hussein. The area was being secured by impromptu checkpoints. When a passenger car slowly approached the checkpoint but did not heed the stop signs, U.S. soldiers opened fire, killing a fourteen-year-old boy and wounding his seventeen-year-old brother and sixteen-year-old cousin. The three teenagers had been picking up food rations, did not see the soldiers flagging down their car, and did not recognize the checkpoint as such because the roadway was clear. The two wounded teenagers were dragged from the car and were repeatedly beaten (Human Rights Watch 2003:35–36).

This particular instance may have been the result of unfortunate circumstance and cultural miscommunication, but the substantial number of checkpoint killings hints at more structural problems. U.S. forces came to regard Iraqi males as suspects and treated them with hostility at checkpoints, in their homes, and after armed encounters. As David Kilcullen (2009:124), the chief strategist of the Office of the Coordinator for Counterterrorism in the U.S. State Department and a counterinsurgency advisor in Baghdad to General Petraeus, admitted, "Rather than working with the population so as to protect them from the insurgents, some units, because of their lack of situational awareness and personal relationships with the people, tended to treat all Iraqis as a potential threat and thus adopted a high-handed approach that alienated the population." The aggressive raids on Iraqi homes by U.S. troops searching for Iraqi insurgents, foreign mujahideen, and key members of Hussein's regime angered many civilians and caused them to regard the American presence as a military occupation. The abuse of inmates in Abu Ghraib prison shocked the world, but detainees in other U.S.- and British-run facilities in Iraq were also treated badly. Add to this maltreatment the vengeance killing of twenty-four civilians in Haditha by U.S. Marines in November 2005 after one of their comrades died in a roadside bombing. It is clear that there has been a systematic propensity to human rights violations that cannot be dismissed as incidents caused by individual soldiers stepping out of line.

Ordinary Iraqis have suffered most from the mainly nationalist Sunni, Shi'i militia, former Ba'thist, and foreign and Iraqi Islamist insurgents (Human Rights Watch 2005b). Even though insurgents have killed twice as many civilians as U.S.-led forces between May 2003 and March 2005, U.S. and Coalition troops have been largely blamed for the political violence in Iraq and resented for the abuses and humiliations suffered through the counterinsurgency campaigns. The hostility is greatest among Sunni Arabs in central Iraq, growing among Shi'is in southern Iraq, while Sunni Kurds tolerate the foreign troops in the north as long as they can maintain their semi-autonomy (Herring and Rangwala 2006:201–6). A bipartisan study group of prominent retired U.S. politicians concluded in November 2006, "The level of violence is high and growing. There is great suffering, and the daily lives of many Iraqis show little or no improvement. Pessimism is pervasive" (Baker and Hamilton 2006:9).

The deteriorating reputation of the Multi-National Coalition Force and its failure to deal with the insurgency led in 2004–5 to a creeping Iraqification of the counterinsurgency campaign and combined operations by U.S. and Iraqi troops (Hashim 2006:310–18; Kilcullen 2009:129; West 2008:71). Former American Special Forces advisors, the very same men who taught brutal interrogation methods to Salvadoran troops during the 1980s, began training a five-thousand-man-strong Iraqi commando force (Maass 2005; Packer 2005:304). The Volcano Brigade is part of this force. By 2005, it had acquired one of the worst reputations for "swooping into Sunni neighborhoods and killing civilians and kidnapping them. Every morning, more and more young Sunni men were turning up dead, in ditches and trash dumps, handcuffed, drilled with holes, burned with acid, shot in the back of the head" (Filkins 2008:120).

The Iraqi counterinsurgency forces may continue to employ the abusive practices against suspects in post-Saddam Iraqi prisons by U.S. and Iraqi personnel that were already common before the advisors arrived. Iraqi detention centers hold suspects in degrading circumstances that resemble Latin American practices of the 1970s and 1980s. Forced to lie handcuffed on prison floors for days, detainees have been whipped with hosepipes, kicked in the groin, tortured with electrical shocks, and hung from their wrists for hours. Many were denied legal counsel and visits from relatives. The 2005 country report of the U.S. State Department and a 2006 Amnesty International report have confirmed the human rights violations by Iraqi forces. Iraqi policemen are involved in torture, enforced disappearances, and degrading prison conditions (Hashim 2006:314; Herring and Rangwala 2006:186–92; Human Rights Watch 2005a). An unannounced inspection of the Iraqi Police Commando Division Central Facility in Baghdad discovered that this police station "held 625 detainees in conditions so crowded that detainees were unable to lie down at the same time" (U.S. Department of State 2006:4). Some detainees had been tortured with electric shocks or had their fingernails torn out. In 2004 at least one hundred so-called ghost detainees were held in U.S. detention facilities in Iraq. These disappearances were justified out of "military necessity" (Amnesty International 2006:13). In other words, suspects were held incommunicado and probably subjected to lengthy coercive interrogation to gather the intelligence deemed necessary to combat the insurgents. The deficient monitoring of prisons under the de facto responsibility of U.S. and Coalition forces enabled the unacceptable treatment of detainees, while the weak civilian oversight of military operations overall failed to curb abuses and halt a decline into human rights violations.

In addition to massive sweeps of neighborhoods and the destruction of cities after the forced removal of their populations, the counterinsurgency war in Iraq was causing similar human rights violations as were endemic in Latin America during the 1970s and 1980s. What was the dynamic behind this deterioration of counterinsurgency operations? What does the outcome of Argentina's dirty war and human rights violations foreshadow about Iraq? Were the abuses in Iraq related to the tactical nature of military swarming?

U.S. Swarming and the Argentine Counterinsurgency Warfare

According to U.S. military doctrine, there are many tactics to deal with insurgents and terrorists, ranging from large-scale to small-scale operations, and from beleaguerment to surprise attacks. Large-unit offensive operations may be announced in advance so that civilians can leave town before the massive attack begins. They involve thousands of soldiers, armored vehicles, tanks, artillery, and air support to kill insurgents. The November 2004 assault on Fallujah is an example. Large-unit encirclement and clearing operations aim to isolate a town and control the entry and exit of people and weapons. In the summer of 2005, Tal Afar was cordoned off by an eight-foot berm, after which small units were sent in to conduct house-to-house searches (FM 3–24 2007:83). Finally, large-unit raids involve several divisions that descend in a three-pronged movement on a city without prior notification to the inhabitants, and disperse into companies and small units to enter hundreds of targeted houses to detain insurgents. This tactic was used in Ba'qubah in November 2005 (Greer 2006).

Small-scale operations are generally carried out by battalions, companies, platoons, and especially squads, use less military force, and leave foot soldiers less protected than do large-scale operations. Cordon and search operations consist of sealing off a neighborhood, raiding houses for insurgents and weapons, and then withdrawing to base. Mounted and foot patrols may follow a planned trajectory to establish military presence, carry out reconnaissance missions to detect insurgents, engage in random cordon and knock operations, or swarm at will in the hope of catching enemy combatants red-handed. Finally, there are a number of surprise tactics (ambushes, impromptu checkpoints) and population control measures (roadblocks, permanent checkpoints, curfews, identity cards) to limit the insurgents' freedom of mobility.

The operational idea behind the swarming tactic is that the combination of advanced surveillance, detection, and communication technologies will provide a significant edge over the enemy in terms of mobility, initiative, surprise, and situational overview by small combat units. "Tactics adopted by a modular unit organised in semi-autonomous teams resemble 'swarming'—the teams cooperate through a few simple decision rules, shared situational awareness, and self-protection by accessing joint combined arms effects" (Kilcullen 2004:16). The swarm units are not directed by a central command but operate as a network of independently operating nodes that keep each other electronically informed about their actions. Questions have been raised in military circles about regarding such technology as a panacea for dealing with an enemy who fights with low-tech means and guerrilla tactics dating back to Mao Zedong. Others point out that insurgents are adapting quickly to U.S. tactics and are becoming increasingly adroit at exploiting the World Wide Web to acquire information about U.S. capabilities and to mobilize international support. Critics recommend a major shift from the narrow reliance on sophisticated military technologies to better human intelligence gathering and flexible networks of political, economic, military, and security agencies (Hammes 2004; Nagl 2005; Smith 2005). However, whether the solution is sought in improved technical or better human resources, the soldier's conduct in combat continues to be the Achilles' heel of counterinsurgency. Even worse, the combination of increased operational freedom by swarming units and the transformation of a guerrilla war into a war among the people are making abuse an ever-present possibility, all the more so when justified by Manichaean convictions.

The military term "swarming" draws a biological analogy with the erratic foraging movements of wasps, ants, and wolves. Combat swarming has been around since Scythian horse archers engaged Alexander the Great's phalanxes. A recent example is the hit, hide, run, and hit again attacks by Somali militiamen against U.S. troops trapped at three defensive positions in Mogadishu when two Blackhawk helicopters were downed after an assault force had captured a group of aids to warlord Aideed (Edwards 2000). Swarming in today's counterinsurgency operations is defined as follows: "A network of swarm units dispersed over an area can perform such COIN

[Counterinsurgency Operations] missions as conducting frequent and random cordon search operations; establishing checkpoints that vary from location to location at random times; quickly reacting to suspected areas of insurgent activity when needed; and constantly gathering human intelligence" (Edwards 2000:83). The U.S. Army in Iraq has used aerial images from drones and helicopters, local information, and intelligence gathered through interrogation to track and capture insurgents through impromptu checkpoints, through aggressive house raids, and by roaming the streets in search of chance encounters with insurgents. This approach is showing a striking resemblance to the counterinsurgency tactics employed by the Argentine armed forces in the 1970s.

The Argentine task groups captured many suspects through swarming. They would cruise by car through city streets or take up temporary positions near a railway station, bus terminal, harbor, or airport. They often forced captured guerrillas to collaborate in pointing out political activists and guerrilla combatants. Even children were forced to identify their parents' comrades. Just as Iraqi civilians have been detained by mistake, so Argentine collaborators pointed out complete strangers to protect their comrades. They hoped that the interrogators would quickly determine their innocence. The opposite was often the case. The captives could not supply any information because they had no information to offer, thus leading to more torture.

"Mimesis" is another term that connects biological phenomena to military practices. "Mimesis" refers to an evolutionary defense mechanism whereby one animal or insect species comes to resemble another. Mimesis has been an important principle of counterinsurgency warfare. It refers to a process in which opposed parties begin to imitate one another. U.S. armed forces deploy combat units that mimic the loosely networked units of al Qaeda and Iraqi insurgents in mobility, improvisation, and surprise tactics. Swarming is so appealing because the Iraqi insurgency does not have the numbers, logistics, or technical means (although the value of mobile phones should not be underestimated) to match the swarming capabilities of U.S. forces. "Crushed in frontal combat, by the summer of 2004 the insurgents had adapted to shoot and scoot tactics and persisted in launching small attacks" (West 2008:131). The complication in imitating these fighters is that they are unlike classical guerrilla insurgencies, which try to create liberated areas and eventually assume power. Precisely because the principal strategic objective of Iraqi insurgents and foreign mujahideen has been to create general insecurity in Iraq, they can swarm against domestic and foreign targets with suicide attacks, political assassinations, and car and road-side bombs at the spur of the moment and without well-coordinated battle plans. "Modern insurgents operate more like a self-synchronizing swarm of independent, but cooperating cells, than like a formal organization" (Kilcullen 2006b:123). There is an interesting parallel here between al Qaeda's global strategy against the United States and the on-the-ground tactics in Iraq: just as the 9/11 attack was intended to draw the "infidel" U.S. forces into the Islamic world to engage them in a guerrilla war leading to many Muslim casualties, and eventual military defeat and the withdrawal of polit-ical support for the autocratic Middle Eastern regimes, as Danner (2005) has argued, so the Iraqi insurgents lured the counterinsurgency troops into urban neighborhoods where civilian casualties became inevitable and human rights violations a likelihood, thus eroding any support for the for-eign troops among the Iraqi population.

Mimesis made military sense in the past when the strategic objective of guerrilla insurgencies was to evolve into standing armies, but it carries too many detrimental effects in the case of today's new insurgencies. Swarming is morally vulnerable because young officers have to make life-or-death decisions in combat situations that are often complicated by the presence of civilians. Inexperience, poor judgment, and a still underdevel-oped sense of responsibility and understanding of the wider implications of lethal force can lead to fatal mistakes with a global impact. The U.S. Army's most up-to-date counterinsurgency manual realizes this: "Indeed, young leaders—so-called 'strategic corporals'—often make decisions at the tactical level that have strategic consequences" (FM 3–24 2007:50). A picture of one U.S. Marine with his boot on an Iraqi civilian, lying prostrate on the ground, reaches every Iraqi through the media and gives worldwide sympa-thy to the insurgents.

Combat errors may evolve into human rights violations when mimesis becomes reinforced by ideological fanaticism or a Manichaean worldview. The belief that the enemy is a force of evil, and that one is fighting for the good of humanity, can lead to misconduct by commanders and soldiers receptive to such ideas. In both Argentina and Iraq the idea set in among certain commanders that terrorists were not only willing to achieve their politico-military objectives with violence but also attempting to destroy a whole way of life and abolish values believed to be universal. If leading poli-ticians and high-ranking officers declare that the enemy is evil, nonhuman, and a worldwide threat, then such Manichaeism may influence troops on the ground into indiscriminate violence against armed opponents and against civilians suspected of aiding them. The operational mimesis of pitting small, mobile units against similar small, mobile insurgent units acquires then an ideological load with grave moral consequences.

Guerrilla insurgency warfare was successful in several post–World War II anticolonial struggles in Africa and Asia. French officers who had experienced defeat in Indochina were among the first to develop a new military doctrine based on the mimesis of guerrilla insurgencies. These French officers spoke in the same way about antirevolutionary warfare as President Bush speaks of the war on terror as a new form of warfare that demands a radically new approach. The French counterrevolutionary approach consisted of three innovations that decisively influenced Argentine military thinking: (1) grid pattern territorialization; (2) imitation; and (3) intelligence. The steadfast faith in the latest communication technologies has given these characteristics a renewed relevance in today's swarming doctrine.

Grid pattern territorialization was developed by French officers in Algeria to combat urban insurgents in the alleyways of Algiers. They advocated the division of Algeria into large sectors and smaller zones, and Algiers into sectors, subsectors, and blocks. Regular troops were to patrol the major roads and guard the principal installations while mobile urban combat units sought out insurgents in each sector with intelligence provided by block wardens. Detainees were tortured during interrogation, and captives were disappeared (Horne 2006). French advisers to the Argentine military suggested precisely this approach in the late 1950s when a sabotage movement had emerged in reaction to the 1955 military coup against the popular leader Juan Domingo Perón (Robben 2005; Robin 2005).

The Argentine military rulers who assumed power in March 1976 employed an updated version of the older grid pattern, organizing Argentina into five defense zones, which were divided into subzones and further divided into areas. Regular troops controlled the major infrastructure (roads, waterways, airports, key installations) and manned checkpoints, while special task groups or combat units pursued guerrillas and political opponents in their designated areas. The regular troops and special task groups had separate command structures that became visible during joint operations. Whenever the presence of guerrillas was suspected, the neighborhood would be sealed off with makeshift checkpoints controlled by uniformed troops in licensed army trucks. The members of the task group would drive in unmarked passenger cars and were dressed as civilians. The regular troops would return to base after the operation ended, whereas the task group took the captives to a secret detention center for interrogation. They tortured them to fill in the organigrams of the guerrilla organizations, and thus dismantled the cell-like networks (Robben 2005:193–97). Such grid patterns, social network analyses, and link diagrams continue to be valued tools in assessing the connectivity and structure of insurgent groups in Iraq (FM 3–24 2007:317–28).

The imitation or mimesis of the guerrilla tactics by the Argentine armed forces was intentional. French instructors stated that guerrillas had to be fought with their own methods, namely by operating in small, highly mobile units. The French colonel Chateau-Jobert even admitted in 1968 that tactically speaking there was no difference between guerrilla forces and counterinsurgency forces. The only difference, he concluded, was the spirit of the fight, namely to be fighting on the side of God against an evil force (1977:117). This spiritual dimension created an ideological context to the mimetic tactics that opened the way to torture, first in Algeria and later in Argentina. Counterinsurgency warfare and coercive interrogations turned into dirty warfare and state terror when the Argentine military went after the political opposition and the civilians supporting the guerrillas. The military objective of state terror was to isolate the guerrillas, their supporters, and political opposition, and use dirty war tactics such as abduction, torture, disappearance, and assassination to defeat, eradicate, and traumatize them.

From Counterinsurgency to Dirty War

The 1975 counterinsurgency operations mounted by the Argentine military against Marxist insurgents who were trying to establish a liberated zone in Tucumán province were not restricted to armed combatants. The urban rear guard was attacked by abducting, torturing, disappearing, and assassinating collaborators and sympathizers of the Marxist guerrillas. This approach was a dress rehearsal for the dirty war that became national strategy in 1976 when the Argentine military took power. Whereas the rural guerrillas were uniformed troops organized in combat platoons, the urban guerrillas lived dispersed across Argentina's cities, were organized in cell-like structures, and carried out assaults disguised as civilians. How to operate against such an invisible enemy living among the people?

According to General Videla, who became the leader of the military junta in March 1976, the armed forces presented the Argentine president in

1975 with four options to combat the revolutionary insurgency, ranging from lengthy and gradual to short, total, and virulent. The first option implied a respect for law, due process, and human rights. The latter option "Implied attacking en masse, with everything, throughout the entire terrain, taking them from their hide-outs" (quoted in Seoane and Muleiro 2001:52). This option was chosen and succeeded in defeating the guerrilla insurgency in about four years. The human and social suffering was high, traumatizing people and Argentine society alike, while eventually leading to the prosecution of hundreds of military officers, NCOs, and policemen. A slower, more paced and careful tactic might have also been successful if the Argentine military had been willing to invest in civil-military relations and employ the minimum force necessary, but they decided otherwise because their dirty war was not just about defeating a revolutionary insurgency but about annihilating a political opposition movement that had been defined as an evil force. This strategic objective implied that the Argentine military transformed the counterinsurgency war into a dirty war because the enemy was not just the guerrilla insurgency but a much broader and loosely defined enemy inserted among the Argentine civilian population.

Everyone became a potential target and society the war zone in what began as a classic guerrilla war in the sparsely populated Andean foothills of Tucumán province and turned into a war among the people in Argentina's industrial zones. Urban guerrillas assassinated businessmen and union leaders, while task groups abducted guerrilla combatants and their relatives, friends, and sympathizers. The ideological justification of violence is crucial here because it blurred the boundaries between combatants and civilians, resulted in excessive violence, and led the military to torture practices against dehumanized captives. Both parties were determined to destroy one another in what was perceived by all to be a long and hard struggle. They regarded the conflict as a cultural war whose outcome determined the future of the Argentine people and was therefore fought with so much tenacity. Their mimesis established a social contract of annihilation and the promise of an exclusionary cultural order.

The belief in an existential struggle—call it cultural war, clash of civilizations, or good against evil—between two armed and determined opponents resulted in a violent confrontation. The guerrillas can be blamed for assassinating numerous noncombatants but the Argentine military surpassed them by far with the assassination of around ten thousand disappeared, and the temporary disappearance and torture of tens of thousands of others.

Captives were taken to secret detention centers where they would spend anywhere from a few days to a few years before being released or assassinated. Coercive interrogation or torture was justified for, supposedly, matters of expediency in an intelligence war where time was crucial to detect the location of bombs planted in public places. However, the majority of the tens of thousands of captives were not guerrilla combatants but either their relatives and sympathizers or political activists and critics of the dictatorship. Torture served more often than not to traumatize captives and thus take away their political agency by instilling distrust in the social world, by humiliating and dehumanizing captives before others, and by burdening them with lifelong memories about being tortured.

The comparison with the prison regime in Guantánamo Bay and Abu Ghraib is easily drawn. The brutal "softening up" practices at Abu Ghraib were blamed on a few low-ranked prison guards, but the abusive treatment had been approved by the highest ranks of government. A U.S. Senate investigative commission concluded that

The abuse of detainees at Abu Ghraib in late 2003 was not simply the result of a few soldiers acting on their own. Interrogation techniques such as stripping detainees of their clothes, placing them in stress positions, and using military working dogs to intimidate them appeared in Iraq only after they had been approved for use in Afghanistan and at GTMO [Guantánamo]. Secretary of Defense Donald Rumsfeld's December 2, 2002 authorization of aggressive interrogation techniques and subsequent interrogation policies and plans approved by senior military and civilian officials conveyed the message that physical pressures and degradation were appropriate treatment for detainees in U.S. military custody. What followed was an erosion in standards dictating that detainees be treated humanely. (Senate Armed Services Committee 2008).

Humiliation and dehumanization were deliberate strategies to break suspects of terrorism/insurgency, even though grave doubts have arisen about the utility and truth value of the intelligence gathered. Furthermore, the torture and abuse undermined the credibility of U.S. forces worldwide (see Danner 2004; Gourevitch and Morris 2008; Ratner and Ray 2004; Rose 2004; Strasser 2004).

The Argentine dirty war strategy of abducting, torturing, disappearing, and finally assassinating more than ten thousand Argentines was effective in the short run. The guerrilla organizations and the leftist political opposition were defeated in less than five years, but at an unacceptable human cost and with long-term detrimental consequences for Argentine society. The guerrilla organizations were decimated, surviving members went into exile, and the political left was shattered. The victorious military enjoyed their success for only a short while. The dictatorship fell in 1983 after growing human rights protests and losing the 1982 Falklands War. Several military junta commanders were convicted in 1985 for gross human rights violations, and more than six hundred officers were awaiting trial. Tensions in civil-military relations led to sweeping amnesty laws in 1986 and 1987, and presidential pardons in 1989 and 1990. Intermittent public protests, the call for accountability and truth, and the public disclosure by officers about the kidnapping of children made the Argentine Supreme Court overturn all amnesties and pardons by 2007. Around 250 officers returned to prison or were placed under house arrest. Argentine society has been held hostage by these military officers, who are unwilling to come clean with the past. Surviving relatives have to rely on forensic investigations, archival work, oral testimonies, and DNA testing to recover the remains of the assassinated disappeared and to find the hundreds of kidnapped infants of whom less than one hundred have had their real identity restored.

The geopolitical context of the wars in Iraq and Argentina is different but the incarceration regimes, the counterinsurgency tactics, the coercive interrogations, and the ideological frameworks have much in common. The Manichaean justification of war has a negative effect on the counterinsurgency efforts and the treatment of suspects when the principle of mimesis, so typical of classic antiguerrilla warfare, becomes the guiding tactic in a war among the people.

The insurgency in Iraq is not a classical guerrilla insurgency that strikes at military targets and tries to take political control of the country, as was the case in China or Vietnam, but resembles more the urban guerrilla warfare of Argentina in tactical and operational ways, while differing significantly in strategic terms. It consists of many different groups of combatants who plant roadside bombs against military convoys, carry out suicide attacks on Iraqi policemen and citizens, abduct and assassinate Iraqi civilians and foreign civilian contractors in reprisal attacks, and wage ethnic and religious feuds. The war among the people in Iraq is more about the constant harassment of U.S., Coalition, and government troops to lower morale, and more about preventing the institutional and infrastructural reconstruction of the Iraqi state, than about winning military victories, building an insurgent army, and ultimately grabbing power, as was the case in the Argentine revolutionaries (Hashim 2006:178–79).

Mimetic counterinsurgency warfare becomes tempting when the insurgents are hard to locate and identify. Dispersed swarming imitates the surprise tactics of the mobile insurgency units. As Kilcullen (2006a:33) has written about training local counterinsurgency forces, "Local forces should mirror the enemy. . . . They should move, equip and organize like the insurgents." The networked swarm units pursue chance encounters by cruising through dark city streets and raising impromptu checkpoints. This tactic turns swarmers into unpredictable predators who will leave a trail of civilian casualties on the hunt for an elusive enemy, and will therefore receive the hatred of the Iraqi people and sow sympathy for the insurgents as happened on Christmas night in 2006. In December 2006, a U.S. swarming patrol was attacked with a grenade. The response came with helicopters, tanks, and missiles. Six civilians were killed, and ten houses were severely damaged after a four-hour assault. The reason for throwing the grenade became clear later: security guards had mistaken the patrol for a militia.[5]

Cultural awareness, high ethical standards, and precise rules of engagement will reduce but not eliminate civilian casualties because the swarm units become part and parcel of the surprise tactics pursued by the insurgents and become chaotic agents themselves and foreign chaotic agents to boot. The one-time liberators became undependable occupiers who shouted commands at civilians in an unintelligible language, barged with excessive force into people's homes, and disappeared and tortured suspects while being unable to provide overall security, prevent ethnic violence, and guarantee public utilities.

The worsening of the violence in Iraq, the declining support for the war in the United States, and the Democratic victory in the congressional elections of 2006 caused a change of strategy. Contrary to public opinion and facing heavy political opposition, President Bush decided to commit "more than 20,000 additional American troops to Iraq. The vast majority of them—five brigades—will be deployed to Baghdad. These troops will work alongside Iraqi units and be embedded in their formations."[6] In addition, 4,000 Marines were given another tour of duty in Anbar province to help Sunni nationalists and the Iraqi army fight al Qaeda mujahideen. The main objectives were to improve the security situation in Baghdad and Anbar province and to train more Iraqi soldiers, officers, and policemen. The U.S. troop surge began in February 2007 and was completed in June 2007. The Multi-National Coalition Force commander in Iraq, General David Petraeus, told Congress in September 2007 that the surge was successful in reducing Sunni-Shi'i deaths in Baghdad by around 80 percent since December 2006 and in developing the capabilities of the Iraqi Security Forces (Petraeus 2007:3). By May 2008 around 4,700 Iraqi Special Operations troops were operative (Department of Defense 2008:35). General Petraeus (2007:2) reported that Iraqi counterinsurgency troops are "living among the people they are securing, and accordingly, our forces have established dozens of joint security stations and patrol bases manned by Coalition and Iraqi forces in Baghdad and in other areas across Iraq." The around-the-clock presence of troops enhanced the predictability of their conduct for the population, reduced civilian casualties, and lessened the need for mimetic counterinsurgency operations. A May 2008 assessment by the Department of Defense (2008:25) stated that "This partnership has provided the ISF [Iraqi Security Forces] with greater exposure to routine counterinsurgency operations, emboldening them to become more proactive in their own operations and improving their overall effectiveness."

The long-term effects on Iraqi society of the war and its Iraqification are unknown, but the Argentine experience suggests several worrisome consequences, especially because the death toll has been so high and because U.S. advisors have been training Iraqi forces in aggressive swarming operations that might be employed again in the future if the violence increases (Greer 2006). The randomness of the swarming operations and the danger of unreliable information acquired through coercive interrogation affected many Iraqi bystanders, as reporter Peter Maass (2004) observed during the first year of the Iraq War: "Yet for every raid that finds its target, there seem to be nine that don't, and in those nine, soldiers often point weapons at civilians, drive through fields and backyards, break down doors and detain people who are later released." The one-to-ten ratio might be an exaggeration, but the social suffering has been great nonetheless. Media-reported civilian deaths rose to over 40,000 by June 2006, while a demographic survey estimated that around 601,000 Iraqi civilians had died from the violence by that time (Burnham 2006:1426).[7] By December 2008 the Iraq War had killed at least 89,600 civilians, forced over two million people to flee their homes to safety abroad, killed 4,209 U.S. and 177 British troops, and caused 167 U.S. troops to commit suicide.[8] If we add these civilian deaths to the tens of thousands of maltreated inmates suspected of insurgent activities, the daily humiliations suffered at checkpoints, the overall insecurity, the infrastructural collapse, and the political vacuum caused by an ineffective government, then we can imagine a traumatized society in the making or at least a society that will suffer the long-term negative consequences of the war.

Conclusion

The skeptical reader might argue that this extrapolation from Argentina's counterinsurgency/dirty war to the war in Iraq is flawed because of one fundamental difference: the Argentine state terror and human rights violations were a deliberate policy of a ruthless authoritarian military regime, whereas the abuses by U.S. and Coalition troops have been excesses in a war waged by democratic governments to bring freedom, justice, and democracy to Iraq. The officially sanctioned aggressive interrogation practices deserve condemnation but their examination and subsequent outlawing by the U.S. Congress show the strength of an open society with democratic checks and balances. This argument is an example of the wrong-actions-for-the-right-reasons logic. When the security rationale of the war was proven false because no weapons of mass destruction were found, then the humanitarian urgency to overthrow Saddam Hussein became the principal justification of war for Bush and Blair. They received support from liberal-humanitarian internationalists, including prominent opinion makers, politicians, and human rights leaders who argued that the U.S. and Coalition governments were morally right to liberate the Iraqi people by force from their brutal tyrant, even though the reconstruction of Iraq had been poorly planned. As one critical supporter argued: "it is important to see the bigger picture: while much of the attention of critics of the war was focused on Abu Ghraib, there has been a tendency toward moral equivocation in which the abuses of a small coterie of soldiers were seen as comparable to the magnificent and glaring atrocities of Saddam Hussein and his regime" (Cushman 2005:20).

Without denying the terror unleashed by Saddam Hussein's regime on the Iraqi people, I find it too easy to dismiss the tens—some sources say hundreds—of thousands of civilians who died violently during the years after the March 2003 invasion, and to trivialize the Abu Ghraib scandal, the checkpoint killings, and the existence of CIA prisons on foreign soil by arguing that the war has been a just war because of the overthrow of a repressive dictatorship, just as it would be too easy to whitewash the human rights violations of Argentina's dirty war by arguing that it succeeded in defeating the guerrilla insurgency. The string of human rights violations during the Iraq War was neither accidental nor the side effect of an undermanned invasion force or insufficient post-victory planning. The invasion was ill conceived from the outset because it was founded on a misleading cause of war about unproven weapons of mass destruction, directed by a Manichaean worldview, the suspicion of Islam as a retrograde religion, an appraisal of Iraq as a backward society in need of modernization, an attitude of cultural superiority, and an ethnocentric mission of spreading Western values believed to be universal, while ignoring that non-Western societies may create alternative political systems that are not necessarily repressive and unjust. The U.S. and Coalition forces did not show a genuine concern for the civilian rights of the Iraqi people, demonstrate a sincere intention to work with them as equals toward a better Iraq, or have much respect for Iraqi history and culture to begin with. The failure to protect the National Museum in Baghdad from plunderers is a glaring demonstration of such indifference. U.S. foreign policy toward Iraq was guided by imperial hubris. As Mark Danner (2006:96) has observed astutely, "the wave of change the President and his officials were so determined to set in course by unleashing American military power may well turn out to be precisely the wave of Islamic radicalism that they had hoped to prevent."

The Iraqi victory celebrations about the fall of Saddam Hussein soon turned into widespread disenchantment because of a failing infrastructure and the rising political violence. The U.S. government might have prevented the escalation of post-invasion violence if they had not dismantled the Iraqi army, had not fired all Ba'th Party members from government offices, and had defined clear postwar objectives about political representation, ethnic-religious relations, accountability and justice, security, and infrastructural reconstruction (Chandrasekaran 2007; Danner 2006; Hashim 2006:288–97). Unfortunately, the Coalition Provisional Authority decided otherwise. This critique is of course wisdom after the fact, but less excusable is that after the first and most fatal mistake of invading Iraq on the wrong grounds, the U.S. government and its military commanders made a second mistake: resorting immediately to military force once U.S. troops encountered armed opposition. Instead, the volatile situation might have been defused through consensus building and finding comprehensive political solutions to the rising ethnic and religious tensions—slow and difficult as it might be to formulate such policies. Despite the lip service paid to such political solutions by prominent politicians and military analysts (Baker and Hamilton 2006; Nagl 2005), the emphasis was on repression rather than state-building (Hashim 2006:271–76; Herring and Rangwala 2006:172–75).

The third mistake has been employing counterinsurgency tactics, based on the imitation of the insurgency and encased in good-versus-evil thinking, that were bound to result in human rights violations. The mimetic reaction to the armed insurgency led to intelligence gathering through torture and unpredictable swarming operations that heightened the risks to the Iraqi people. Great suffering was imposed on the civilian population and played into the insurgents' hands and paradoxically helped them achieve their objectives by enhancing people's feeling of chaos, insecurity, and fear, and turning the initial approval for the overthrow of Saddam Hussein into a widespread rejection of the foreign presence on Iraqi soil. "The more the measures to impose order involve terrorizing the population the more the position of the opponent as their defender is enhanced," British general Smith (2005:380) has argued. The occupation turned into a quagmire that deteriorated even further by grim counterinsurgency tactics that caused severe human rights violations and the unnecessary deaths of tens of thousands of civilians. The lesson to be learned from Argentine history is that when a war among the people is fought with a lack of concern for human rights and due process with the argument of military expediency, and justified by a Manichaean rhetoric of fighting "a brand of evil, the likes of which we haven't seen in a long time in the world,"[9] then fear among a civilian population will eventually turn into hostility.

Trying to improve the combat situation, the 2006 Iraq Study Group recommended: "Military priorities in Iraq must change, with the highest priority given to the training, equipping, advising, and support mission and to counterterrorism operations" (Baker and Hamilton 2006:51). The change of strategy in 2007 was a direct result of the Iraq Study Group's critical observations. However, instead of following the report's comprehensive strategy about launching a regional diplomacy, involving the international community, promoting national reconciliation, restoring the criminal justice system, maximizing oil production, and rebuilding the infrastructure, the choice fell narrowly on the suggestion of "a short-term redeployment or surge of American combat forces to stabilize Baghdad, or to speed up the training and equipping mission" (Baker and Hamilton 2006:50). The troop surge of 2007 significantly lowered the violence and number of dead. The merit of this impressive success detracts from its price, namely the ethnic cleansing of Sunnis by Shi'i militias in Baghdad and the payment of $360 a month per combatant to over ninety thousand former Sunni nationalist insurgents who became U.S. allies against al Qaeda mujahideen. These Sunni Awakening groups or Sons of Iraq are supposed to integrate eventually into the Iraqi Security Forces (Department of Defense 2008:23; Simon 2008). Unfortunately, a resurgence of violence in Iraq continues to be imaginable as long as religious tensions and political quarrels remain unresolved. The growing political confidence of the well-armed former Sunni insurgents might clash with the ambitions of Shi'i militias, and either party might decide to take on the Iraqi Security Forces to wrest power from the national government. The burden to quell the renewed violence will then fall squarely on an Iraqi military trained and equipped by the U.S. armed forces.

The Iraqification of the counterinsurgency carries the danger of worsening the situation for the Iraqi people, as the Iraqi Security Forces are likely to step into the same trap of mimicking the insurgency, as did U.S. commanders, with swarming operations to try to beat the insurgents at their own methods, thus further alienating the Iraqi population as civilians continue to be killed. The Argentine dirty war shows the danger of a mimetic counterinsurgency tactic in a war among the people. The unlimited operational freedom of small combat units, roaming streets and squares, breaking into homes, and torturing captives for intelligence, is a wrongheaded imitation of chaos-producing insurgents that only enhances public insecurity. Were the political violence in Iraq to develop into a civil war between Shi'is and Sunnis, then the swarming tactics planted by U.S. advisors during the occupation will be turned on fellow citizens and increase the number of human rights violations. It can further traumatize Iraqi society and shut the door on the reconciliation that was so much desired after decades of repression and state terror.

Notes

Different versions of this essay were presented in 2007 at a conference honoring Ulf Hannerz at Stockholm University, Sweden and as a keynote address at the annual meetings of PACSA (Peace and Conflict Studies in Anthropology) held at the Max Planck Institute in Halle, Germany, and in 2008 at the annual meetings of the Netherlands Society of Anthropology in Arnhem, the Netherlands, and the American Anthropological Association in San Francisco. I was given many valuable suggestions at these occasions, and I want to thank in particular Eyal Ben-Ari of Hebrew University for his thoughtful comments on this chapter's final draft.

    1. General Galtieri quoted in *Somos*, April 11, 1980.

    2. "Address to a Joint Session of Congress and the American People," September 20, 2001, http://www.whitehouse.gov/news/releases/2001/09/print/2001 0920-8.html (accessed March 2, 2006).

    3. Address to the nation by President Bush, March 17, 2003. http://www .whitehouse.gov/news/releases/2003/03/print/20030317-7.html (accessed December 1, 2006).

    4. Address to the nation by President Bush, January 10, 2007, http://www

.whitehouse.gov/news/releases/2007/01/print/20070110–7.html (accessed December 23, 2008).

    5. http://aliveinbaghdad.org/2007/01/08/americans-xmas-operation/ (accessed March 4, 2008).

    6. Address to the nation by President Bush, January 10, 2007. http://www.whitehouse.gov/news/releases/2007/01/print/20070110–7.html (accessed December 23, 2008).

    7. http://www.iraqbodycount.org (accessed June 25, 2006).

    8. http://www.iraqbodycount.org; http://icasualties.org/oif and http://www.justforeignpolicy.org/iraq/iraqdeaths.html (accessed December 10, 2008).

    9. President Bush at O'Hare International Airport, September 27, 2001. http://www.whitehouse.gov/news/releases/2001/09/print/20010927–1.html (accessed March 2, 2006).

Bibliography

Amnesty International. 2006. *Beyond Abu Ghraib: Detention and Torture in Iraq.* March 20, AI Index: MDE 14/001/2006.

Arquilla, John, and David Ronfeldt. 2003. Swarming: The Next Face of Battle. *Aviation Week & Space Technology*, September 29.

Baker, James A., and Lee H. Hamilton, co-chairs. 2006. *The Iraq Study Group Report.* Washington, D.C.: United States Institute of Peace.

Blair, Tony. 2005a. Full Statement to the House of Commons, March 18, 2003. In *A Matter of Principle: Humanitarian Arguments for War in Iraq*, ed. Thomas Cushman, 329–39. Berkeley: University of California Press.

———. 2005b. The Threat of Global Terrorism. In *A Matter of Principle: Humanitarian Arguments for War in Iraq*, ed. Thomas Cushman, 340–51. Berkeley: University of California Press.

Burnham, Gilbert, Riyadh Lafta, Shannon Doocy, and Les Roberts. 2006. Mortality After the 2003 Invasion of Iraq: A Cross-Sectional Cluster Sample Survey. *The Lancet* 368 (October 21):1421–28.

Chandrasekaran, Rajiv. 2007. *Imperial Life in the Emerald City: Inside Iraq's Green Zone.* New York: Vintage.

Chateau-Jobert, P. 1977 [1968]. *La Confrontación Revolución-Contrarrevolución.* Buenos Aires: Editorial Rioplatense.

Cooper, Robert. 2004. *The Breaking of Nations: Order and Chaos in the Twenty-First Century.* London: Atlantic Books.

Cushman, Thomas. 2005. Introduction: The Liberal-Humanitarian Case for War in Iraq. In *A Matter of Principle: Humanitarian Arguments for War in Iraq*, ed. Thomas Cushman, 1–26. Berkeley: University of California Press.

Danner, Mark. 2004. *Torture and Truth: America, Abu Ghraib, and the War on Terror.* New York: New York Review of Books.

———. 2005. Taking Stock of the Forever War. *New York Times Magazine*, September 11.

————. 2006. Iraq: The War of the Imagination. *New York Review of Books*, December 21.

Department of Defense. 2008. *Measuring Stability and Security in Iraq*. Report to Congress, June 13. http://www.defenselink.mil/pubs/pdfs/Master_16_June_08%20FINAL_SIGNED%20.pdf (accessed December 23, 2008).

Edwards, Sean J. A. 2000. *Swarming on the Battlefield: Past, Present, and Future*. Santa Monica, Calif.: RAND.

Filkins, Dexter. 2008. *The Forever War: Dispatches from the War on Terror*. London: The Bodley Head.

FM 3–24. 2007 [2006]. *The U.S. Army–Marine Corps Counterinsurgency Field Manual*. Chicago: University of Chicago Press.

Gourevitch, Philip, and Errol Morris. 2008. *Standard Operating Procedure*. New York: Penguin Press.

Greer, James K. 2006. Operation Knockout: Counterinsurgency in Iraq. *Military Review* (special edition: Counterinsurgency Reader) (October):41–44.

Hammes, Thomas X. 2004. *The Sling and the Stone: On War in the 21st Century*. St. Paul, Minn.: Zenith Press.

Hashim, Ahmed S. 2006. *Insurgency and Counter-Insurgency in Iraq*. Ithaca, N.Y.: Cornell University Press.

Herring, Eric, and Glen Rangwala. 2006. *Iraq in Fragments: The Occupation and Its Legacy*. Ithaca, N.Y.: Cornell University Press.

Horne, Alistair. 2006. *A Savage War of Peace: Algeria, 1954–1962*. New York: New York Review Books.

Human Rights Watch. 2003. *Hearts and Minds: Post-War Civilian Deaths in Baghdad Caused by U.S. Forces*. 15 (October):9(E). http:/www.hrw.org/en/reports/2003/10/20/hearts-and-minds (accessed April 14, 2009).

————. 2005a. *The New Iraq? Torture and Ill-Treatment of Detainees in Iraqi Custody*. 17 (January):1(E). http:/www.hrw.org/en/reports/2005/01/24/new-iraq (accessed April 14, 2009).

————. 2005b. *A Face and a Name: Civilian Victims of Insurgent Groups in Iraq*. 17 (October):9(E). http:/www.hrw.org/en/reports/2005/10/02/face-and-name (accessed April 14, 2009).

Kilcullen, David. 2004. Complex Warfighting. *The Australian Army, Future Land Warfare Branch*. http://www.defence.gov.au/army/lwsc/Publications/complex_warfighting.pdf (accessed July 16, 2008).

————. 2006a. Twenty-Eight Articles: Fundamentals of Company-Level Counterinsurgency. *Iosphere, Joint Information Operations Center*. http://www.au.af.mil/info-ops/iosphere/iosphere_summer06_kilcullen.pdf (accessed July 16, 2008).

————. 2006b. Counterinsurgency Redux. http://smallwarsjournal.com/documents/kilcullen1.pdf (accessed July 16, 2008).

————. 2009. *The Accidental Guerrilla: Fighting Small Wars in the Midst of a Big One*. New York: Oxford University Press.

Maass, Peter. 2004. Professor Nagl's War. *New York Times Magazine*, January 11.

————. 2005. The Salvadorization of Iraq? *New York Times Magazine*, May 1.

Nagl, John A. 2005. *Learning to Eat Soup with a Knife: Counterinsurgency Lessons from Malaya and Vietnam*. Chicago: University of Chicago Press.

Neiman, Susan. 2004. *Evil in Modern Thought: An Alternative History of Philosophy*. Princeton, N.J.: Princeton University Press.

Packer, George. 2005. *The Assassins' Gate: America in Iraq*. New York: Farrar, Straus and Giroux.

Petraeus, David H. 2007. Report to Congress on the Situation in Iraq. September 10–11. http://www.defenselink.mil/pubs/pdfs/Petraeus-Testimony20070910 .pdf (accessed December 23, 2008).

Ratner, Michael, and Ellen Ray. 2004. *Guantánamo: What the World Should Know*. White River Junction, Vt.: Chelsea Green Publishing.

Robben, Antonius C. G. M. 2005. *Political Violence and Trauma in Argentina*. Philadelphia: University of Pennsylvania Press.

Robin, Marie-Monique. 2005. *Escuadrones de la muerte: La escuela francesa*. Buenos Aires: Editorial Sudamericana.

Rose, David. 2004. *Guantánamo: America's War on Human Rights*. London: Faber and Faber.

Senate Armed Services Committee. 2008. Inquiry into the Treatment of Detainees in U.S. Custody. December 11. http://levin.senate.gov/newsroom/supporting/ 2008/Detainees.121108.pdf (accessed December 15, 2008).

Seoane, María, and Vicente Muleiro. 2001. *El Dictador: La historia secreta y pública de Jorge Rafael Videla*. Buenos Aires: Editorial Sudamericana.

Shadid, Anthony. 2005. *Night Draws Near: Iraq's People in the Shadow of America's War*. New York: Henry Holt and Company.

Simon, Steven. 2008. The Price of the Surge. *Foreign Affairs* 87 (3):57–76.

Smith, Rupert. 2005. *The Utility of Force: The Art of War in the Modern World*. London: Penguin/Allen Lane.

Strasser, Steven, ed. 2004. *The Abu Ghraib Investigations: The Official Reports of the Independent Panel and Pentagon on the Shocking Prisoner Abuse in Iraq*. New York: PublicAffairs.

U.S. Department of State. 2006. *Iraq: Country Reports on Human Rights Practices— 2005*. Bureau of Democracy, Human Rights, and Labor. March 8.

West, Bing. 2008. *The Strongest Tribe: War, Politics, and the Endgame in Iraq*. New York: Random House.

Epilogue

Ibrahim Al-Marashi

Prior to 1980, Iraq and Afghanistan provided fascinating case studies for anthropologists. By the 1980s, the Ba'th government of Saddam Hussein had consolidated power and declared war on Iran, and the Soviet invasion of Afghanistan had sparked a tenacious resistance movement. Both conflicts resulted in chronic instability that would preclude anthropologists from conducting fieldwork in those countries for decades. As a result, the study of both countries by anthropologists declined, in addition to that of other academic disciplines. When the United States went to war with Afghanistan in 2001 and Iraq in 2003, there were perhaps no more than a dozen genuine experts on either country.

The United States would experiment with nation-building in two states, unaware of their pasts of continuous insurrections. America had failed to appreciate that previous attempts to do the same in both Iraq and Afghanistan were spectacular failures. Despite the dearth of academic research conducted on Iraq or Afghanistan, this volume demonstrates that valuable lessons could have been gleaned from other insurgencies or political conflicts in Afghanistan, Northern Ireland, Algeria, Cambodia, and Palestine.

I was first introduced to the ethnosectarian diversity of Iraq and Afghanistan by anthropologists. Growing up as an Iraqi American, there were few books available about Iraq. The book *Guests of the Sheik*, an ethnography written by the academic Elizabeth Fernea (1965), the wife of a social anthropologist, introduced me to life in an Iraqi village. Her work also taught me a valuable lesson about studying the peoples of Iraq. Well before the 2003 Iraq War, the Iraqis were viewed by foreign governments and the media through a "tri-ethnic prism." One myth they expounded was that Iraq's communities could be viewed through an ethnosectarian prism, breaking them up into the "the Arab Shi'is, the Arab Sunnis, and the Kurds" when in fact the groups are divided within themselves by class differences, tribal affiliations, varying levels of religious belief, and those who fled and those who stayed. It has been a fashion in the foreign media to essentialize Iraqis into three "ethnic" categories, which leads to erroneous notions such as viewing Iraq's Shi'is as an "ethnic" group or neglecting to recognize that the majority of Kurds are also Sunnis as well, or that there is another major ethnic group in Iraq called the Turkmens. When reading Western media during and after the war, it seemed to me the outside world wanted to divide up Iraq into three pieces well before the war started.

However, Iraq is not a puzzle of three pieces that can be broken up in a tidy fashion. It is a collage or mosaic of sorts. Iraq is home to the Yazidis, whose adherents believe in a Creator God, who is now resting, and Malak Ta'us, the Peacock Angel and current organ of divine will. The Peacock Angel is familiar to the world's monotheists, Muslims, Christians, and Jews; they call him the Devil. Hence the Yazidis would be known as "devil worshipers" and were the targets of a devastating car bomb attack in August 2007. There are also the Ibrahimiyya who live near Tal Afar, also in the north of Iraq. They are ethnically Turkish and believe in a trinity of Allah, Muhammed, and Ali. Finally, there are also the Shabak who live in villages near the northern city of Mosul. They seemed to me to be the most Middle Eastern people of the region because of their language, which is a combination of Turkish, Persian, Kurdish, and Arabic.

My fascination with Afghanistan was sparked during my first year of undergraduate studies, a decade before the events of September 11. Nazif Shahrani, an anthropologist, introduced me to the complexities of "Afghanness," an all-inclusive nationality that incorporated Tajiks, Hazaras, Uzbeks, Turkmens, and Baluchis, ruled by a Pashtun elite who used Persian as a court language.

The aforementioned cultural complexities and cultural nuances of Iraq and Afghanistan were cherished by anthropologists but often lost on policymakers. Anthropologists certainly could have contributed to the public debate about the post-9/11 global war on terror, not as experts on behalf of the U.S. government but as those able to inform publics woefully ignorant of the vast diversity of these states.

As a historian in the fields of communication, film, and propaganda, I found numerous analytical similarities in the contributions to this volume. The authors' examination of languages of power and the clash of diametrically opposed narratives has accentuated the importance of the study of discourse in the "war on terror." They have demonstrated that insurgencies are fought not only on the streets with bullets but on the discursive level with rhetorical ammunition.

At the same time this volume offers a valuable history of insurgencies, popular resistance movements, and counterinsurgencies, providing a comparative perspective of similar events in Argentina, Northern Ireland, Algeria, Palestine, Iraq, and Afghanistan. Furthermore, they document the changing geography of the Middle East as a result of the war on terror. The separation wall between Israel and the Palestinian Authority, the divisions of Iraq into "swarm zones," the dichotomy between NATO-held urban centers and the rural periphery held by the Taliban in Afghanistan all attest to the transformation of physical space in these insurgency zones. The human geography of the region has also been affected, ranging from women barred from public space in Iraq to Palestinians barred from traveling to see their families in either the West Bank or Jerusalem.

Historical Memory and the War on Terror

As a historian, I believe that the historical context for the chapters demonstrates how the post–September 11 events are a continuation of struggles that began well before 2001. The conflicts in Iraq and Afghanistan that erupted in the aftermath of the war on terror form an integral part of the historical memory of its inhabitants. Both countries were created to secure the interests of the British Empire. However, these states were formed as a matter of colonial expediency and the conquerors ignored the cultural sensitivities of the inhabitants that made up the mosaic of peoples inhabiting the Hindu Kush range that later made up Afghanistan, as well as those of the peoples of the Mesopotamian basin that formed the state of Iraq. The British created Afghanistan as a buffer state between a southern expanding Russian Empire to protect its crown colony of India. The borders of Afghanistan separated Pashtun tribes that straddled the border with Pakistan, ensured that Persian-speaking Tajiks were separated from Iran, and resulted in Turkmen and Uzbeks being cut off from their ethnic brethren who were subjects of a Russian czar. The British designed the borders of Iraq to create a state that could secure the overland route to India and unite oil-rich areas in the south and north of the country under the administration of a pro-British energy cartel. The often perfectly straight lines that form the borders of Iraq separated Shi'i tribes inhabiting Kuwait and southwest Iran, as well as Kurdish tribes that straddled the borders with Turkey and Iran, and severed economic and cultural links between Sunni Arabs in Iraq and Syria.

In Julie Peteet's chapter, "The War on Terror, Dismantling, and the

Construction of Place," she writes how resistance to foreign domination has been consistent across the region, and thus "it is stunning that U.S. policymakers did not foresee an Iraqi insurgency." Jeffrey A. Sluka in his chapter, "Losing Hearts and Minds in the 'War on Terrorism,'" reaffirms Peteet's point that failing to learn from history resulted in dire consequences for post-Ba'thist Iraq: "Because the military did not anticipate and did not intend to fight an insurgency in either country, they did not plan or prepare for it and were thus caught on the back foot with having to cope with this reality—namely, large and growing guerrilla wars in both countries."

Indeed, insurgencies and counterinsurgencies also have their historical precedent in both Afghanistan and Iraq. A BBC documentary series that highlights the experience of British soldiers combating the Taliban in Afghanistan serves as an example of the "militainment" that has erupted since September 11, often blurring reality with Hollywood escapism. The soldiers depicted in this series fight over territory that their great-grandfathers fought over more than a century ago. The idea of the British propping up a regime in Kabul was not new to this land (even though the United Kingdom may have been doing the same under a NATO mandate since 2001, as opposed to a colonial mandate). In January 1842 British troops supporting a regime friendly to Britain's interest sparked a revolt, precipitating their withdrawal. As the British forces withdrew through the rugged snow-covered mountain passes of Afghanistan, they were constantly harassed by Pashtun Ghilzai warriors. Out of more than sixteen thousand people who made up this foreign contingent, only a single Briton survived to tell the tale of the massacre. The British-backed government of King Shuja collapsed without foreign support. The Ghilzai tribal warriors who took part in the attack against the British would form an organization years later that would continue in this tradition of resisting foreign occupation—the Taliban.

Just as the American-led Coalition forces met with resistance in post-2003 Iraq, the British presence in Iraq after World War I was also troubled by a similar insurgency. In fact, the term "insurgent" was also used in the 1920s to describe those who opposed the political center in Baghdad with violence. The British and the Iraqi military it created dealt with its insurgency on and off for fifteen years. The insurgency was finally crushed by the general Bakr Sidqi, who used unrestrained military might. His success, however, did not mean stability for Iraq. Sidqi proved that the Iraqi government could not survive against the insurgents without the Iraqi armed forces, and he launched the first military coup in the Middle East in 1936. What followed was a series of military coups that only ended with the rise of Saddam Hussein in 1979 and a unique set of authoritarian tactics that brought the military under his control. Hussein's most successful tactic was busying the armed forces with foreign adventures such as the Iran-Iraq War and the 1991 Gulf War, which ushered in its sequel, the 2003 Iraq War, which ultimately led to another sequel—the second Iraqi insurgency.

Collective traumas form an integral part of the historical memory of this region. Peteet describes a Palestinian family from Jerusalem who lived in the city for a millennium. When they compared their current status to the Crusader occupations that their ancestors lived through, it reminded me of Iraqi writer and academic Sinan Antoon's "They Came to Baghdad." He lists a series of occupations of Iraq's historic city:

945 Buwayhids; 1055 Seljuks; 1258 Mongols led by Hulagu; 1340 Jalayrs; 1393 & 1401 Mongols led by Tamerlane; 1411 Turkoman Black Sheep; 1469 Turkoman White Sheep; 1508 Safavids; 1534 Ottomans under Sultan Sulayman the Magnificent; 1623 Safavids; 1638 Ottomans under Sultan Murad IV; 1917 British; 1941 British again to depose pro-German government; 2003 Anglo-American invasion. (Antoon 2003)

Antoon's words highlight Peteet's assessment: "These invasions and occupations and those of the contemporary era are not disparate unconnected events; for many in the region they are part of a long historical pattern and narrative of unequal relations with the West." Peteet's reference to the Crusades is similar to that of an Iraqi nationalist colonel named, ironically enough, Salah Al-Din Al-Sabbagh (the name of the Arab liberator of Jerusalem during the Crusades). Al-Sabbagh controlled Iraqi politics from 1937 to 1941 until he was deposed by a British "regime change" after a month-long war. Al-Sabbagh viewed the events in the Middle East in the 1930s as a continuation of a greater clash between Islam and Christianity. Al-Sabbagh's vision of a new Crusade resonated with the neo-Crusader themes of al Qaeda in Iraq, in addition to those of a variety of Iraqi nationalist groups opposed to the U.S. role in their country (Al-Marashi 2006:219).

The aforementioned cyclical interpretation of history in Iraq and Afghanistan is also demonstrated by the history of events in Argentina, Northern Ireland, and Palestine. The contributors to this volume provide an important historical lesson—that those who fail to learn history are doomed to repeat it.

Language and Counterinsurgency

The counterinsurgency campaigns in Iraq and Afghanistan employed rhetorical tools that were also used to justify military actions and discredit enemies. Along with the vast arsenal at the disposal of the United States, the United Kingdom, and NATO, the language of power used during the conflict also emerged as a crucial weapon. The Western media was influenced by and absorbed such terminology, complementing these governments' efforts to vilify the "enemies" in a "war of words." The media have adopted many elements of the Bush administration's political rhetoric, ripe with symbols and narrative devices employed to link the attacks of September 11 with the Saddam government in order to justify an offensive war against Iraq as a "defensive action." In both the war in Afghanistan and the Iraq War, U.S. and British governments and select media attempted to define the battle and the actors for the viewers by conscientiously appropriating labels, titles, categories, and catchphrases to the various politicians, foreign policy initiatives, and weapons that made up the drama of the war on terror.

Peteet coins the term "terrorology," the "lingo" that emerged in the aftermath of September 11. I would suggest that what has emerged years after the events in 2001 can be described as the "banality of terrorology," where catchphrases and titles produced by the war have become so pervasive in the news, in the entertainment industry, and in education that people often use them without understanding their implication.

All of the chapters gathered in this volume deal with Manichaean thinking and binary oppositions, ranging from Argentina's generals protecting their country and civilization from evil communists, to the Khmer Rouge safeguarding its order from evil imperialists, to Bush's invocation of a fight of good nations versus evil advocates of terrorism. An example of this language of terrorology was crystallized in the 2002 State of the Union speech, which declared the threat from an "axis of evil." In using this terminology, the Bush administration hoped to alienate the parties named, Iran, Iraq, and North Korea, and set them apart from the rest of the "good" countries in the world. Not only did the title succeed in creating an identifiable enemy bloc, it also succeeded in working an entire political agenda into its listeners' memories.

In Alexander Laban Hinton's chapter, "'Night Fell on a Different World': Dangerous Visions and the War on Terror, a Lesson from Cambodia," he encapsulates the episodes in the war on terror from the viewpoint of its entertaining nature, framed as a film or TV miniseries. Because Hinton is also attentive to film history, his analysis emerges in the language of terrorology. The Hollywood system is characterized by the single-line concept, where a film has to be summarized in a few words. A lengthy description indicates that the film is too complex, hence too complex for audiences and thus denied support from production companies. Most U.S. government initiatives, wars, and villains could be summarized in catchy two- or three-word titles on par with the single-line concept and titles used for Hollywood films. This trend presaged 2001, with terms like "Cold War," "Red Scare," and "New World Order," and followed with "axis of evil," "war on terror," and "Operation Iraqi Freedom." The problem with these concise, catchy titles is that they repackage complex phenomena into deceivingly simple components. A war on terror implies that terror is something that can be targeted, fought, and defeated when in reality such a title is so broad and so ill defined that it becomes essentially meaningless. "Terror" is a worldwide problem that underrepresented parties have resorted to for ages in their struggle for agency, whether it be in Northern Ireland, Gaza, or Iraq. The Bush administration could have more aptly declared "War on Osama bin Laden," a "War on UBL," or, better yet, "A War on al Qaeda" to fit into the Hollywood-inspired three-word formula. However, it was clear that such a broad name was intentional. There were those in the Bush administration who wanted to target not just al Qaeda but Iraq and Iran, and a war on terror gave them free reign to justify any military action in the name of seeking out terrorists wherever they may be. Furthermore, once Bush had created the villain of the axis of evil, he would be compelled to act against them.

Antonius C. G. M. Robben's "Mimesis in a War Among the People," on Argentina's "dirty war," compares Argentina's experience with that of the United States in Iraq. His chapter ultimately raises the question of how the United States sanitizes a "dirty war" into a "clean war." Counterinsurgency operations develop a lexicon used to sanitize the conflict, such as "shock and awe," "swarm," and "surge." This lexicon had also made "smart bombs," "stealth fighters," and "cruise missiles" household terms but rarely shows the Iraqis who are on the receiving end of these weapons. These weapons were marketed as simply "degrading" Iraq's fighting capability. The United States attributes the insurgency to "sectarian militias," "foreign fighters," and "Ba'thist dead enders" and rarely blames it on Iraqi nationalists resisting an occupation. Even the term "foreign fighters," used to describe Arab volunteers who came to Iraq to combat Coalition forces, is an anomaly, as technically American and British troops are also foreign fighters in Iraq.

Robben's analysis of the use of terms such as "shock and awe" fits into Peteet's use of the term "terrorology," which she compares to a "discourse of monstrosity." Robben argues that "swarm" in a sense anthropomorphizes the conflict. This theme is implicit throughout the Iraq War. The war had begun with an air attack on a meeting place of the Iraqi leadership in an attempt to "decapitate" Saddam Hussein's government, which was described as a "surgical strike." Even the term "Operation Iraqi Freedom" suggested that the war was a medical, surgical procedure that sought to remove the cancer of Saddam Hussein through decapitation. "Shock and awe" was used by U.S. military war planners to describe how the showcase of American firepower would intimidate the Iraqis into submission. Those words would also become a banality pervading everyday life; even the American TV series *Desperate Housewives* described one of the characters, Bree Van de Camp, as using "shock and awe" against one of her rival housewives. It is often forgotten that the term "blitzkrieg" used to describe an American football maneuver was adopted from Hitler's use of "lightning" firepower to overcome the Low Countries, France, and Poland. The term "shock and awe" proved so catchy that even Muhammed Said Al-Sahhaf, the Ba'thist minister of information famed for his exaggeration of Iraqi battlefield successes, appropriated this term during a press conference: "The shock has backfired on them. They are shocked because of what they have seen. No one received them with roses. They were received with bombs, shoes and bullets. Now, the game has been exposed. Awe will backfire on them. This is the boa snake. We will extend it further and cut it the appropriate way."[1] The importance of the term "shock and awe" is that it has ramifications for the counterinsurgency that developed after 2003. The "shock" of the war settled after major combat was declared over, but the "awe" campaign still continued. After traveling to Iraq one year after the conflict, I could not help but notice the heavy U.S. military presence. The Iraqis I spoke with pointed out helicopters flying overhead, armored carriers rumbling down the motorways, and tanks parked on major intersections, and I wondered if the array of weapons was meant to intimidate the Iraqis or "awe" them into submission. Jeffrey A. Sluka discusses the role of winning over local populations during counterinsurgency campaigns in his chapter, "Losing Hearts and Minds in the 'War on Terrorism.'" America postwar shock and awe was losing hearts and minds in Iraq.

Sluka defines four main elements that alienate popular support from the civilian population during insurgencies: civilian casualties, political murder or "extrajudicial" killings, everyday human rights abuses under military occupation, and torture and other repressive measures such as arbitrary detention. The battles for Fallujah in April and November 2004 resulted in civilian casualties, the attempt to arrest or kill in the process the cleric Muqtada al-Sadr in April 2004 was an extrajudicial killing, human rights abuses against civilians have been widely documented, and a torture regime was discovered at the Abu Ghraib prison—these are but a few examples that demonstrate that all four acts have occurred in Iraq, alienating the civilian population. In Iraq, "Fallujah," "Muqtada," and "Abu Ghraib" have emerged as single-word concepts that form a counterdiscourse to the American rhetoric designed to sanitize its counterinsurgency operations. While the United States has tried to clean the image of its "dirty war," Iraqis have also employed language to depict the counterinsurgency as becoming even dirtier.

In Hinton's comparison of rhetoric used by Cambodia and the United States, he describes a "sense of national community through the constant use of first-person plural ('we') and possessive plural pronouns ('our')." The use of the collective pronoun is a common practice in political communication and the mainstream media. For example, when James Woolsey, former director of the Central Intelligence Agency, was interviewed on a Fox News program by Greta Van Susteren, he was asked about the possibility of Saddam's attacking the United States during the buildup to the war.

Van Susteren: All right, we've talked al Qaeda. What about Saddam? Do you fear Saddam is going to strike here in the United States as *we* sort of get geared up for war?

Woolsey: I think what he's likely to do is provide something like, you know, anthrax or something like that to terrorist groups, al Qaeda or some other. He and these terrorist groups are sort of like Mafia families, particularly the ones that are religiously based, in part, like al Qaeda. They hate each other and they kill each other and they criticize each other, but they're willing to work together on this and that because they hate *us* more. (Fox News Network 2003)

While some news channels challenge their pundits, Van Susteren does not ask Woolsey if he "believes" or "is there a possibility" of Saddam Hussein striking in the United States but whether he "fears" such an attack, a feeling that keeps the audience tuned in to the program. Her use of fear and the collective "we" in the phrase "we sort of get geared up for war" and Woolsey's use of "they hate us more" are common tools used to link the American audience to both the interviewer and interviewee. In less than thirty seconds of air time the clashing parties in this war had been defined.

Like Hinton, Peteet also refers to a "dualism" in the war on terror, "a split between us and those like us and those others—terrorists and lawless evildoers." By constructing the "them," the ethnosectarian diversity of Iraq and Afghanistan is reduced to a monolithic unit to be vanquished. Groups like al Qaeda and Hezbollah are linked together as a collective terrorist threat, even though the Salafi ideology that imbues bin Laden's organization deems the Shi'is like those in the Lebanese group as a repugnant apostasy.

The Geography of the War on Terror

The war on terror has produced new geographical contours, bringing obscure towns such as Kandahar in Afghanistan or Fallujah in Iraq to the attention of the consumers of terrorology. In her chapter Julie Peteet writes that "Many Middle Easterners have narrated the war on terror as a contemporary attempt to fragment the region's space and reorder national borders, structures of governance, and the organization of power, human mobility, and ethnic and sectarian organization and identities. Local narratives invoke comparisons to 1916 when the French and British carved the region into their respective mandates." Her assessment describes the nexus between geography and historical memory. The mind-set that established the Middle East's arbitrary borders is just as prevalent in the war on terror as it was in post–World War I Britain and France. An article by Ralph Peters titled "Blood Borders" published in the *Armed Forces Journal* in 2006 serves as a reflection of this mentality of arranging Middle Eastern borders to suit the interests of a foreign power. His article seeks to inform policymakers as to what "a better Middle East would look like." He describes Iraq as "A Frankenstein's monster of a state sewn together from ill-fitting parts. . . . [it] should have been divided into three smaller states immediately." The author has no quips about the United States' redrawing the map of a Middle East to serve American interests: "And by the way: A Free Kurdistan, stretching from Diyarbakir through Tabriz, would be the most pro-Western state between Bulgaria and Japan" (Peters 2006).

Peteet argues in her chapter that there is a Middle Eastern perception of the war on terror as a scheme to impose American hegemony in the region through the establishment of U.S. military bases. U.S. bases had radically changed the geography of the Gulf. The American naval base in Bahrain is situated on most of the southern territory of the small Gulf island. The roots of the war on terror emerged as a campaign by Osama bin Laden to oppose American bases in Saudi Arabia. The prospect of establishing bases in Iraq has also served as a rallying cry for Iraqis. During the British Mandate and after Iraq's independence in 1932, the British presence in Iraq was represented by two military bases in Habbaniyya and Shuayba. In fact, the Habbaniyya base was the first to be attacked during the monthlong 1941 Anglo-Iraqi war. The possibility of American bases in Iraq after the 2003 war was also viewed by the Iraqi public as a violation of military sovereignty. This view was expressed by Adnan Al-Dulaymi, an Iraqi politician who formed his own party, which generally represented Sunni Arabs in Iraq. In an interview with a Jordanian paper, Al-Dulaymi declared that the Americans would stay in Iraq by confining themselves to specific bases, but they would not remain in the streets of the cities like the British had done when they occupied Iraq in 1917. He said of the British, "In the early years they interfered in everything, and then they had advisors until 1954. They did not have armies. They had two bases, one in Basra, and Al-Habbaniyya. They had consulates in Basra, Mosul, and Baghdad." He argued that the Americans would do the same by establishing military bases just as they did in Japan, Italy, and Germany.[2]

Peteet, when referring to the Crusades, writes, "After Saladin liberated the city [of Jerusalem] in 1187, Christians and Jews were able to practice their religions and synagogues were rebuilt. For nearly eight hundred years under Muslim rule Jerusalem was a site of religious pluralism and tolerance." The status of Jerusalem alludes to a historical victim in the region: the multiethnic and multireligious space. Cities like Sarajevo and Beirut have endured episodes of violence that have marred their cosmopolitan pasts. The question remains as to whether the Iraqi city of Kirkuk, which is divided among Kurds, Arabs, and Turkmen, Sunnis, Shi'is, and Christians, will meet the same fate as Jerusalem.

The war on terror has also transformed the human geography, in particular that of women in Iraq. In "The War on Terror and Women's Rights in Iraq," Nadje Al-Ali analyzes how the role of women in Iraqi society was transformed after 2003. During the years of the Iran-Iraq War, Iraq had the highest percentage of women in the workforce as a result of the conscription of men between the ages of eighteen and forty-five. Yet during a three-week visit to Iraq in April 2004, I saw only one Iraqi woman, working in a hotel in the Green Zone. I realized that she was the first female I had seen since I entered the county and she would probably be the last. After the war, Iraq was touted as a "free Iraq." It was free for only half of the population. The other half—women—were locked in virtual prisons: their homes. In some cases it was a forced imprisonment, in others it was voluntary. Women had no protection from sexual violence, abduction, and rape, which have become increasingly common during the postwar chaos. The Iraqi police were too busy protecting themselves from insurgents to offer any protection. Al-Ali offers a firsthand account of the status of woman in Iraq and the ordeals that affect their everyday life, in both the workplace and educational establishments.

Al-Ali discusses the binary oppositions that have marked the war on terror from the perspective of gender. In the "us" versus "them" dichotomies, Iraqi women become a cultural marker to define the Iraqis opposed to the occupation forces. In this environment, I would argue that hypermasculinity has emerged in Iraq, where insurgent groups deem women in Iraq an asset to be protected. A case that demonstrates this hypermasculinity emerging in Iraq is that of Sabrin al-Janabi, an Iraqi Sunni Arab woman. On February 19, 2007, she claimed on the Al-Jazeera channel that she was raped by the Iraqi security forces after they raided her house in the south of Baghdad. While the Iraqi government claimed that medical reports did not corroborate her story, soon she emerged as a political symbol in the Iraqi discourse.

The Iraqi Al-Tawafuq Front, whose primary constituents are Sunni Arabs, declared the party's "concern for women's honor." A spokesman said, "The women are Iraqis, and all parties are Iraqi parties that are extremely eager to safeguard their honor, especially since the whole Iraqi people guaranteed the protection of honor, property, and lives when the security plan was announced."[3] Each party thereafter jostled for prominence in declaring their efforts to protect Iraqi women, whether the parties were in the government or opposition. The director of the Sunni Muslim Bureau Shaykh Al-Samarra'i declared, "This is a major incident and painful tragedy, the rape incident, took place. But, I cannot understand how an Iraqi lady would agree to appear before the media. I saw many Iraqi ladies, who swore to me by the Koran that they were raped. I asked them to appear on television and the news media, but they said we prefer to die than appear on television."[4] His statement is a testament to the exclusion of women from the Iraqi public sphere, especially television. Most of the Arab media pundits discussing the Al-Janabi incident and the security of women in Iraq were men.

Al-Janabi had also emerged as a potent symbol for the Iraqi insurgents. On February 22, the Call and Encampment Brigades vowed to punish the "Crusaders" (a euphemism for the American, British, and other Coalition forces) and "Safavids" (a derogatory term referring to Iranians) for the alleged rape of Al-Janabi. "Sabrin Al-Janabi's rape is one of thousands of similar cases executed by the occupation's armies in the Abu-Ghurayb Prison and the rest of the occupation's prisons two years ago and the raping of men before women in the prisons of the so-called Ministry of Information in Al-Ja'fari's former government" (Open Source Center 2007a). Even though the Iraqi security forces were accused of raping Al-Janabi, insurgent groups utilized the violation of the honor of an Iraqi woman to attack the United States and its "surge" plan to secure Baghdad. Another insurgent group issued the following statement regarding the case of Al-Janabi:

The rapists of Sabrin al-Janabi are those who could have provided support to save and protect the women, elderly men, and children of Iraq by volunteering themselves, providing money, or at least praying for them, and who did not do anything.

The rapists of Sabrin al-Janabi are those who enjoyed the taste of humiliation, accepted degradation, and abandoned jihad and did not rebuke themselves for doing so.

The rapists of Sabrin al-Janabi are those policemen, soldiers, and officers of the Arab states who imprisoned and tortured the mujanidin, and stood as a barrier to hinder their advances against the Zionists and the Americans. (Open Source Center 2007b)

This insurgent group also used Sabrin Al-Janabi as a symbol of opposition to the United States in addition to Israel.

In the aforementioned statements, the Iraqi insurgent groups support Al-Ali's assertion that conflicting parties create an "us," the Iraqi forces engaged in armed opposition to the "them," the Iraqi government, the United States and its allies, and Iraqis who have failed to endorse and support their movement. The symbol used to create this dichotomy is the Iraqi woman, whom these groups claim to seek to protect.

Entertainment

The war on terror has emerged as a form of militainment, of which Peteet writes, "Ominously, a discourse of monstrosity pervades contemporary

America's war on terror." An example is provided by Hinton, when he describes how Saddam Hussein had emerged as "The evil archenemy and 'wild man,' who was the 'ace of spades' in the government-issued deck of fifty-five cards of the 'most wanted' Iraqi leaders and upon whose head a $25 million bounty had also been placed." He "had finally been 'smoked out.'" The U.S. Defense Intelligence Agency produced its first "Iraqi Most Wanted" cards, printing and cutting out two hundred decks by hand. They were initially created for use by U.S. soldiers in Iraq to identify and capture high-ranking Ba'thists. Various companies such as Great USA Flags started to market these cards over the Internet, selling over a million Most Wanted decks at $5.95 apiece. The cards not only were a profitable venture; they also added to the militainment of the war on terror. The capture of the former Iraqi Ba'thists became a game, enhancing the entertaining nature of this conflict. The cards of Iraqi officials, many of whom were war criminals, could be collected as if they were baseball cards. Former general-turned-pundit David Grange was asked about the ongoing hunt for members of Saddam's ousted regime. He responded:

Well, what we can talk about on Task Force 20, it's a special operations force made up of several services that all bring different capabilities to this task force. It could even have Coalition members from British forces as an example. Its primary missions are to go after the *card deck of fifty-five*, the top people, to kill or grab these enemy leaders, hostage rescue, and also sensitive or highly sensitive possible WMD sites. (Cable News Network 2003)

Thus, the hunt for some of the members of the most odious regime in the history of the Middle East was reduced to a game of cards.

Hinton also portrays the war on terror as having a cinematic quality, with a plot, heroes, and a villain, " 'a collection of loosely affiliated terrorist organizations known as al Qaeda' who 'practice a fringe form of Islamic extremism' and are led by 'a person named Osama bin Laden.'" In an episode of the American news parody program the *Daily Show*, one of the comedians/commentators compares the entertainment value of the war on terror to the political drama the *West Wing*, describing how Osama bin Laden emerged as a character in the "first season," only to disappear in the "second season." The entertainment provided by this conflict has become integral to the "9/11 Imaginary" and was prevalent throughout the 2003 Iraq War.

The villainization of "Saddam" and his family emerged into an elaborate soap opera of family intrigue with the stories of the abuses of 'Uday

Hussein, Saddam's eldest son, featured prominently in men's entertainment magazines such as *Maxim*, detailing stories of his excess drinking and love of sports cars and beautiful women. Given that his interests are basically the topics of these magazines, such a figure may have appealed to its readership. However, 'Uday was not a key actor during the 2003 war, whereas someone like 'Abid Hamid Mahmud, the Iraqi presidential secretary who was responsible for Iraq's security apparatus and Hussein's personal protection, and was perhaps the second most powerful man in the government, received little attention in the U.S. media. His title of "presidential secretary" and his long Arabic name did not have a sinister tone as "'Uday, the son of Saddam." 'Uday Hussein did command an Iraqi militia known as the Fidayin Saddam, depicted in the international media as a frightening group of unprofessional bandits and mercenaries in the service of the "dictator Saddam" opposed to the "professional," "technologically" advanced American and British armed forces.

Saddam, 'Uday, the Republican Guards, and the Fidayin emerged as the array of icons and symbols throughout the media. As Hinton writes, just as in any film, the characters, villains, and heroes emerged throughout the conflict. Along with the sinister list of regime "cronies," there were other characters such as Dr. Huda 'Ammash, known as "Mrs. Anthrax" or the odious title of "Chemical Sally," while Dr. Rihab Taha was known as "Dr. Germ." The use of nicknames to describe the members of the "Saddam" regime was an inherent part of the entertainment that the war provided but obscured the fact that these two women developed some of the deadliest weapons of the last century that were used eliminate large segments of Iraq's Kurdish population. 'Ali Hassan Al-Majid, Saddam Hussein's cousin, was usually referred to with the euphemistic title of "Chemical Ali," a sinister nickname to acknowledge his use of chemical weapons against the Kurds. However, "Chemical Ali" was soon overshadowed by "Comical Ali," Muhammed Sa'id Al-Sahhaf, the Iraqi minister of information whose exaggerated claims of Iraqi battlefield successes won him international recognition and celebrity. Al-Sahhaf emerged as the master of Iraqi public diplomacy during the 2003 war. Not only was he a frontline soldier for Iraq during the "war of words," he provided entertainment for international audiences. His overly optimistic press briefings were referred to by one source as "The al-Sahhaf Show" (Reid 2003). The media's fixation on him was because of his bombastic press conferences, but he also served some networks' desire to present the Arab and the Iraqi as ridiculous.

The anthropologists who have contributed to this volume provide analysis not only of the tactical campaigns used against insurgencies in various conflicts but of the rhetorical tools, labels, and terminology used in the war on terror. Such analysis is significant, as this discourse changed the perceptions of its viewers, particularly in the United States, by soliciting their support for war, convincing audiences that Iraq and the al Qaeda threat were one and the same. The language and tactics used during the current insurgencies in Iraq and Afghanistan demonstrate that the remnants of the 2001 and 2003 war discourses continue to resonate as the U.S. and British governments attempt to justify troop deployments in both countries. This volume, which compares the conflicts engendered by the war on terror, is a testament to the intractability of both parties. Both parties have a teleological vision of their struggle, where good will ultimately triumph over evil, suggesting that the war on terror can continue indefinitely on a battlefield, both symbolic and physical.

Notes

1. WeLovetheIraqiInformationMinister.com.
2. *Al-Ra'y*, August 25, 2005, 5.
3. *Al-Iraqiyah*, 1530 GMT, February 21, 2007.
4. *Al-Arabiyya*, 1900 GMT, February 21, 2007.

Bibliography

Antoon, Sinan. 2003. Of Bridges and Birds. *Al-Ahram Weekly Online* 634:17, April 23. http://weekly.ahram.org.eg/2003/634/bo1.htm (accessed September 17, 2007).

Cable News Network. 2003. Hunt for Saddam: American Morning. June 23, Transcript #062302CN.V74.

Fernea, Elizabeth Warnock. 1965. *Guests of the Sheik*. Garden City, N.Y.: Doubleday.

Fox News Network. 2003. *Fox on the Record with Greta Van Susteren*. February 26, Transcript #022602cb.260.

Al-Marashi, Ibrahim. 2006. Iraq's "Cyber Insurgency": The Internet and the Iraqi Resistance. In *Cybermedia Go to War: Role of Non-Traditional Media in the 2003 Iraq War*, ed. Ralph Berenger, 213–31. Spokane: Marquette Books.

Open Source Center. 2007a. Document GMP20070221342006, February 21. https://www.opensource.gov/public (accessed September 15, 2007).

———. 2007b. Document GMP20070223030001, February 21. https://www.open source.gov/public (accessed September 15, 2007).

Peters, Ralph. 2006. Blood Borders: How a Better Middle East Would Look. *Armed Forces Journal*, June. http://www.armedforcesjournal.com/2006/06/1833899 (accessed September 16, 2007).

Reid, Tim. 2003. Comical Ali Makes His TV Comeback. *The Times*, June 27.

Contributors

Nadje Al-Ali is reader in gender studies and chair of the Centre for Gender Studies at the School of Oriental and African Studies (SOAS), University of London. Her main research interests revolve around gender theory; feminist activism; women and gender in the Middle East; transnational migration and diaspora mobilization; and war, conflict, and reconstruction. Her publications include *Iraqi Women: Untold Stories from 1948 to the Present* (Zed Books, 2007); *New Approaches to Migration* (Routledge, 2002); *Secularism, Gender and the State in the Middle East* (Cambridge University Press, 2000), *Gender Writing—Writing Gender* (American University in Cairo Press, 1994), and numerous book chapters and journal articles. Her most recent books (coauthored with Nicola Pratt) are *What Kind of Liberation? Women and the Occupation in Iraq* (University of California Press, 2009) and (co-edited) *Women and War in the Middle East: Transnational Perspectives* (Zed Books, 2009). She is also a founding member of Act Together: Women's Action for Iraq (www.acttogether.org) and a member of Women in Black UK.

Alexander Laban Hinton is director of the Center for the Study of Genocide and Human Rights and associate professor of anthropology and global affairs at Rutgers University, Newark. He is the author of *Why Did They Kill? Cambodia in the Shadow of Genocide* (University of California Press, 2005), which received the 2008 Stirling Prize, and editor or coeditor of six collections, including *Genocide: Truth, Memory, and Representation* (Duke University Press, 2009), *Annihilating Difference: The Anthropology of Genocide* (University of California Press, 2002), and *Genocide: An Anthropological Reader* (Blackwell, 2002). He is currently working on several other book projects, including a co-edited volume on the legacies of mass violence, a book on 9/11 and Abu Ghraib, and a book on the politics of memory and justice in the aftermath of the Cambodian genocide.

Ibrahim Al-Marashi is associate dean of international relations and assistant professor of communication history and politics at the IE School of Communication, IE University, Spain. He obtained his D.Phil. at the University of Oxford, completing a thesis on the Iraqi invasion of Kuwait, parts of which were used by the British government to justify the war against Iraq. His publications include *Iraq's Armed Forces: An Analytical History* (Routledge, 2008). He is an Iraqi American who has lived at various times in Saudi Arabia, Yemen, Egypt, Morocco, and Turkey and has traveled extensively throughout the Middle East.

Julie Peteet is chair of the Department of Anthropology and director of Middle East and Islamic studies at the University of Louisville. Her research has focused on Palestinian displacement, refugee camps, space and identity, and, more recently, the policy of closure in the West Bank. She has authored two books: *Gender in Crisis: Women and the Palestinian Resistance Movement* (Columbia University Press, 1991) and *Landscape of Hope and Despair: Palestinian Refugee Camps* (University of Pennsylvania Press, 2005). She has published in a variety of journals, including *Signs, American Ethnologist, Cultural Anthropology, Cultural Survival, International Journal of Middle East Studies,* and *Middle East Report,* as well as numerous chapters in edited volumes. Her research has been funded by SSRC, Wenner-Gren, Fulbright, the Mellon Foundation, CAORC, and PARC. She serves on the editorial board of MERIP and was an associate editor of the *Encyclopedia of Women and Islamic Cultures.*

Antonius C. G. M. Robben is a professor of anthropology at the Department of Cultural Anthropology, Utrecht University, the Netherlands. He has a Ph.D. from the University of California, Berkeley, and is a past fellow of the Michigan Society of Fellows, Ann Arbor, past fellow of the David Rockefeller Center, Harvard University, and past president of the Netherlands Society of Anthropology. His publications include *Fieldwork Under Fire: Contemporary Studies of Violence and Survival* (University of California Press, 1995; coedited with Carolyn Nordstrom), *Cultures Under Siege: Collective Violence and Trauma* (Cambridge University Press, 2000; coedited with Marcelo Suárez-Orozco), *Death, Mourning, and Burial: A Cross-Cultural Reader* (Blackwell, 2004), *Ethnographic Fieldwork: An Anthropological Reader* (Blackwell, 2007; coedited with Jeffrey Sluka), and the ethnography *Political Violence and Trauma in Argentina* (University of Pennsylvania

Press, 2005), which received the 2006 Textor Prize from the American Anthropological Association.

Jeffrey A. Sluka is associate professor in the Social Anthropology Programme at Massey University, New Zealand. He received a Ph.D. from the University of California, Berkeley (1986), is a fellow of the American Anthropological Association, and is a former chairperson of the Association of Social Anthropologists of Aotearoa/New Zealand. A political anthropologist, he is an expert on political violence and the cultural dynamics of armed conflicts between states and ethnonationalist movements and indigenous peoples. He is author of *Hearts and Minds, Water and Fish: Popular Support for the IRA and INLA in a Northern Irish Ghetto* (JAI Press, 1989) and edited *Death Squad: The Anthropology of State Terror* (University of Pennsylvania Press, 2000) and (with Antonius Robben) *Ethnographic Fieldwork: An Anthropological Reader* (Blackwell, 2007).

Index

Abu Ghraib prison: abuse of detainees, 19, 51, 63–64, 115, 121, 122, 139, 148, 167; women detainees, 63–64

Adversary Cultural Knowledge and National Security Conference, 127

Afghanistan, U.S.-led war in: civilian casualties, 111–13, 119; constant warfare, 124; cost of war, 124–25; expanded Islamic resistance, 125; human rights violations, 115; increased insurgency, 109–10, 115, 119–20, 121, 125; military fatalities, 110; NATO forces, 110, 117, 119; prisoner abuse by Special Forces units, 113; refugee situation, 118; shifting popular perceptions of troops, 115, 121; Taliban resurgence, 109–10, 117, 118, 119–20; "warlordism," 117. *See also* civilian support for counterinsurgency wars

Ahmadinejad, Mahmoud, 47, 120

Ahmed, Akbar, 4

Al-Ali, Nadje, 3, 7, 10, 13–14, 57–79, 169–71, 175. *See also* women's rights in post-invasion Iraq

Alcalay, Ammiel, 90

American Anthropological Association, viii, 127

American Civil Liberties Union (ACLU), 63

'Ammash, Dr. Huda, 173

Amnesty International, 109, 115, 116, 140

anthropology at a distance, vii–viii, 1–23; anthropology of violence and suffering, 8–9, 21; and anthropology's marginal place in Iraq War debates, 20; and Benedict, 2; Cold War–era methodology, 2; comparative approach and methods, 2–3, 9–11, 20–21; and "the compassionate turn," 4–5, 21; and constructions of difference invoked in war narratives, 50, 52; contradictions of, 8–9; early anthropological fieldwork, 1–2;

effect of 9/11 and Bush's war on terror, 6–7; and empathy, 4; ethnographic imagination, 3–11, 20–21; and "ethnographies of empire," 84; and globalization, 5–6, 8; Gough in the late 1960s, 2–3; imagined geographies, 88; methodological alternatives, 4, 9–11, 20–21, 49–50; moral implications, 5; and multisited fieldwork, 5–7, 10; new disjunctions and exclusionary zones, 6–7; Peteet on anthropological insights into war on terror, 81, 84–88; and "preventive diplomacy," 85; the public anthropological voice, 85; sources for research, 8–9; and the spatialization of conflict, 7–8, 51; World War II–era fieldwork, 1–2, 8

Antoon, Sinan, 163

Appadurai, Arjun, 6

Argentina's dirty war, 18–20, 135–36, 145–51, 155; counterinsurgency swarming tactics, 18–19, 143, 145–46, 155; effect on Argentine society, 149; grid pattern territorialization approach, 145–46; and ideological justification of violence, 147–48; and Manichaean good-versus-evil thinking, 147, 154; and "mimesis," 145–46; secret detention centers and coercive interrogations/torture, 148–51. *See also* counterinsurgency war in Iraq

Asad, Talal, 84

Association of Social Anthropologists (Great Britain), 127

Badr Brigade, 66

Bagram prison (Afghanistan), 113, 121

Barak, Ehud, 81, 98

Bauman, Zygmunt, 93

Beamer, Todd, 31, 37

Been, Aluf, 91

Benedict, Ruth, 2